Dispatches from the Land of Flowers

A Snake Man, a Sad Poet, a Lightning Stalker and other stories about Real Florida

Jeff Klinkenberg

Down Home Press, Asheboro, N.C.

Dedication

For Frank and Eleanor Lash,
my other parents,
with love.

Acknowledgments

Nobody writes a book without help. I got tons of support from the *St. Petersburg Times*, Richard Bockman, Chris Lavin, Nancy Waclawek, Gretchen Letterman, Mary Jane Park, Paul Tash, Neil Brown, Susan Taylor Martin, Andy Barnes, Jeanne Malmgren, Mary Evertz, Jack Reed, Bill Stevens, Bryanna Latoof, Roy Peter Clark, Don Murray, Chip Scanlan, Vic DeRobertis, Mimi Andelman, Anne Hull, Tom French, Gabe Horn, Kitty Bennett, Barbara Hijek, Stephen Klemawesch, Antoinette Falk, Bob Stone, Scott Hiestand, Randy Wayne White, and Jerry Bledsoe.

Thanks for marrying me, Suzanne. After 25 years I still can't believe my wonderful luck.

Permissions

Grateful acknowledgment is made to the following for permission to quote copyrighted material:

Totch: A Life in the Everglades, by Loren G. "Totch" Brown, with permission of University Press of Florida.
The Birdlife of Florida, by Henry Stevenson and Bruce Anderson, with permission of University Press of Florida.
Sanibel Flats, by Randy Wayne White, with permission of the author.
Okeechobee Hurricane, by Laurence E. Will, with permission of The Glades Historical Society.
The Orchids of Florida, by Dr. Carl Luer, with permission of the author.
Tell Me Why You Like Roosevelt, by Willie Eason, with permission of the songwriter.
The Choice, by W.B. Yeats, reprinted with the permission of Simon & Schuster from **The Poems of W.B. Yeats: A New Edition**, edited by Richard J. Finneran. ©1933 by Macmillan Publishing Company, Renewed 1961 by Bertha Georgie Yeats.

Recommended reading:

Travels of William Bartram, by William Bartram
Moby Dick, by Herman Melville
Journals, by Henry David Thoreau

Recommended visits:

The Museum of Florida's Art and Culture, Sebring.
Big Cypress Gallery, Ochopee.
The Florida Folk Festival, Stephen Foster State Park, White Springs, Memorial Day weekend.

Introduction

The Florida I know and love is like the royal poinciana tree that shaded my front yard when I was a boy growing up in Miami.

For most of the year the tree was easy to take for granted. It was brown, skeletal, ugly—unless you looked closely.

Then it became interesting and beautiful. Inch worms crept up the trunk and mockingbirds zoomed between branches to pick them off. If you watched the mockingbirds long enough you might notice a yellow rat snake trying to shed its skin on rough bark. Some nights, if the windows were open, you could hear the hoots of the barred owl that liked our tree. Our poinciana was bursting with life.

In the spring, even folks who paid little attention to nature had to notice our tree. It blossomed with thousands of spectacular flowers, burnt-orange blooms the color of the most fantastic sunset. Every once in a while, someone driving by would stop and gape. Occasionally, somebody would knock on our door and ask permission to take a photograph.

I always was tempted to shout "Welcome to the land of flowers."

But I never did.

I do now, not because I have a poinciana tree, but because I want people to pay closer attention to Florida, which is absolutely bursting with life. A lot of people who have lived years in Florida, or vacationed in Florida for a few short weeks, have no idea what's here. Once they've visited the famous theme park, or walked on a crowded, overdeveloped beach, they think they have seen everything. Often they pronounce themselves disappointed.

"Florida has no seasons," they say. "Florida has no culture. How do you stand living here?"

I try not to scream.

I tell them about the essays I have written during my years at the *St. Petersburg Times*, the essays contained in this book. I tell them about the Real Florida available to anyone who takes the time and the effort to look, the Real Florida found in the Fakahatchee Strand and the Big Cypress and the Everglades. I tell them about our gospel music, and the starving but remarkable landscape artists known as the Highwaymen. I point them toward the always amazing—and inexpensive—Sponge-O-Rama in Tarpon Springs.

I tell them about the beach where sea loggerhead turtles still nest by the thousands, and order them to go tubing, not tomorrow but today, on the spring-fed Ichetucknee. The least I can do is share with them my secret for finding a luscious tomato or a delicious sweet potato pie. I tell them where in the Florida Keys they can feed tarpon by hand, and where they might take a walk in a good swamp and see a stunning ghost orchid.

"One more thing," I tell to them. "Welcome to the land of flowers."

Contents

FALL

WINTER

SPRING

SUMMER

Fall
Okeechobee Gourd

Modest plans for a Florida autumn

October 1995

Summer seemed as if it would hang on forever, but fall has finally shown up on our doorsteps.

If I could write poetry, perhaps I'd try to knock out a verse on Florida's autumn.

I know. I know. We supposedly have no fall. We don't have a spectacular show of dying leaves, we can't buy apples from roadside stands, and some years our sweaters remain in the closet until Christmas.

Blah, blah, blah.

Florida's fall has subtle beauties, and some overwhelming ones, but for the most part they don't reveal themselves easily to people who spend their lives indoors, shopping at the mall, typing at a desk, or sitting on a couch.

City folks with a passive lifestyle are the most likely to complain about missing our fall, like a person who sits in a room full of wonderful books and says "I'm bored," because there is no TV. Enjoying our fall is a matter of becoming literate about the many pleasures Florida has to offer, and then actively seeking them out.

To me, our fall is most like a northern spring. It celebrates the beginning of a six-month reign of pleasant weather. Having survived another rough summer, there is much to do, see and taste in the fall ahead.

Here are modest plans for a Florida autumn:

I intend to celebrate fall's arrival with a feast. I'll buy stone-crab claws—the season just opened—spread newspaper on the floor, grab a hammer, and have at them. I pick the white meat out of the cracked claws, dip it in melted butter and try to forget any worries about cholesterol. Forgive me, Doc, but I can't help myself. It's fall.

I have to visit Sawgrass Lake Park in St. Petersburg, where I live, and look for rose-breasted grosbeaks. They're a northern bird, one of my favorites when I visit North Carolina in the summer. During our fall, they migrate through Florida. They're a stunning species: dramatically red, white and black, with heavy bills. Sometimes they hop among the oak branches above the interpretive center, sit still and preen. Lights, camera, action!

When I go to bed in the fall, I hope it is cool enough to open the windows. We have screech owls in the neighborhood, and on quiet evenings I sometimes go to sleep listening to their distant high-pitched warbling.

On fall mornings, buttered grits—stone-ground, never instant!— taste especially grand.

On fall Saturday afternoons, I like to sit in my backyard, spy on the red-bellied woodpeckers in the live oak and listen to college football on the radio.

As soon as I can, I want to camp at Lake Kissimmee State Park, near Lake Wales, in Central Florida. After breakfast (heart-clogging bacon, eggs and grits!) I will hike the Buster Hammock Trail and look for deer. The males grow big antlers during the fall. Before supper, I'll ride my bike to the park office and maybe see a scrub jay.

A great pleasure of Florida's fall is angling for kingfish. This time of year, they migrate south through the Gulf of Mexico and hang around the Suncoast for a spell. Most anglers are too secretive to tell you where to look, but I don't mind spilling the beans. Take a boat a few miles west of the Don Cesar Resort on St. Petersburg Beach and drop anchor where the bottom is rocky. Chum—I mean throw into the water little chunks of sardine minnows or catfood—and wait for a kingfish to pick up the trail.

With your fishing pole, cast out a live sardine and wait. Watch the pelicans. Watch the terns. Mostly watch your line.

If you are lucky, if the water is the right temperature—about 68 degrees is perfect—a kingfish will come along. A kingfish is a giant mackerel. Sometimes they grow 40, 50 even 90 pounds, though I will be happy to make the acquaintance of a 10-pounder.

Sometimes a kingfish will leap out of the water like a silver-green missile and land mouth-first on your bait. Anglers call the phenomenon "skyrocketing." When a skyrocketing king feels the hook it bolts for the blue. Its life energy surges up the line and through the rod and into your hands. You feel connected to the wild heart of the Earth.

You can let the kingfish go if you want. If you are hungry you may want to fire up your grill.

I don't mind telling you where to catch kingfish, but I am sworn to secrecy about my friend Elmo's kingfish sauce recipe.

Now that fall is here, I plan on riding my bicycle on the Withlacoochee State Trail, which rolls 40 miles through rural Pasco, Hernando and Citrus counties, in North Central Florida. As I pedal among the oaks, I'll be watching for wild turkeys scavenging for acorns. Passing through open fields, I hope to see bluebirds on pasture fenceposts. I will settle for a cool wind on my face.

Any minute now, I'm going to jump into my truck, drive across Tampa Bay's Sunshine Skyway to Terra Ceia and buy naval oranges. It is part of my fall ritual.

Sometime in late November, my own tree will be ripe with tangerines. When I walk into my back yard, I will feel rich.

On my next fall visit to Northwest Florida, I will drive US 19 and look for that little hand-painted sign near Perry that says: "Firewood." Last time, big bundles of just-sawed oak logs were piled high along the road, and on sale for only $5 each.

Nobody was there to take my money, so I put $10 in a jar and selected two bundles. Used the wood in my fireplace for two or three winters.

On my next South Florida fall visit, I'll certainly need to spend a couple of days in Everglades National Park. Maybe there will be another short-tailed hawk at Mahogany Hammock, or a snail kite hovering over the marsh behind the Miccosukee Indian Restaurant at Shark Valley Slough. If nothing else, it is very dark in the Everglades at night, so dark I sometimes can see my favorite deep sky object of the fall, the Andromeda Galaxy—two million light years away—without binoculars.

If everything goes right, I hope to squeeze in another camping trip before Christmas, this time to Paynes Prairie State Preserve, near Micanopy, in North Florida. Every November, greater sandhill cranes by the thousands fly here from the Great Lakes. "Gar-roo, gar-roo," they trumpet from the marshes and the pastures and the prairies. At night, over a campfire, I will celebrate the day's great crane triumphs by sentimentally roasting my year's only marshmallow.

It is fall, and I don't plan to miss a moment.

Good times at the Desert Inn

YeeHaw Junction
November 1994

"You got to have some of my chili."

I have just wolfed down the luncheon special, meat loaf, when Beverly Zicheck sits on the nearest stool at her restaurant, the Desert Inn, in the town of Yeehaw Junction, and tells me I need to pretend I'm still hungry. Yes, I say, of course I'm famished, and she walks over to a hot plate and ladles me out a bowl.

Beverly Zicheck, who has short brown hair, blue eyes and a horsewoman's callused hands, cooks an outstanding chili, it turns out, spicy but not too spicy, hearty and flavorful, and without the dreaded kidney beans.

"If you want my chili hotter, you can make it hotter," she says, and points to a jar containing Jamaican peppers. They're scattered about the counter between the larger jars filled with pickled sausage and pickled hard-boiled eggs.

You can get just about anything at the Desert Inn, including a good scare, a hangover and a splendid donkey. Beverly sells them, too. It is not for nothing that her restaurant is a landmark at Yeehaw Junction, a speck on the map that some truckers still call by its former name, Jackass Crossing.

For more than a century, the Desert Inn has been a gathering place and a watering hole for travelers. They drive through Central Florida on State Road 60 or U.S. 441 past phosphate mines and white-faced bulls with egrets on their backs, past trailer parks and fish camps and squashed coyotes, until, up ahead, they see the familiar green and white clapboard building, and maybe stop for a bite or a belt.

Customers who have laughed and cried and cussed and bled and loved and got drunk inside the cypress-walled restaurant include truck drivers, tourists, bass fishermen, good ol' boys, wild hog hunters, motorcycle mamas, Seminole Indians, donkey fanciers and lots and lots of lonely cattlemen. The Desert Inn traces its roots to Cracker Florida, when grizzled cowhunters drove wily cattle across open ranges from one side of the state to the other, and needed a spot to wet their whistles or maybe go upstairs with one of the ladies of the evening.

Those were the good old days. Now ranges are fenced and highways are paved, and the wolves and panthers are gone. The Kissimmee River down the road is not a real river anymore, it's an Army Corps of Engineers canal. About an hour north is Disney World and a half hour east are the splendid mansions of Vero Beach. The Desert Inn, pink lights flashing, remains, pretty much intact, except now it has water and electricity and no prostitutes. Last year, the federal government added it to the National Register of Historic Places.

"Frog legs."

As I finish my chili, the man on the stool across from me leans over and recommends his favorite dish. Bob Davis, who lives in Belle Glade, near Lake Okeechobee, has been stopping for lunch at the Desert Inn at least 40 years. He pushes the cowboy hat back on his head and lights up a cigarette—non-smokers are welcome here, too—and leans his elbows on the Formica counter and rubs his hand mindlessly across a frosty can of Busch. He says again, "I like the frog legs here. My wife, she never lets me order frog legs when we go out together, so whenever I stop here, I got to order them."

Bob says he is going to head west after lunch until he gets to the Oasis Fish Camp on the river and fish in a tournament for bass. He'd rather fish in the Rim Canal around Lake Okeechobee, he wants me to know, but it's not like he can tell tournament organizers where to have their contest. So he'll fish in the Kissimmee River, even if the engineers did mess it up. Then he remembers something else that needs mentioning.

"The onion rings are the best here," he says.

Beverly Zicheck, the owner, hears the compliment as she comes back again to sit on the stool and says thanks. "We do bread our own onion rings," she adds, and a guy down the counter who is wearing a red cap that says Marlboro across the front says he likes the sweet tea, and Beverly says, "We sell sweet tea like it's going out of style."

Beverly, who looks to be about 45 but refuses to tell her age, took over the Desert Inn nine years ago from her parents, who throughout their lives bought, ran and sold restaurants. Beverly grew up in Brandon, near Tampa, and loved riding horses, but was probably even better in math, and after high school studied to be an accountant, working for many years as an internal auditor for a motel chain, which sent her around the world. Beverly eventually studied for two more college degrees, hotel management and bovine and equine science, and so when the Desert Inn presented itself, she was ready.

She fixed it up, but not too much, working hard to keep unchanged its colorful character. As you spoon your chili, as you munch your frog legs, you can gaze in wonder at Beverly's rattlesnake skins, at her pencil sketch of John Wayne, her sign advertising the weekend's clogging dance, her bullhorns sticking out of the wall, and her inevitable jackalope, a taxidermist's stuffed rabbit onto which somebody glued an antelope's antlers. Because the Desert Inn has always sold donkeys, a bunch of hand-written jokes about jackasses hang over the bar. The adult beverage of the house, and please excuse me for even mentioning it, is a form of liquid TNT known as the "Ass Grinder." It contains 151-proof rum, blackberry brandy and prune juice.

"We got one guy who comes here once a week and has two and chases it with a beer," says Suzy Davey, one of Beverly's waitresses, admiration in her twang. And then, all bets are off.

"We like to have fun here," Beverly says, which explains the rubber spiders and bats hanging from near invisible fishing lines above the tables. If you study the fishing lines, you'll notice that they run back to the bar, where Beverly or Suzy can manipulate them and drop the spiders and bats onto unsuspecting customers. They do.

"I dropped a spider on this biker, he musta weighed two hundred fifty pounds, when he was over at the juke box," Suzy says. It's a great juke box, by the way, full of real country songs, from the likes of Patsy, Waylon, Merle, and Hank, the father not the son. But that's another story.

"So I drop the spider on him," Suzy says, "and, like, he did a jig, only he stayed in the same place, and then tried to bolt, and I thought he was going to run through the juke box."

"He was mad," Beverly says. "We were just having fun."

They try, they try. Across the bar, near the side door, is a funny box onto which somebody wrote "The Mongoose will bite." Beverly walks to a table, where a father and a son are eating hamburgers, and invites the son, a boy about 10, to open the mongoose box. He looks at the box and he looks at his father, who nods yes, go ahead. He starts to open the box but then backs off. Then he returns and opens it just a little. Beverly loses patience and says, "Here, let me" and opens it dramatically and . . . well, I won't give it away. But as Beverly says, "If the walls could only talk."

Beverly and I amble outside so she can show me her donkeys, which she sells for $150 a head, and also she'd like me to get a look at her mule, already 1,400 pounds and likely to stand 16 hands before too long. But they're clean on the other side of the pasture, so I admire her grapefruit trees and the inn part of her establishment, 11 motel rooms, which she rents for $33.30 night and a little less for truckers, who get a discount.

She jumps to another topic, the roads that go by her business, and complains that she has a bone to pick with the Department of Transportation on account of they put a traffic light about 10 feet from her restaurant, which makes it near impossible to get out of the parking lot if there's traffic. And then we go inside so I can pick up my things, and I encounter a giant piece of lemon pie on the counter at my stool.

"You got to try the pie," Beverly says. I obey her. Her lemon pie, as I suspected, is absolutely delicious. "It's made from scratch," she goes on. "We also make peach, blueberry, pecan and cherry." I write all her pies into my notebook and try to say my goodbyes. Beverly asks, "Did I tell you about George?"

How could she have forgotten? George is the male mannequin inside the women's restroom. Naturally I ask to see him. He stands, next to the sink, covered with the signatures of many women, a leer on his face. As I leave the restroom, Beverly enters, while Suzy, the waitress, sneaks out from behind the bar and starts fiddling with a switch on the ceiling. Suddenly, an alarm pierces the quiet of the Desert Inn.

"We got the dummy rigged," Suzy explains. "If a lady touches his zipper, the alarm goes off."

Seeds of doubt

Gainesville
November 1993

On the eventful week in 1774 that William Bartram discovered the mystery squash, a squash botanists have wondered and argued and speculated about for the two centuries since, his mind quite possibly was occupied by more fundamental matters. Razor-toothed alligators were on the prowl and headed his way with jaws agape.

As his little boat sailed across a lake adjacent to North Florida's St. Johns River, the famous naturalist grabbed his paddle and drove away two ferocious crocodilians. Others charged, opening and closing their mighty jaws with horrifying snaps, before sinking mercifully from sight.

It is hard to fault the Philadelphia resident for not paying more attention to the pretty gourd he saw a few hours later, what with all those ravenous alligators trying to polish him off. In the influential 1791 book he published about his journey, considered a work of literature and science—*Travels of William Bartram*—he spent one stingy sentence on the gourd and hundreds on alligators, snakes, birds and Indians.

Twentieth-century botanists do not begrudge Bartram his alligators, birds and Indians. But living plants are their reason for being. The world may not shiver in delight when a scientist of Bartram's stature describes a mysterious gourd—a squash that more than likely was inedible—but certain botanists, squash men, if you will, do get misty-eyed. It is the 1990's, man, and they want to know more.

What the blazes did Bartram see in the woods of the St. Johns River? Was it a *Cucurbita peregrina* as he had speculated? Or could he have seen—for crying out loud, could Billy Bartram have seen the rare *Cucurbita okeechobeensis*?

Whatever he saw isn't there now.

Anyway, that's what squash men thought.

The Okeechobee gourd—*cucurbita okeechobeensisssp, okeechobeensis* to scientists in the know—is among the rarest plants on Earth. Last summer, the United States listed it as an endangered species. On the brink of extinction, the orange-size gourd is restricted to Florida. Its last known stronghold is in the islands of southern Lake Okeechobee—about 200 miles south of where Bartram discovered his gourd.

At one time, the South Florida gourds were found by the thousands along the rim of the huge lake, growing among vast groves of pond apple trees. But by 1930 they were all gone. And if they were growing along Bartram's St. Johns River, nobody saw them.

As farmers along Lake Okeechobee replaced the pond apple groves with marketable crops, the Okeechobee gourds disappeared. Then a terrible hurricane washed over the lake and drowned 1,800 people, resulting in a long dike that prevented future floods while incidentally keeping the Okeechobee gourd from re-establishing along the lake shore. In the decades that followed, vegetation from foreign lands—Australian pine, melaleuca and Brazilian pepper—moved in, shading out native plants, including the gourd.

In truth, nobody much cared except for people who study obscure plants. Like most wild squashes, the gourd is too bitter for the human palate. It has no known medicinal qualities. It lacks the snuggly appeal of a furry animal or the attractive danger of something with big teeth. Bartram, who knew how to tell a story, may have had good reason for short-shrifting his gourd discovery. A good squash story—even one about the rare Okeechobee gourd—is no guaranteed page turner.

"In the 1980s, we pretty much thought they were extinct from Lake Okeechobee," says Terrence Walters of Fairchild Tropical Gardens in Miami. "You just couldn't find them."

Walters, a gourd man through and through, wondered. In 1991, on behalf of the United States Fish and Wildlife Service, he mounted an expedition to Lake Okeechobee to look for them. If he found them, he intended to do some genetic testing. The federal government wanted to know if the Okeechobee gourd was the same gourd found commonly in Mexico. If it turned out to be Mexico's *Cucurbita martinezii*, it deserved no federal protection.

Not far from Clewiston, Walters and an assistant shoved a canoe into the lake. They began exploring nearby islands. As they glided onto a muck-laden island, a large alligator abandoned its nest and slipped into the water, reminding Walters of Bartram's trials: Bartram had found his gourd near alligator nests, too. Walters looked up. Growing on the vines that enveloped nearby trees were Okeechobee gourds.

"It was an exciting moment," Walters says.

Back in his Miami lab, Walters and his wife Deena began their genetic work on the plants. The Okeechobee gourd was related to the Mexican gourd, they determined, and at one time may even have been the same species. But the plants had been separated for half a million years and evolved separately. The Okeechobee gourd, Walters said, was now a distinct sub-species.

The federal government declared it endangered.

"The way the lake is going, I don't see any hope," Walters says, referring to the explosion of exotic plants and the unnatural lake shore. "There's so much going against it."

But that raises other questions.

What if the Okeechobee gourd exists somewhere else?

Could Bartram's St. Johns River gourd have been the Okeechobee variety?

His description more than two centuries ago sounded much like an Okeechobee gourd. Orange-shaped. Found near white moonflowers and alligator nests. He called it a *Cucurbita*, the correct genus. But he thought it was some other species. And there is another nagging thing: The Okeechobee gourd is green like a watermelon, with vertical white stripes; Bartram's beauty was supposedly yellow.

"When they dry out," Walters says, "they get brown. But they're not yellow.

So Bartram's description doesn't seem to fit. Unless he made a mistake. It's easy to make a mistake in the field, especially if you're writing down a lot of stuff about a lot of plants."

William Bartram was 35 when he made his 2,400-mile trip through the South. He was a gentle Quaker, the son of a famous botanist, John Bartram, who was a friend of Thomas Jefferson, Benjamin Franklin and George Washington. John Bartram was also an ambitious businessman. He had once made a trip to Florida, too, for the purpose of public relations and real estate. He considered his son a failure.

William Bartram, called Billy by his family, had no head for business. Like Thoreau, another famous pacifist who preferred nature to commerce, William enjoyed walking in the woods, drawing the plants that he saw and gathering seeds for later experiments. As the rest of the continent braced for war with mother England, Billy missed the American Revolution by vanishing into the southern wilderness to collect plants, document wildlife and meet Indians.

"Billy had an interesting mind," says Charlotte Porter, a University of Florida historian whose specialty is science.

During the next four years, he saw many wonders. He identified 358 plants, 150 of which were new to him, and hundreds of mammals, reptiles, amphibians, birds and fishes. He was the first white naturalist to describe the gopher tortoise and the black vulture. Florida's Lower Creek Indians, who became known as Seminoles in the next century, called him Puc Puggy—the Flower Hunter. He described their way of life and their kindness toward him in loving detail.

The book was a bigger success in the Old World than in the New, and it was more popular in literary circles than in scientific ones. William Wordsworth used Bartram's prose in his poem, "Ruth." Samuel Taylor Coleridge liked it well enough to use its imagery in his "Rime of the Ancient Mariner." Although Bartram was a trained scientist, he sometimes is called the father of the Romantic Movement in literature. He considered himself a writer first and foremost.

Some scientists, who prefer precision over dramatic narrative, have been troubled by the literary qualities of *Travels*. Did he make honest mistakes or did he take literary license?

Bartram provides an excellent description of the mating dance of sandhill cranes on Paynes Prairie and even provides a highly accurate drawing. But then he has them dramatically roosting, at dusk, in the trees. Sandhill cranes avoid trees. They roost on shallow water prairies.

He describes the howling wolves he encounters, but he says they were black. Florida had red wolves.

And then there was his famous account of his first encounter with an alligator:

"Behold him rushing forth from the flags and reeds. His enormous body swells. His plaited tail brandished high, floats upon the lake. The waters like a cataract descend from his opening jaws. Clouds of smoke issue from his dilated nostrils. The earth trembles with his thunder."

Male alligators during mating season sometimes bellow. Sometimes water droplets are expelled into the air. If the light was right, and an observer were watching from an ideal position, those water droplets might look like smoke. Bartram drew a picture, too. No doubt about it, his alligators look like steam-breathing dragons. At the same time, he describes their mating and nesting behavior with a scientific accuracy that holds up today.

Still, those discrepancies gnaw at scientific minds.

Can you trust a writer who pictures an alligator as a fire-breathing dragon? Was the gourd he discovered green or yellow?

"I don't worry about the few mistakes he made," historian Charlotte Porter says. "He was describing hundreds of species and putting them into ecological context. Some of his writings and drawings he did from notes; some of it he may have done from memory years later. Most of his work holds up scientifically.

"His value was not his precision but his vision, his grasp of the complexity, the beauty, the danger and the mystery of nature. He used literature to describe it. He didn't think science was a sufficient tool to understand the whole of nature."

Marc Minno works for the St. Johns River Water Management District. Among other things, he conducts field surveys to identify plants.

In October, he and two other men were on a routine mission. They were making a plant survey in the woods and wetlands adjacent to the St. Johns River—smack in the middle of William Bartram territory.

Finding an Okeechobee gourd was the last thing on their minds.

They walked into the woods. There were pop ash and cypress trees. There were moonflowers like the ones Bartram saw in 1774. There were vines tangled over everything. Hanging from the vines were green gourds.

"This is strange," Minno remembers thinking. "What are gourds doing here?"

He wondered if somebody on a houseboat had thrown supper leftovers into the river and if some kind of squash had taken root. Minno studied the gourds. They resembled no squash he had ever seen. Like many Florida naturalists, he is steeped in Bartram. Suddenly he wondered if this could be the mystery gourd of Bartram's travels.

It was not a question he felt comfortable answering. The man he needed to talk to was at the University of Florida.

Dan Ward is a 65-year-old botanist who arguably knows more about endangered plants than anyone in the state. In 1979, he wrote the book on them, *Rare and Endangered Biota of Florida*. He's updating the work now.

In Gainesville, Minno handed the professor a gourd. Ward's eyes widened. He asked to be taken to the place on the St. Johns where the gourd was growing.

A week later, they jumped into a 14-foot Boston Whaler and roared down the river that Bartram had described more than two centuries ago. Not far from Hontoon Island State Park they hacked their way through the damp underbrush. Gourds hung like Christmas tree ornaments.

Okeechobee gourds.

Ward remembers feeling a deep joy.

"This confirms the discovery of the Okeechobee gourd in the St. Johns River in 1774," Ward says now.

"Two hundred and nineteen years later we can say, 'Billy Bartram, you were right.'"

Ward sent two of the four gourds he collected to Terrence Walters at Fairchild Tropical Gardens for genetic testing. Walters agrees that the gourd is an Okeechobee gourd. Now he wants to see if it has evolved differently from the gourds found on Lake Okeechobee.

The discovery of a new population of the gourds is unlikely to change their endangered species status. Their presence in the St. Johns River basin will probably mean the state will protect them on public land along the river.

In South Florida, nursery owner Richard Moyroud is growing them commercially in an experiment. He notes that Okeechobee gourds, unlike domestic squashes and pumpkins, are resistant to fungi and mildew. Farmers who grow edible squashes spend thousands of dollars on chemicals to control fungi and mildew.

"The Okeechobee gourd could be important to agriculture," Moyroud says. "If farmers could cross-breed it with edible squashes, they could end up with something that doesn't need chemicals. That could save thousands of dollars."

Meanwhile, in Gainesville, Dan Ward has two Okeechobee gourds hanging in his office. Every once in a while he takes them down and admires them and thinks about William Bartram.

A friend recently asked to have one of the gourds. Ward, an unusually generous man, shook his head no.

"If you went into a jewelry store, and asked if you might have a diamond, would they give it to you?" Ward asks. "I'm keeping these. They're my diamonds."

Milford Myhre
plays his carillon

Lake Wales
October 1990

What Milford Myhre likes is the quiet. In fact, he demands it. When he plays his carillon at Bok Tower Gardens, one of Central Florida's loveliest places, he wants to hear the bells, and he wants his audience to hear the bells.

Shhhh. Mr. Myhre is about to begin.

Up in his tower, which overlooks the gardens, he sits at a giant wooden keyboard and works it with fists and feet. Keys are wired to clappers, which strike the bells, which produce the magical music that rings through the gardens. Groundskeepers extinguish fountains when he performs, and they switch off other machinery that might distract from the music. Tower doors are neither opened nor closed during his performance. Nothing is allowed to break the spell.

"Any noise," Milford Myhre will tell quietly, "is the enemy of music. Music should be heard from the background of silence. And that is the point of this place. It's where you get away from the mad rush of civilization."

It is quiet at Bok Tower gardens, the 128-acre wildlife sanctuary that Dutch immigrant and Pulitzer-prize winning author Edward Bok opened in 1929. It is so quiet you can hear an acorn drop. From the branch of a live oak, a careless gray squirrel looks down as if to apologize for nearly beaning you.

A gentle breeze blows through the trees, and you can hear it as well as feel it. The fronds of sabal palms rustle, and somewhere a dead branch from an orange tree creaks. A blue jay scolds a mockingbird.

But when Milford Myhre puts on a carillon concert, even nature seems to know enough to hush. At 50, he is snow-haired and formal in manner. He has been playing the carillon at Bok Gardens since 1968, and he is not to be trifled with. Shortly after lunch on a Monday, the fountains go off, the birds stop singing and Sir Arthur Sullivan's *Roses White and Roses Red* floats through the trees.

Only when the last bell has tolled does a bullfrog in the pond dare croak.

"What Mr. Bok intended as a sanctuary for wildlife," a visiting carillonneur once wrote, "has become a sanctuary for the carillon as well."

Carillons are rare in North America. Fewer than 200 exist, and many are out of tune, broken or otherwise neglected. Some have nobody to play them. Many institutions that own carillons have no money with which to pay carillonneurs. Milford Myhre is one of three full-time carillon players on the continent.

Most carillons are in the hearts of cities, where bells are drowned out by sirens, motorcycles and booming car radios. They are overpowered by the roar of lawn mowers and the neighbor's television. Air conditioners hum and the new kid on the block just got a set of Ludwig drums.

But real Floridians are lucky. We can escape noise pollution. We can drive to the very heart of the state, pay a few dollars and enter the gardens. We can bring a picnic lunch, if we wish, or buy a meal at the cafe. We can walk through an awesome collection of exotic and native vegetation. We can look at swans in the ponds, or, if we are lucky, encounter a bobcat as it hunts raccoons along the nature trails. The view of the surrounding countryside is as fine: At 295 feet, the gardens are about as high as it gets in Florida.

"I come here to find myself," a naturalist named John Burroughs once wrote Edward Bok. "It's so easy to get lost in the world."

The Bok Tower Gardens are a place for quiet reflection, and listening, too. *We Thank Thee, Lord*, the Johann Sebastian Bach cantata, opened a recent carillon recital. It seemed absolutely right.

Edward Bok spoke no English when he arrived in the United States in 1870. But he learned quickly, and saved his money to buy encyclopedias that would teach him other skills. He was 19 when he began working for book publishers, and he was 27 when he began editing *Ladies' Home Journal* and printing the works of Mark Twain and Rudyard Kipling. His autobiography, *The Americanization of Edward Bok*, won the Pulitzer.

Bok, whose green-thumbed grandfather had once transformed a barren North Sea island into a lushly vegetated bird sanctuary, began buying Central Florida property in the 1920s. Like his kin, Bok liked gardens, too. He also remembered, with fondness, the carillons of his native Netherlands. He wanted a carillon for his garden.

He hired a famous architect, Philadelphia's Milton B. Medary, to design the tower, and Horace H. Burrell & Son to build it. The marble, pink and gray, came from the best Georgia quarries. The tan coquina rock, the same kind Spaniards used when they settled St. Augustine, was the best local mines could produce. The tower, 205 feet tall, is covered with elaborate carvings and ironwork. Experts consider it a work of art.

Near the top, hanging in the belfry, are 53 tuned bronze bells. The smallest treble, whose pitch is the third A flat above middle C, weighs 17 pounds. The largest bell, pitched to the second E flat below middle C, weighs 22,300 pounds.

"It's an awesome instrument," says Milford Myhre.

Myhre, who was born in a Nebraska farming town, heard his first carillon by accident. He was a teen-ager driving the family car to piano lessons when a carillon concert came over the radio. Later, at the University of Nebraska, where he was an organ major, he got the opportunity to play the bells. He also studied in Paris, Belgium and at the University of Michigan. Since 1982 he has served as president of the World Carillon Federation. During summer, he usually tours the world and plays carillons where he can find them.

He was teaching music at an Indiana military academy, and refining his technique on the carillon, when he visited Bok Tower and Gardens in 1966. As a guest artist, he made what some people would call an impression. Anton Brees, the only carillon player the tower had ever had, died in 1967 and Myhre was appointed to the post.

Every day at Bok Tower, he either plays the carillon or puts on a tape recording of previous performances. Recitals begin promptly at 3 p.m., though he sometimes schedules concerts when the moon is full. As Shakespeare wrote: "Here will we sit, and let the sounds of music creep in our ears. Soft stillness and the night become the touches of sweet harmony."

Myhre favors the classics, both in his literature and his music, although he also includes original material and folk music in his repertoire. The other afternoon, for example, he included *Listen to the Mocking Bird* and *Swing Low, Sweet Chariot*. He played nothing from the new pop music albums—not because he hates popular music, but because the carillon is better suited for quieter numbers that offer some space between notes. Bells resonate, after all, sometimes for more than a half a minute.

For that matter, you are unlikely to hear *Flight of the Bumblebee*. Boogie-woogie would kill a carillonneur. Playing the instrument, among other things, is an athletic endeavor. The keyboard that Myhre plays with his hands, and the bass keyboard he strikes with his feet, both measure almost seven feet across. On numbers where he must play both bass and treble simultaneously, he literally stretches his body like a first baseman straining for an errant throw. When a concert is over, Myhre is typically drenched with sweat.

Recovering, he postpones meeting his public until he can shower. Then he rides the elevator to the ground floor, passes through double doors, takes a sidewalk around the moat, opens the gate and greets people at the information booth. There, he shakes hands with the people who may have come to hear him, answers their questions and thanks them for their kind words.

Carillon players, locked in their towers, seldom have contact with their audience at all. "You usually can't hear the applause," Milford Myhre says. "In some countries, people climb into their cars and honk their horns in appreciation. But that wouldn't be appropriate here. It's too quiet and peaceful to allow it."

Goose

Cortez
November 1993

Fall is Goose Culbreath's favorite time of year. When temperatures start dropping, when the air begins to feel crisp, he climbs into his ancient wood boat, cruises into Sarasota Bay and waits for the mullet to move. He drops his net, encircles the school and strikes hard. A man who knows mullet will never starve. Not in the fall.

"It's the onliest time a year I fish now," he says. "There's enough mullet and you can make some money. How I love to fish. I thank the Lord he's let me fish."

At 76, he is the grand old man of Cortez, the rustic Gulf Coast commercial fishing village of 1,450 people in west central Florida. He has walked the streets and worked the waters of Cortez for going on seven decades. Beloved for his stories about the good old days, he also is a popular musician whose lively fiddling has spiced up weddings, square dances and fish fries for generations.

"Cortez is a special place," Goose says, running his hands through thick white hair. "Wonderful, hard-working people always lived here. Even in the Depression, nobody went hungry in Cortez. There was a world of fish to eat, clams, oysters and even good scallops. I think we was the onliest town around not to go on relief."

Now hard times have come to Cortez and to commercial fishers throughout Florida. The industry is under siege from environmentalists, recreational anglers and government agencies. Although habitat destruction and pollution have damaged fish populations, many hold commercial fishers more responsible. Some groups want to ban netting. For Goose and his netting brethren, the great fall mullet seasons may be a thing of the past.

Goose has seen struggles before. When he moved as a boy from North Florida to Cortez, the village was trying to recover from the devastating 1921 hurricane that rolled across the waterfront and destroyed homes, docks and boats. "But we came back," he says. "People in Cortez are tough. They know how to survive."

Goose is not the complaining type. There was no electricity or running water when he was a child, but he remembers it as a wonderful, exciting time. Candles lit the night and cisterns collected the rain. Smoky fires chased away mosquitoes. There were gardens everywhere, and some of the fishermen cultivated coconut trees. His parents never made him wear shoes. The commercial fisherman down the sandy road had a pet cormorant that looked like a goose. The boy Julian played with it so much he got nicknamed. Even today, in the phone book, he's listed as Goose Culbreath.

When he was little, the gin-clear bays and bayous were filled with what seemed an endless supply of fish. There were no condominiums or huge housing developments or vast parking lots to funnel pollution into the water. Instead there were acres and acres of thick mangrove forests, whose decaying leaves begin the marine food chain.

Microscopic organisms ate mangrove leaves, shrimp ate the microscopic organisms, fish ate the shrimp and commercial netters caught the fish. Life had rhythm, life had purpose, life was predictable—and commercial fishers were regarded as hardworking heroes who supplied America with fresh food.

"All I ever wanted to do was fish," Goose says. "I went to school through sixth grade but I didn't like it. I just kept lookin' out the window 'cause fishin' was on my mind. . ."

He netted mullet, mackerel and pompano. He hook-and-lined for sheepshead and redfish. And when the fishing was over he took out his fiddle and played up a storm. A musical family, Culbreath men fiddled, strummed guitars, blew harmonicas and played the piano. Friends and neighbors collected on the porch and listened. Some would sip moonshine and get up and dance.

"We was known as the Cortez Grand Ole Opry," Goose says.
They would play *Orange Blossom Special, Boil Them Cabbage* and *Arkansas Traveler.* "We couldn't read a lick of music, we didn't know a flat from a sharp, but if we heard it on the radio or the juke box, we'd learn it."

He picks up his fiddle, purchased when he was a boy with $12 he earned from a job gutting Spanish mackerel. Cradling the fiddle under his chin lovingly, he readies the bow and says, "I made this here tune up fifty years ago. Just wanted to learn a new tune, you see. Call it *The Cortez Rag* . . . ."

Eyes closed, a grin on his face, he attacks the fiddle, upper torso bobbing and feet tapping. *The Cortez Rag* fills the room and drifts out the open window, a joyful gift to his neighbors. "I just love to play the fiddle," he announces. "I can still saw on a fiddle."

In the fall he would rather net mullet. A silver, cigar-shaped fish that jumps frequently and grows as big as a loaf of french bread, mullet long have been a staple of the Florida cracker diet. They are easiest to catch in the fall, when they begin gathering by the millions as part of the spawning ritual. Filled with roe and sperm, they swim in vast schools and wait for a passing cold front to trigger migration. Then they swim out of creeks, rivers and canals, through bays and bayous into the Gulf of Mexico to spawn.

Commercial fishers in modest wooden boats maneuver their monofilament nets, some 1,200 yards long, around the mullet. Terrified, the mullet try to swim through the near-invisible net and become trapped at their gills.Then the fishers, one or two to a boat, haul in the catch by hand or by winch and return to any number of waterfront businesses, where mullet are processed, iced and packed onto trucks.

When Goose was young, mullet were worth only a few pennies a pound and less desirable than pompano, mackerel and other lucrative species. But everything changed about two decades ago when Asian markets developed a taste for mullet roe.

During the fall today, mullet are worth as much as $1.50 a pound, and the waterfront is jammed with boats, nets and fishermen who are convinced they are going to get rich. A netter who hits a motherlode of fish—5,000 pounds or more—can earn in a few hours what fishers of Goose's vintage once earned in a year. Mullet bring an annual $13-million to fishers.

Yet few individual mullet fishers become wealthy. Most are independent businessmen with no corporation to support them when fishing is poor. When they fail, they don't eat. Many lack life or medical insurance. Although mullet are worth more than in the past, the costs of gas, nets and boat maintenance have also risen. Full-time fishers, at least during the fall mullet run, have to compete with an army of part-timers with their own boats and nets and dreams of easy money.

"Fishin' is feast or famine," says Goose, who owns a modest home a block from the waterfront. "A fisherman is always going to know hard times. But you learn to love the life anyway. I like to be on the water. I get fresh air to breathe. And I got nobody bossin' me."

Fishing is not getting better, for reasons that include habitat destruction, pollution, overharvesting and the new regulations. In 1964, netters landed 35-million pounds in West Florida. Last year, they got about 20-million pounds. Conservationists believe mullet stocks are dwindling. They worry that a decline will harm countless other marine species that eat mullet, which could destroy the food chain.

"There's probably too many fishermen fishin' for mullet now," Goose concedes. "But the state can't just say, 'Stop fishin'.' Don't they know people got to make a livin'?"

In his opinion, some people have no idea. On his last fishing trip, a waterfront homeowner hollered at him for netting near the entrance to a canal. "He didn't realize I been fishin' there longer than he's been alive," Goose says. "A lot of the places we used to fish ain't there anymore. Houses are. The more people you have, the worse it seems to get."

The commercial fishermen understand. Late in the day, Goose walks to the waterfront and greets old friends at the Fulford Fish House. They talk about fishing and boats and how what happened in the past was better than now.

Next he visits the pier where his 23-foot skiff is berthed. He and his friend Boogie Taylor will need it soon, state willing, to pursue mullet. Goose used to fish by himself, but two years ago he had a heart attack. He is better now, but he is afraid to pull the heavy net by himself.

"It's a good boat," he says. Fifty years old, it belonged to Goose's wife, Maida, who was among the best trout fishers in Cortez. She died eight years ago.

"Goodness, a lot of us have passed on," Goose Culbreath says. "Smiley Guthrie. Leo Taylor. Buck Jones. Woodrow Green. Jesse Williams. Tink Fulford. My, oh my. So doggone many. All gone."

Clyde's World

Ochopee
November 1993

Clyde Butcher's new yard is different than yours. Last fall, as he trudged down his driveway in the Big Cypress National Preserve, a Florida panther walked out of the trees and looked him in the eye. Clyde was flabbergasted, Clyde was thrilled, Clyde felt he was the luckiest man on earth—but Clyde also found himself thinking about sharp claws and teeth.

He said to himself: "I hope he isn't hungry."

A panther, the nation's rarest mammal, a living symbol of the wild, provokes a natural apprehension even among people who know the species has no appetite for human flesh. As his feline neighbor vanished into the cypress like a brown ghost, the man who deserves to be called the photographer laureate of natural Florida was caught without his camera. Next time, perhaps.

Clyde, who is 51, has chronicled what remains of wilderness Florida, in stunning black and white photographs, since 1986. Until recently, the former Californian drove, hiked or boated into the wild places, set up the large wood box that serves as his camera, and pressed the shutter. The result was haunting landscapes of beaches, woods and swamps.

Now, deep into a new fall, he predicts his work will change in substantial ways. He recently moved from the suburban sprawl of Fort Myers into one of America's great wilderness areas. No longer will he be just another visitor with a camera to the Big Cypress. He'll be a resident. He will be home.

"I'm going to understand this country better," he says, walking an overgrown path as mosquitoes hover. "I'm sure I'll still be doing the broad landscapes I'm known for, but I think I'll be taking more close-ups as I get to know the place a little more intimately."

The Big Cypress, which stretches for more than a half-million acres, sits in the middle of Florida's wild heart, the Everglades. Cypress trees grow out of black swamp. Otters slip between the roots—cypress roots that look like black knees—and hunt bream and catfish. Alligators stalk garfish and otters, too. Barred owls hoot from the treetops, and panthers moan. Clyde's house and gallery on the Tamiami Trail, halfway between Miami and Naples, is in the middle of it all.

"I'm so lucky to live here," he says.

He looks like a swamp man He has a beard like Spanish moss and walks through the water in bare feet. On land, he grudgingly wears sandals. The rest of his uniform is likely to be shorts held up by suspenders and maybe a work shirt. He weighs 300 pounds, but he moves almost as nimbly as his burliest neighbors, the black bears that roam this hard country.

Taking photographs the way he does constitutes an athletic feat. He does not shoot pictures from a road or a bridge or from a vehicle. Sometimes he and his wife, Niki, row a creaking skiff a mile through cypress knees to find a beautiful spot. Other times he hauls his 60-pound camera on his back and wades through waist-deep water.

He'll set the camera on a tripod in the water and wait. Sometimes he stands for hours at a time, very conscious of the alligators and the water moccasins lurking nearby. Mosquitoes cover his face and arms. He counts patience among his virtues.

He waits for the light to get right—he favors overcast days without shadows—and he waits for inspiration. What inspires Clyde Butcher? He knows it is difficult to explain: "It's not the composition of a photo. It's the emotion. The emotion I want is the feeling you get when you first walk into the woods or put your canoe into the water. I'm talking about that inner glow.

"Does that make sense?"

Out in a swamp, he'll put his head under a black hood—imagine Matthew Brady, the Civil War photographer, at work—and focus. He opens the shutter for one minute, two minutes, maybe 45 minutes. Long exposures bring out tiny details and exaggerate motion.

"The thing that's exciting about Florida is change," he says. "The water, the clouds, the diverse vegetation. It's different every time out."

A favorite spot is the Loxahatchee River, which flows out of the eastern Everglades. It's a primeval haunt where cypress trees stand like dinosaurs and shaggy ferns spring from decaying logs. But the otherworldly thing about his Loxahatchee photographs is the water. The long exposures make the slow-moving current look like molten silver.

The Loxahatchee photos—many of his photos, in fact—seem gloriously sad even as they capture the lush fertility of a Florida wilderness. The photos inspire regret in some viewers because the Loxahatchee, and places like it, are endangered by Florida's rapid development.

"My job is to record these places before they're gone," Clyde says.

Once he was a prominent California architect who helped design, among other things, San Francisco's most prominent building, the TransAmerica Tower. His hobby was photography, and Ansel Adams, the famous photographer who captured Yosemite National Park in black and white, was his inspiration.

Clyde sold enough photos in California to quit his architecture practice and take pictures full time. Soon, his savings were gone and he and Niki and their two children were homeless, living in their camper in any number of state parks.

Things improved after a wealthy businessman encountered a Butcher black-and-white in an art gallery. Believing he had discovered the next Ansel Adams, the businessman began promoting Butcher's work. Department stores, looking to sell framed photographs, bought more than a half-million pictures. Butcher soon had more money than he ever dreamed.

In 1982, he moved his family to Florida and sold his California pictures from his Fort Myers home. He investigated his new state, but only dabbled with photography. He was told that there was no market for black and white photography in Florida. Color photography didn't interest him—in his opinion, it tends to duplicate more than interpret nature—but he went out and took color pictures. Still, he felt indifferent about his own work.

It was a tragedy, in 1986, that changed his life and his art.

His 17-year-old son, sweet, introspective Ted, was killed by a drunken driver. The Butcher family plunged into depression. Clyde's father passed away two weeks after Ted's death of what seemed to be a broken heart. Ted's 19-year-old sister, Jackie, lost many of her childhood memories. Niki barely hung on. Clyde's grief was total.

He disappeared, days at a time, into the Everglades. Even summer's heat, high water and the vicious mosquitoes failed to stop him. Eventually, he brought his camera. After four months he was working in black and white again.

The result was art.

"Life is too short not to do what you want to do," he says now. "I wanted to take black and white photographs even if they didn't sell."

But they did. Butcher today is among Florida's most successful nature photographers. His photos grace the homes of United States senators, movie stars and ordinary people who respond to the mystery and beauty he captures.

He always wanted to live within the beauty and mystery of the Big Cypress. Yet he knew it was probably impossible. It's federal land with limited commercial enterprises. There was a restaurant, a gas station, a modest airstrip and an orchid business that had endured on the trail for 42 years.

Orchid Isles was owned and operated by an 84-year-old Everglades eccentric named Louis Whilden. No ordinary entrepreneur, he sometimes roamed his property along the Tamiami Trail quite nude. He had no use for New Yorkers, men with beards and families with children. Sometimes he chased them away from his door with shotgun or machete.

Twice he lumbered after the bearded Clyde, who further enraged the old man by trying to take pictures of the beautiful creek in front of the store without paying the two dollars admission. But he liked Niki, who always stepped out of her car waving admission money. On a visit more than a year ago, she learned that he planned to sell his 13-acre homestead.

In 1992, the Butchers bought it. They built a home. They opened the gallery.

On a damp, overcast day Clyde launches the canoe behind his house into the swamp. It's been raining a lot, and the swamp has come up. There is enough water for canoeing.

Clyde gingerly climbs into the stern—his great weight challenges even more stable watercraft—and points ahead. Paddles dip into the slick, dark water. The canoe slices through the cypress knees. When Clyde talks, his voice sounds too loud, as if he's shouting in church.

"Oh look at those cypress trees! Aren't they beautiful? Yeah, yeah. Resurrection Fern! Last time I was in here it was all dried up. Now it's all green! It's the rain, you know, we've had some rain. Isn't this great? Isn't this great? I love this place! LOVE IT!"

It is his church, after all. It is home.

A lethal paradise
for bears

Naples
November 1992

Pam Hawley loves nature. That is why she lives near the Everglades. But the black bear that climbed over her barbed wire fence near the clothesline tested her limits.

Inside the fence, the bear proceeded to disassemble the pen that housed the Hawley family's pet pygmy goats. Then it disassembled a goat and ate it for supper.

Pam Hawley was afraid the bear might next target her two small children, her pot-bellied pigs, llamas, chickens and peacocks. It returned the next night and feasted on another goat.

"Having a bear in your yard is in no way romantic or exciting in any way, shape or form," says Hawley, who had to protect her property with electrified fences and stronger pens. "When a wild animal eats a pet you love, you feel a sense of violation. I love wild animals, I really do. I'd feed them if I knew when they were coming. I just don't want them eating my pets."

People who have seen black bears only in zoos are often surprised to learn that Southwest Florida has bears at all, much less bears that may stand seven feet and weigh more than 600 pounds. But civilization crashes head on with wilderness in booming Collier County, where the human population has increased almost 900 percent during the last three decades and pushed farther and farther into bear territory.

It is possible to buy a compact disc player at the busy Coastland Center Mall and 10 minutes out of town see a very wild bear lumbering across the highway. In Mrs. Hawley's woodsy Golden Gate Estates subdivision, which bumps up against a national wildlife refuge, a quiet evening spent watching a *National Geographic* special about bears might be interrupted by the real thing looking for a snack in the back yard.

Bears have yet to be as common as squirrels in Collier County, of course. Most people never see them. But in some areas, an increasing number of residents are encountering them, and their delight is sometimes tempered by fear. Although there is no record of a bear attack on a human being in Florida, the state's largest native land animal has big teeth, sharp claws and an unpredictable disposition. Domesticity does not suit the very essence of wilderness.

It is early morning on the western fringes of the Everglades, Florida's last frontier, home of rattlesnakes, panthers and bears, oh my. I'm driving with Dave Maehr, a Florida Game and Fresh Water Fish Commission biologist who has roused me from slumber to accompany him on his mission.

"Today I hope I can share with you the elation of finding bear scat," he says, much too cheerful for 7 a.m.

Maehr, who is 37, hopes to show me more than bear droppings. For the last 15 months, he has been catching bears, outfitting them with radio collars and tracking their movements through the forests, swamps and even residential neighborhoods of Southwest Florida. Learning the biology of bears, how they behave and how encroaching civilization affects them are goals in Maehr's three-year project.

Few Florida counties have more undeveloped wilderness than Collier, and Maehr spends much of his time looking there for bears. Collier is home to the 570,000-acre Big Cypress National Preserve, the 70,000-acre Fakahatchee Strand State Preserve, the 24,310-acre Florida Panther National Wildlife Refuge, National Audubon's 11,000-acre Corkscrew Swamp Sanctuary, 6,500-acre Collier-Seminole State Park and a piece of 1.4-million-acre Everglades National Park. It would seem to be a bear paradise.

"All that public land is amazing," Maehr says. "But it still may not be enough."

A tide of people is sweeping from the heavily developed Collier County coast through sparsely developed bear-friendly land toward the publicly owned wilderness on the edge of the Everglades. Among the fastest growing counties in the nation, Collier in the last three decades jumped from 19,000 residents to 170,000. The population is expected to double by century's end.

Where civilization and wilderness collide so dramatically something is bound to give. Usually that something is wild animals. The Florida panther, the symbol of Florida wilderness and an animal Maehr has studied extensively, is the classic example.

Even with all the public land, panthers are in trouble. On extinction's brink, panthers have disappeared because of habitat destruction, decades of persecution by landowners and hunters, and collisions with speeding automobiles. Several have been found dead from mercury poisoning. And panthers fight and kill each other all the time.

Down to about 50 adults, the species has been further weakened by genetic problems caused by inbreeding. State and federal wildlife agencies have started a captive breeding program designed to manage reproduction and increase the population. But nobody knows whether it will work, and if it does, where additional panthers might be released. Panthers require vast wilderness territories, far away from people, and Florida is running short of those places.

South Florida's bears, designated a threatened species by the state, require vast stretches of wilderness, too. But unlike panthers, which are much more rare and intolerant of any human activity, bears can learn to make the best of shrinking territory and even learn to live within close proximity of people.

In parts of Collier County, they have little choice. "For sale" signs dot privately owned wooded tracts where bears now live. Bulldozers are knocking down slash pines. Subdivisions are on the march. New roads are going in. Convenience stores and gas stations are popping up at new intersections. Twelve thousand acres of citrus have been planted on good bear habitat since 1984. As civilization pushes into bear territory, more people are encountering what puts the wild into wilderness.

"Panthers are secretive and so interactions with people are rare," Maehr says. "But bears are different. They can get into trouble."

Hungry bears walk through yards and knock over garbage cans. Delighted homeowners rush out to offer them doughnuts. Pretty soon, the novelty wears off, and the homeowners stop feeding, but the bear has learned to associate people with food and shows up anyway.

The family cat disappears, and the game commission is called. Sometimes the game commission catches and releases the bear, an act that is usually enough to scare the bear away from suburbia forever. But some bears, once they get a taste of doughnuts, or a farmer's chickens, or a beekeeper's honey, are stubborn and return to become nuisances.

Encroaching suburbia has turned out to be a lethal paradise for the several hundred bears that live in South Florida.

About one a month gets killed crossing a highway.

A bear, dead from a gunshot wound, was found recently near a hunter's tree stand. Another was found dead from unknown causes and partly skinned.

Three other bears disappeared under mysterious circumstances. Their radio collars—cut from around their necks—were discovered in canals or on roadsides. Three others bears have been injured, possibily by irate homeowners, beekeepers or shooters. Those bears were missing eyes.

"Some people are delighted to see bears," Dave Maehr says, as we drive out Alligator Alley. "Some people abhor them. And some people are just scared. There's a growing urban sensibility out here that reflects a way of living that may not be compatible with bears."

We turn off State Road 29 into the Florida Panther National Wildlife Refuge, pass through a locked gate and drive along a dirt road. Then we enter the woods of Mud Lake Strand. There are pines and palmettos and cabbage palms. With any luck there will be *Urses americanus floridanus*, a Florida black bear.

Maehr feels the need to issue a warning.

"We've put some bait out to attract bears," he says. "The bait doesn't smell very good." The bait is a bobcat a biologist found dead on a road a few days ago. Bears are omnivorous, which means they will eat almost anything.

Maehr has placed his smelly bait, and set a series of snare traps, in an area frequented by bears. A snare is a plastic-covered steel rope. One end is attached securely to a tree. The looped end is placed on a path and covered by dirt and leaves. In the middle of the loop is a hidden spring. If a bear puts a foot inside the snare it also steps on the spring. The spring throws the snare up the bear's leg. When the bear tries to run, the snare tightens. A snare angers and frightens a bear more than hurts it.

Once and sometimes twice a day Maehr checks his snares. When he catches a bear, he tranquilizes it with a hypodermic needle attached to a long pole. When the bear is asleep, he measures and weighs it using a portable winch. Maehr, who has never been hurt by a bear, removes a tooth—he can age bears by their teeth—and tags their ears with an identifying number. Then he attaches a radio collar. The radio collar allows him to track the bear for up to three years. Fifty bears wear radio collars in Collier County. Maehr thinks the total population might number more than 100.

Maehr has worked with animals ever since he can remember. Growing up in Ohio, he caught tadpoles so he could watch them mature into frogs. He had pet box turtles and raccoons. He studied birds until he could identify them on sight and draw their pictures. He got a wildlife management degree from Ohio State, earned his master's at the University of Florida and joined the game commission in 1980.

A man of many talents, he is the co-author of *Florida's Birds*, the popular field guide. He recently illustrated a textbook called *Parasites and Diseases of Wild Mammals* in Florida. He contributed an article about bears and solar-powered electrified fences to the *American Bee* Journal. He is a national authority on Florida panthers. He coaches his son's soccer team, he can play the trumpet and he has a very strong stomach.

"Well, let's see what we've got," Maehr says, parking his truck.

What we have is the overpowering stench of decaying bobcat. Walking behind Maehr, I cover my mouth and nose and try to take short breaths. Still I gag.

"The problem with using rotten bait is that the bear will smell like that, too," Maehr says. "And I'll have to handle it."

We find no bear. Eyes watering from the smell, stomach playing roller coaster, I don't know if we're lucky or not. Maehr checks his bait at uncomfortably close quarters—he neither gags nor covers his nose—and checks his snares. Everything is okay.

"Let's look somewhere else," he says.

We return to State Road 29, where Maehr points to a place a car killed a panther last year. Heading south, we turn into a pocket of private land, owned by hunters, within the panther refuge. Panthers and bears are protected from hunting here, but the hunters are allowed to shoot deer, hogs and turkey during the fall season.

It is wilderness. Cypress trees line a pond. A snapping turtle creeps across a Jeep trail. Oaks and cabbage palms grow thickly. Bears like it here. They eat acorns and the delicate soft tissue beneath cabbage palm fronds.

Maehr has placed a culvert trap. It's a big, round pipe he has baited with corn and sardines. If a bear crawls into the trap and touches the bait, a door slams shut. Alas, we have caught no bear. Maehr adds fresh bait: six glazed and chocolate doughnuts. Maybe next time.

Maehr is disappointed with the lack of bears, but he is always delighted with bear scat. Bear poop may not seem interesting to you, but it fascinates bear biologists. Maehr kneels next to the scat and pokes it with a stick. Then he smells the stick.

"I can tell by the smell that the bear has been eating aquatic plants," he says. "Probably alligator flag." South Florida bears eat different foods than other bears, including saw grass, the dominant plant in the wetland Everglades, and berries from palmettos, an important plant found in pine forests. They also eat beetles and ants. They will take a deer or a small hog if they can catch it. They consider armadillos a gastronomic delight. Maehr scoops scat into a zip-lock plastic bag. He has collected 300 scat specimens since 1991.

"We're learning how bears behave," he says.

Sometimes, a quiet biologist can follow the radio signals emitted by a bear's collar and get close enough to observe the animal. One biologist watched a discriminating bear sniff the unripened berries of a Brazilian pepper plant and turn up its nose. Another biologist watched a bear rip apart a log and eat the termites.

Maehr recently sneaked within 30 feet of a collared, female bear. When she saw him, she woofed and ran in fright. As Maehr's eyes adjusted to the shade of the hammock, they beheld a surprising sight: a 350-pound male bear, lazing under a tree, looking at him.

"It didn't woof and it didn't snap its teeth like most bears would do in that situation," Maehr says. "That concerned me." A bear that is unafraid of people has the potential to be dangerous. Maehr retreated.

Buck Flowers moved to Rattlesnake Hammock in 1966. A fourth-generation Floridian, Flowers loved hunting and fishing and carved himself a home out of 10 fine acres in southeast Naples.

"But it's changed a whole lot," Flowers says when I telephone. "There's quite a few houses. We got lots of Yankees here now."

Flowers, 61, also has bears. Not long ago, two showed up on his property. Flowers and a few neighbors were overjoyed. They set out bowls of Cheerios, doughnuts and pancakes swimming in syrup. They trained the bears to visit on schedule.

"Sometimes I'd lie on the floor next to the sliding glass door and watch the bears on the patio," Flowers says. "They'd come right up to the door like they were trying to sniff me."

Sometimes, after filling up on doughnuts, the bears would scour the neighborhood in search of additional snacks. Some people fed them. But others were frightened to have bears in their yards, and they were angry at the bear feeders for creating a nuisance.

"Some Yankees are leery of bears," Flowers admits.

The game commission is leery about people who feed bears. One, bears are healthier when they eat natural foods. Two, bears that are fed overcome their natural fear of humans, become pests and have the potential to be dangerous.

"It's like with alligators," says Jim Schortemeyer, a commission biologist who works with Dave Maehr. "Twenty years ago you could tell people that alligators don't attack and kill people. Now you can't tell people that."

In the last two decades, there have been numerous alligator attacks on people and several fatalities. In most instances, the attacking alligators were domesticated by feeding. Black bears have killed 25 people in North America during this century, but there is no record of an attack in Florida.

"I'm not saying bears are going to attack people," Schortemeyer says. "But there's potential. We could have some serious encounters here."

Commission files are filled with records of Collier County bear encounters. Golden Gate Estates, wedged between Naples and federal and state land, is where most encounters happen. At 173 square miles, Golden Gate once was hailed as the world's largest subdivision.

A Golden Gate resident walks outside his home in his undershorts to do a quick chore. When he returns to his modest house, a bear is blocking the only door and his access to pants. The scantily clad fellow is compelled to visit his neighbor, who doesn't call the vice squad but kindly notifies the game commission, which tranquilizes and moves the bear.

A bear claws through a screened porch to get at garbage. A bear kills a cat. A dog disappears shortly after bears have shown up in the neighborhood to take advantage of free food.

A bear shows up in the yard of a Golden Gate homeowner and is chased up a tree by two dogs. The homeowner reports: "The bear smelled like an old wet rug."

A bear that has been routinely fed peeps through a window and alarms a homeowner. A game commission biologist chases Peeping Bear into the woods. The bear stops, leans against a tree and looks back. The biologist fakes a charge and the bear scrambles up the tree. The biologist shoots the bear with a tranquilizer dart and the bear slides to the ground. It is fitted with a radio collar and released.

Looking for food, a bear strolls into a residential neighborhood, prompting calls to the game commission. Dave Maehr and a dozen uninvited homeowners give chase. The bewildered bear flees. Maehr fires a tranquilizer dart. Clinging to consciousness, the bear tries to hide in a palmetto thicket.

"I gave everyone a thrill by crawling in after it and injecting it by hand," Maehr says. The bear is fitted with a collar and released.

A black bear destroys a beehive in Bob Best's yard one night, eats the bees and drinks the honey. "It also clawed a pine tree, urinated and left a pile of feces," says Best, whose previous home was on the 23rd floor of a Chicago condominium. The bear returns during the next two nights for additional meals. Until he puts up an electrified fence Best loses $900 worth of hives.

"My experience with bears was limited, unpleasant and aggravating," he says. "I felt hostile and very powerless."

The commission catches a chicken-coop-raiding bear in Golden Gate and outfits it with a radio collar. In the next three months the 200-pound bear travels north nearly 100 miles, crosses major highways, wide-open pastures and the Calasoohatchee River, raids unprotected beehives and chicken coops, and finally ends up near Central Florida's Lake Placid—where it hangs around a Fourth of July picnic unafraid of even the fireworks.

Because the bear shows no fear of humans, because it continues to damage livestock, commission personnel kill it. A subsequent necropsy reveals old gunshot wounds.

Maehr writes in his report: "Clearly, the perceived need for the protection of human life and property versus the ecological or aesthetic value of a single wild animal is a difficult management problem."

At noon we drive along Everglades Boulevard through a part of Golden Gate Estates where there are still more trees than houses. I keep expecting to see a deer or a bobcat jump the road. We're looking for the two big dumpsters that serve the growing neighborhood. The dumpsters are probably the best place in Collier County to see bears.

"Even in the daytime," Maehr says.

The bears have been feasting. The ground is littered with cans, bottles, plastic jugs, cardboard food boxes. Some cans show puncture marks.

From the back of the truck Maehr takes out a radio receiver, dials a number and holds up what looks like a little television antenna. The receiver begins to beep. Maehr says we're picking up a signal from the radio collar of Bear No. 16. She's a young female, about 125 pounds. She's close.

We step off the road and follow a path trampled over the months by the feet of many bears. There are more cans, bottles and jugs. There is a paper plate licked clean.

There is a log shredded by bear claws. There's a pine that's been used as a scratch pole.

Maehr holds his receiver in front of him and listens as he walks. The bear is east of us and seems to be still. Maehr says it's possible to sneak up on a bear if we are quiet and lucky.

I have seen bears only in Great Smoky Mountain and Yellowstone national parks. But I was in a car then, separated from the wild by German steel and Pittsburgh safety glass. It's more exciting to trail a bear through the woods on foot. That's how the Calusa Indians, and the Seminoles who came after, stalked them. They killed bears with spears and arrows for the skin, meat and fat. Modern men chase bears for information. But our hearts still pound.

Sweat drips down our faces as we creep through thickets so dense our feet stay hidden. We pass through cabbage palm and palmetto, swamp fern and Virginia creeper. I hope I don't step on a rattlesnake. I am glad I carry a compass.

Beep. Beep. Beep.

Maehr stops and listens to his receiver. The bear is moving. Above us, a small plane banks and turns. It's a coincidence, but a commission biologist is in the plane, monitoring the position of the bear, too. Maehr waves to the pilot, who circles a thicket ahead. We are close. Very close.

A machete would be nice. But it would make too much noise. Grapevines entangle our legs. I try to fall once, but vegetation prevents me from hitting the ground. We stop, kick away vines, move ahead and stop again to clear vines from our legs. It's work. Maehr stays fit by swimming 10 miles a week.

We're about a half mile in now. Maehr and his radio receiver turn again, north. The bear is just ahead, sitting still, hidden among the vines and palmettos and wild coffee, only 30 feet away. A wild bear. A wild bear trained to eat human garbage. We move as quietly as we can, but we're clumsy humans, and dead branches explode under our feet like cherry bombs.

When a frightened bear runs, it doesn't worry about being quiet. It crashes through the underbrush like a Jeep run amok. It crashes through the palmettos and breaks through the grapevines and barrels through the dog fennel.

"There she goes," Dave Maehr says. "There goes our bear."

The last wild man

Chokoloskee
October 1993

Loren G. "Totch" Brown, Everglades folk hero and former prison inmate, says he is going to run back to the house to fetch his radio. He abandons me at the dock, all alone with the ravenous salt marsh mosquitoes he calls "skeeters" or "swamp angels." As I wait in his boat, hidden in the mangroves, bedeviled by swamp angels, I yield to temptation and douse myself with repellent as if it were holy water.

Totch, wrinkled and brown like an old snapping turtle, never bothers with bug dope. When he was growing up, he learned to tolerate swamp angels, or stand in the smoke of a campfire, or hide himself behind netting, or get his boat up on a plane and speed away from them. The Florida of his boyhood, gone so many years now, was a hard land.

There was no electricity or running water or supermarkets or other signs of civilization. The people who settled here, in the Ten Thousand Islands of Southwest Florida, made do with kerosene lanterns and cisterns to collect rain water. They grew their own vegetables, caught their own fish and killed their own meat, including, on the most desperate of occasions, the gentle manatees that tasted like gamey pork.

Women died in childbirth. Babies, miles from the nearest doctor, succumbed to childhood diseases. During the day, folks prayed to Jesus and helped their neighbors. At night, as the corn liquor took hold, men settled feuds with fists, knives and guns.

Civilized society and its many restraints were a long, long way from this land of moonshiners, smugglers and alligator poachers. Totch, the last wild man in one of the wildest places on the map, learned to ignore laws he disagreed with. Eventually, one of his indiscretions landed him behind bars, but even now, at the age of 73, he does not get misty-eyed about his crimes.

"Hell," he tells folks, "probably not a thing I'd do different."

Totch has a new—and perfectly legal—career now. He is author of *Totch: A Life in the Everglades*, published by University Press of Florida, and the first book he has ever read. In a video documentary, released in English and German, he chats about his adventures in *Tales of the Everglades*. He is a regular guest on the Southwest Florida talk-show circuit, where he is revered as a story teller.

As I stand among the mosquitoes, temporarily protected by an oily sheen of repellent, Totch returns to the dock, grumbling and lugging his VHF radio. "Used to be I never brought a radio," he complains. But after three heart attacks and a quadruple bypass, he is aware of his own mortality. A radio might come in handy even for an old outlaw.

He cranks the engine, adjusts his baseball cap, coughs, spits and points his boat for Everglades National Park, which is still Florida's last frontier and Totch Brown's back yard.

I spent my youth in the Everglades, fishing and fooling with snakes. But I never felt at ease in the Ten Thousand Islands—they were too wild and forbidding and bug-infested for a true city boy. On my rare fishing or canoeing excursions to the water wilderness, I constantly referred to charts and compass and landmarks, certain I would become hopelessly lost the instant I ventured out of a marked channel.

The idea of seeing this part of the Everglades with the last of the wild men was irresistible.

The land where he was born, and has seldom left, is the largest roadless area in the lower 48 states. It is home to alligators, crocodiles, moccasins, panthers, bears and the most ferocious mosquitoes on the planet. It has pine forests, sawgrass prairies and cypress swamps. But his world is dominated by a labyrinthine system of mangroves, dense and forbidding for hundreds of miles.

"I was always in too damn big a hurry to get after them fish and birds and gators to appreciate this when I was young," Totch drawls, as we cut across Chokoloskee Bay toward Turner River. "But I slowed down some, and now I'm smellin' the roses."

"It's gorgeous," I say.

"It is," he agrees, "but it's never gonna be like it was when I was growin' up in the '30s. It was some world back then, a way of life you can hardly explain to civilized folks. They was hardships—all them skeeters and no money an' sometimes nothin' much to eat. But I wouldn't trade them days. It was a life of complete freedom."

His great-grandparents were among the first white settlers in mangrove-choked Chokoloskee Island. Their neighbors were Seminole Indians who came to trade in dugout canoes. His dad built boats and shot bear, panther and alligator, including a hungry 11-footer that once tried to climb into a boat and eat Totch's brother, Peg.

"I hollered and Peg jumped out onto the beach just in time."

As a boy, Totch trapped and hunted raccoons to supply fur to the raccoon coat industry. Sometimes, as he looked for raccoons, he was frightened by the growls of panthers. From his own boat he netted mullet, collected oysters and hauled crab traps.

During Prohibition, when the sale of alcohol was illegal, Everglades smugglers brought rum into the United States from the Bahamas. Once the smugglers made it into the impossible maze of mangroves, they were hard to catch. A federal agent, sent to investigate, once tried. He went out and never returned. After Prohibition, the smuggling stopped, but liquor violations continued anyway. Local people wanted cheap whiskey, and Totch's daddy wanted to make it. A carpenter, boat builder and pillar of the community, he was one of the Everglades' most prolific moonshiners.

"I don't wanna brag on him, but he was always too smart to fish," Totch says. "He had stills hidden all through these woods." He slows the boat and points to a spot in the mangroves where Indians over centuries dumped oyster shells to create high ground.

"Dad had a nice still back there. It was a dandy."

As we leave the Turner River, and approach the entrance to Lopez River, a flock of white ibis flies just above the water. They were a staple of Totch's boyhood diet, especially during the Depression, and they numbered in the thousands. As the Everglades was ditched and drained, as water levels fell, the population of ibis and other wading birds dropped precipitously. Hunting—but not the development responsible for the decline of wading birds—was outlawed.

"We called 'em curlew or Chokoloskee chicken," Totch says.

I ask if they tasted like chicken.

"No way! Never been no chicken that good," he goes on, a little too fondly for the present. "You could fry 'em, you could stew 'em. They was good anyway you cooked 'em. They had a thick breast you had to split in two. Lotsa meat."

A new pair of immature ibis soars over the mangroves and heads upriver.

"We called the young-uns 'fryers.' We'd sit in our skiffs and shoot 'em when they flew over the islands."

I ask if he is ever tempted to bring his shotgun and shoot himself supper.

"Jeff," he says, looking me in the eye. "I'm not only tempted, I do it sometimes. Does that answer your question?"

For years people had been telling Totch he should write a book. So one day, a couple of years ago, after he got out of prison, he picked up a pencil and started. At first, he intended just to put down the history of the Everglades as he knew it. "But the more I wrote 'bout myself, the more excited I become," he says, as we cross Sunday Bay and head for House Hammock Bay and Huston Bay beyond.

With no schooling beyond seventh grade, he stewed about his spelling and grammar. So he gave his manuscript to better-educated friends to fix up. When his current publisher decided to buy his book, new editors worked on it even more. But they have left in enough of Totch's way of saying things to get across his personality.

His advice on dealing with swamp angels:

A smudge pot helps, and a good one can be made by cutting the top of a five-gallon gas can and putting about six inches of shell in the bottom. In this county there's a black mangrove tree. After it's dead for a number of years, the sap part of the tree becomes crumbly. Put some on top of the shell in your smudge pot, light it, and you'll get a good smoke that helps run skeeters off. Once they're gone, don't walk in the woods nearby unless you have to. If you do, you'll bring back a whole new bunch of skeeters every time.

Out in his boat, we're moving fast enough to avoid skeeters, deer flies, sand flies, wasps, honeybees, and other winged denizens; chiggers, too. Totch slows the boat and ties up to a dock on the Chatham River, where all manner of biting insects await.

Totch lived here when he was a boy in a two-story house shaded by a poinciana tree. The house burned years ago, after the National Park Service took over. Now there's a portable toilet and a picnic table swallowed by the grass. It's a park campsite.

Mosquitoes make me part of the food chain.

Invisible predators burrow into my bare arms and legs. Totch, grizzled Everglades veteran, knows better than to wear shorts and T-shirts during bug season. He wades into towering grass looking for something only he would know is here. He shows me Ed Watson's old cane syrup kettle.

Watson lived here at the turn of the century, supporting himself by hunting, fishing and farming. When he visited Chokoloskee, he minded his manners and paid bills on time. Yet his neighbors had mixed emotions about him.

They thought he was a murderer.

Some folks claimed Watson fled to the Everglades after killing the infamous outlaw Belle Starr in Oklahoma. Others were less sure. But they were convinced Watson occasionally knocked off farm workers who toiled on his island and were bold enough to ask for their pay. Totch, who grew up hearing Watson stories, who passed them on to writer Peter Matthiessen for his acclaimed novel, *Killing Mister Watson*, thinks Watson was simply a mean, bad-tempered man with an itchy trigger finger.

"It happened in nineteen-ten," Totch says, beginning a story he has told many times. "Three bodies come a-floatin' down the river. The people in Chokoloskee, they knew Watson done it. So one day they hear him comin'—you could hear his boat motor a long way off—and they get ready. They say, 'Watson, the killin' has got to stop. Give up your arms.' Watson says wait a minute—he didn't kill those people, but he knows who done it. He says he'll bring the killer in.

"A while later, Watson comes back to Chokoloskee. The men in town are waitin' for him on the dock. Watson, he's got a hat with a hole in it in one hand, and his shotgun in the other, when he steps on the dock. Watson says, 'He wouldn't come. I had to kill him.' The men say, 'Watson, that ain't good enough. Give up your arms.'

"Well, he pretends like he's throwin' his shotgun down, but then swings it up on the people on the dock and pulls the triggers for both barrels. The gun pops—shells was made with paper back then and they had got all wet. So Watson reaches for his thirty-eight. A man shoots a hole in him. Then everybody else opens up. They say there was thirty-eight bullets in him when it was over.

"My mother seen it from the beach that day. She was seventeen."

A day with Totch goes like that. He tells stories and points out the sights. We see ospreys, roseate spoonbills and more Chokoloskee chickens than even Totch could devour.

Thinking about Totch's heart condition, and worrying whether I could find my way to civilization if he fell ill, I constantly ask where we are. We see no people, no boats, no signs of civilization except for empty park campsites. We're alone in this mangrove wilderness.

"Everywhere I look I got memories," Totch says, eating a piece of mullet for lunch.

In the 1930s, when the craze for raccoon coats died in northern cities, Totch had no income except for commercial netting. But fishing was good, and he felt prosperous enough to propose to Estelle Demere. Totch was 17 and she was 14 when they married. They have been together 56 years, and she jokes that she married Totch because he was the only man on the island who was not kin. He calls her "the Queen of the Everglades."

They still hold hands.

During World War II, commercial fishers received farm deferments. But Totch enlisted and was wounded in the Battle of the Bulge. After healing, he returned to the front. On April 18, 1945, Totch and his men were pinned down by German machine gun fire. Totch, crawling through the Bavarian thicket like a she-coon hunting oyster crab in the mangroves, heaved a hand grenade among the enemy. He was awarded the Bronze Star.

"The skills I'd learned shootin' and survivin' in the 'glades helped me," Totch tells people.

Back home, he warred against poverty. Fishing and crabbing put food on the table but provided few luxuries. Two of his children died, one in a boat fire and another from having an enlarged heart. Urban Florida, all the while, was growing fast. Miami and Naples pushed toward the Everglades, threatening to overwhelm it and its rugged people.

In 1947, President Truman visited Everglades City, across the bay from Chokoloskee Island, to dedicate a new Everglades National Park. Nature lovers celebrated, but Everglades residents who had long fed their families in the wilderness worried about changes federal ownership might bring.

"The park didn't do the Everglades no good," Totch says now.

Everglades hunters, from the men of Chokoloskee to the Seminole Indians before them, had periodically burned the sawgrass prairies and piney woods to clear dead vegetation and promote new forage for deer and other game. Though scientists consider fire part of the Everglades' natural landscape today, it was different when the park was born. To Totch's disgust, park rangers fought even lightning-caused blazes.

"When they stopped the fires, they changed the woods and chased off all the game," Totch says now. "Good huntin' disappeared. I snuck in once and started a fire, but it wasn't enough."

Fire-fighting rangers were just one problem. Pretty soon, the park began evicting "squatters" who were living on islands within park boundaries; outside the park, the Army Corps of Engineers was constructing 1,400 miles of canals to further drain the Everglades. Some of the evicted old-timers, who had spent their lives on wilderness islands, never felt at home even in tiny, remote villages like Chokoloskee or Everglades City. As water levels went down, wildlife populations plummeted. There were fewer fish to catch. Eventually, the park banned all commercial fishing.

"The park took away our way of life," Totch declares, and we disappear into Alligator Creek.

"Man, did I kill some gators in here!"

Totch is maneuvering his boat through a narrow, winding mangrove creek that is so overgrown we have to duck limbs that stretch over the water. Crabs scuttle along branches. Deer flies hover. With no map to study—Totch's map is in his head—I'm completely lost within the mangrove void. If I were alone, I would have turned back a long time ago. But I am with Totch, and Alligator Creek is one of his favorite places in the world.

"During the summer, during the rainy season, the gators, they'd follow the fresh water down the marshes into mangrove creeks like this," he says.

To me, the creek looks unpromising in every way.

"No, they was huge gators in here," he insists. "I'd go in at night, with my gun, and I'd get a lotta gators."

It was quite illegal.

"Oh, the park started to enforce the law, and I had to be real careful. I gave up my shotgun—it made too much noise—and went down to a twenty-two rifle. It was much quieter.

"I'd float down the creek with a spotlight. You could see the gator eyes a-glowin' back under the mangroves. They'd lie there watchin' you."

"It must have been some difficult shooting."

"Oh, it was," he says, taking advantage of a chance to boast. "You had a target 'bout as big as a nickel. I'll tell you: I liked nothin' better than puttin' a ball right in a gator's eye. It was a real challenge."

Most nights, he'd kill about 30 alligators and take them into the mangroves for skinning. Then he'd smuggle the skins back into Chokoloskee. During the 1960s, the nation's alligator population came close to crashing because of illegal hunting. But Totch, sneaking into the great swamp, didn't notice a shortage.

Rangers knew he was killing gators. But they couldn't arrest him unless they saw him hunting or caught him with the skins. One night, a stubborn ranger—Totch called him Little Eddie—hid outside Gator Creek in Sunday Bay and waited in the dark.

Totch was racing around a bend, his boat loaded with alligator skins, when Little Eddie's boat light illuminated him. Totch accelerated, with Little Eddie on his trail in a faster boat, and headed toward a sandbar that Little Eddie didn't know about. Totch sideswiped the sandbar; Little Eddie ran aground. Totch hid the gator skins and went home to Estelle and the kids. Little Eddie went home without the last wild man.

He was never caught with skins. He was never arrested.

"Funny thing, I don't like to kill nothin' anymore. I mean, sometimes I feel like puttin' a Band-Aid on a grasshopper I run over. But, you know, I guess if I had to do it over, I'd be swattin' skeeters with one hand and shootin' gators with the other."

In the 1970s, drug smuggling came to the Everglades. Totch, and a lot of older men, resisted. But younger men told them marijuana was no more dangerous than moonshine.

Still, Totch's wife cried when he told her what he was thinking about doing. When he pointed out their lack of medical insurance, his need for expensive heart surgery, and the fact that he could no longer earn a living fishing in the park, she said he could try it.

Just once.

But Totch didn't stop after one trip. He made many. He'd take his boat far into the Gulf of Mexico, meet the "mother ship," load marijuana and then return in the dark to the mangroves where he could hide himself better than anybody.

Before long, he went into business for himself, taking shrimp boats to Colombia and loading them with heavy bales of marijuana. He had several close calls, but never was arrested, and when he retired in 1981, he says he was $2-million richer.

Other people were rich, too. A lot of men in Chokoloskee and Everglades City, for the first time in their lives, had real money. Most had no idea how to spend it.

Some bought Cadillacs and gold jewelry. The federal government took notice.

Totch had tried to be discreet with his cash. He'd given much of it to family and friends, paid bills, invested in some Panama tanning parlors and hidden the rest. Still, he had a reputation, and maybe somebody notified the authorities.

One day, two men wearing suits—a startling sight in Chokoloskee—knocked on his door and introduced themselves as Internal Revenue Service agents. He threw them off his property, then called his lawyer.

His lawyer had bad news. Totch was part of a big federal investigation of drug smuggling in the Everglades. After some plea bargaining, Totch admitted to authorities only that he had defrauded the government of tax money—the same crime that landed Al Capone in the iron hotel. A sentencing date was scheduled, and even the *Miami Herald* took special interest.

"How do you sentence a man like Totch Brown?" the editorial asked. "A veteran of the Battle of the Bulge, a Bronze Star winner, with near 50 years of close family ties, who handed out thousands of dollars to his neighbors in need and was never in serious trouble before."

In court, the judge took his background into account:

"Mr. Brown, you rendered your country—my country—a great service in World War II, you've had a good life and you've been a credit to your community. On the other hand, somewhere along the line you got into a business that was a disservice to a lot of people."

The judge fined him $1.25-million—Totch paid in cash—and sentenced him to 15 months. Later, he got 18 months added to his sentence for refusing to testify against his friends. Eventually, federal prosecutors gave up trying to make him talk and dropped those charges. Totch was 64 when he entered a Kentucky federal penitentiary. He was a guest for more than a year.

"I deserved to be punished for my wrongs," he says now. We're in Lostman's River, headed for the gulf. "I don't have no complaints. I couldn't have been treated better in prison."

"But you were accustomed to a free life outdoors," I say.

"I was an old man and had slowed down. I had a good wife who wasn't gonna run out on me. It was harder on the younger men."

As we near Chokoloskee, civilization begins to inturde. High-tech fishing boats roar by. We see an Everglades tour boat stuffed with tourists—now the leading industry in the western Everglades. Along the shore there are convenience stores, marinas, resorts and recreational vehicle campgrounds.

"It's hard gettin' used to," Totch says as we near his modest concrete home, and I understand he is talking about more than all the tourists. The outstanding fishing he knew as a boy is now just a memory. Few modern Floridians are likely to consider alligator poaching, or drug smuggling, very romantic. Old friends are dead. His way of life is, too.

We climb into the car and head for his home.

"I used to see people sittin' on their porches after supper, tellin' the old stories to the young people," Totch laments, looking out the window. "Now nobody's on their porches."

As we pull into his driveway, I am thinking about the changes an old Everglades wild man like Totch Brown has seen during his lifetime.

"Now, after supper, everybody runs for the TV," he thunders. "The other night, I saw people screwin' on TV! People let their kids watch that garbage! TV, it's a terrible thing."

Hugo's crossings

Homestead
December 1993

Hugo Vihlen reads books but says he is no literary man. A literary man might ask himself the question "why." He doesn't—isn't interested.

Why has he twice sailed across the Atlantic Ocean, alone, in tiny boats hardly bigger than a coffin?

"I really don't know," says the 62-year-old retired airline pilot, former Marine, tough guy.

Literary men and their infernal "whys"—their eagerness to psychoanalyze—annoy him. Staring out his car window at South Florida's congested U.S. 1, he pauses.

"I'm a doer," he finally says. "Not a talker."

After his first transatlantic voyage,which took 85 days in 1968, a literary man asked if he would do it again. Hugo said "Hell, no. It was torture." Hugo meant the part about not going again. His boat had been a fraction under six feet in length, he had hallucinated while at sea, and he believed he had set a record that would never be broken.

But there are other adventurous men in the world and they kept trying to outdo him in smaller boats. The thought of them gnawed at Hugo. Two years ago, as he was planning another trip, his worst fear came true when a British sailor crossed the Atlantic in a record five-foot four-inch boat.

Hugo felt he had no choice but to definitely try again. Hugo's wife Johnnie didn't want him to go. In 1968, she was sick with worry and spent the nearly three months he was away hardly five feet from the telephone hoping for a word about him that never came. Hugo's radio had stopped working.

Now her husband was preparing for another dangerous trip. Hugo was an athletic 61, but too old in Johnnie's opinion. Hugo said he was not too old; he was mature and experienced. She just knew the boat was going to sink. No, Hugo said, the boat won't sink. He smashed a ball-peen hammer against the space-age hull material to demonstrate its strength. Johnnie still opposed her husband.

Johnnie said she wouldn't sit at the phone and wait this time. She said she'd travel, get away from home, not worry about him. Hugo said he understood, and he knew he was being selfish, but that he had to go anyway, even if he didn't know why.

"I'm different than most people," he says.

He was born in the little southeast Florida community of Homestead when it was an Everglades outpost. The child of poor farmers, Hugo grew up with no indoor plumbing, and he was 15 before he lived in a house with electricity.

He was the baby in the family and spent much of his time in his own company. Alone he hunted quail in the open fields and shot deer in the deepest woods and hauled in bass from the river of grass. He never worried about encounters with alligators or rattlesnakes. He could take care of himself.

"I didn't mind being alone."

When he was a high school senior, he and a friend built a sailboat on which they explored Biscayne Bay. That satisfied his sense of adventure for a while. Then, after graduating from the University of Florida, he joined the Marines and flew airplanes in the Korean War.

Back home, he had a small business taking people fishing, sailing and scuba diving. Then he started flying airplanes for Delta, which employed him 35 years.

In the late 1960s, he read a book about a man who sailed the Pacific in a 21-foot boat. Hugo thought he might try to sail the Atlantic in such a craft. Then he read about a man who crossed the Atlantic in a 13-footer. Soon, another sailor broke the record in an 11-foot boat.

Hugo almost gave up the idea. Then he saw an eight-foot pram in a marina. Such a boat might be made seaworthy. He built one out of plywood, but sawed almost two feet off the bow so it would be smaller, by far, than any transatlantic boat in history.

His triumph over the Atlantic Ocean made all the newspapers in 1968. He was invited on the "Today" show. President Johnson sent him an autographed picture. The state of Florida honored him. Homestead featured him in a parade. The Miami Seaquarium named its star attraction, a Killer whale, after him. A book followed.

Peace returned to the Vihlen household. Johnnie forgave him. They watched their son grow straight and strong. Dana, an athlete like his dad, was the national acrobatics champion. Once, when the boy fell off his motorcycle and cut his face, Hugo told him, "You can't live in a house all your life. You're going to get hurt." Dana became an Air Force pilot and now flies commercial jets just as his old man did.

Twenty-five years passed and Hugo's glory faded. He bought himself a Harley and broke bones before taming it. He retired from Delta. All the while he was watching over his shoulder for up-and-coming sailors, those daring younger men, poised to steal his record.

Johnnie kept her eyes on Hugo.

Hugo and Dana built the boat in Dana's garage so Johnnie wouldn't have to watch. "We didn't want to rub her nose in it," Hugo says. They were helped by a shipwright who said, "It's the largest model I ever worked on and the smallest boat I ever built."

Hugo's boat, which he called *Father's Day*, resembled a fat turnip. It was five feet four inches and about as deep. It was 30 inches wide and weighed 1,500 pounds. He invested $30,000 in it.

In 1968, Hugo had navigated, badly, with a sextant. This time he had the best electronic navigation equipment. He had solar panels to keep it working. He had airtight compartments to keep dry his Desert Storm "Meals Ready To Eat" food. He had equipment to make drinkable water out of salt.

The U.S. Coast Guard said his boat was unsafe and threatened to confiscate it if he tried to leave a U.S. port. He tried and the Coast Guard towed him to shore but let him keep his boat. Last June 14 he left St. John's Harbor in Newfoundland and headed for open ocean.

Everything went well at first. He was entertained by dolphins and birds and passing ships. He had brought a dictionary to study, *a World Almanac* and a couple of adventure tales, *Return With Honor, The Story of a Shipwrecked Sailor* and *Rowing to the Amazon*. The rowing book fell apart and he threw it overboard. The others he read several times.

Big whales circled him more than once. "I don't know what kind of whales they were. Big-ass whales." He knew the story of *Moby Dick* and worried. "A big whale will ram your boat." They let him be with his lonely thoughts.

In storms, he sealed himself below the deck—at five feet eight he was four inches too tall to stretch out—and waited. His boat was designed to right itself after capsizing, but he never turned over. Salt water leaked into the boat, though, and sponging it out of the cockpit by the hour, his fingernails split. Salt water sores developed all over his body.

"That happens to everyone. You just get used to it."

He tried to think of everything. During bad weather he tried to shut down his digestive system by eating only high-energy candy bars. Anything more and he would risk being washed overboard if he had to hang over the side when answering nature's call.

His expensive radio equipment, damaged by salt water exposure, stopped working. With his weaker shortwave he twice contacted the passing *Queen Elizabeth II* and four times talked to airliners overhead, asking them to message his wife. He felt depressed for her. He knew how she worried.

The wind died, the ocean became as flat as a pond and he made no progress. Then the wind blew against him and he lost ground. For a month he hardly advanced. He tried to shut down his mind because the act of thinking was terrible for his morale. "I stopped focusing on progress. I just worried about that day.

"I became a zombie."

As he neared Europe, and began running out of food, he encountered passing ships who hailed him as a hero. A French ship gave him bread, wine and cheese. A Spanish ship gave him apples and oranges.

On Sept. 27, the 106th day of his voyage, after what he believes was almost 5,000 zig-zag miles of open ocean, he came ashore in the south of England. His legs wobbled. Hugo had always looked with contempt on emotional men, but when he saw Johnnie waiting for him, he cried.

"Don't do that," Johnnie said, startled at his tears.

Hugo Vihlen has been back in the United States about two months now. He has regained the 34 pounds he lost at sea. But he complains about feeling weak and taking naps. It makes him feel foolish.

People—those literary-minded people—keep asking him why he did it. Many suggest there must be something important missing in his life, that maybe he is crazy.

"I hate the word *crazy*," he says.

"I'm not crazy. There are people who run hundreds and hundreds of miles to train for a marathon. Shit! They're crazy."

Driving through Homestead, heading for his home, he stews about these people who dare question him, these couch potatoes, these dullards, these people who go through life as spectators and never accomplish anything worth talking about.

"I'm a doer," he says.

He has gotten media attention, but not like 1968. There has been no letter from the President or testimonials from the Florida Legislature. His home town newspaper, the *Miami Herald*, wrote stories, but not enough to suit him. The "Today" show didn't call this time. Only "Inside Edition," the tabloid television show he dislikes, bothered.

"I wasn't even the highlight. A kid who murdered his parents was. Jesus Christ! You'd think what I did was more interesting than a murder. It's unbelievable what the media thinks is news. AIDS or murder. I'm sick of AIDS and murder."

At home, the press clippings he has managed to accumulate cover a coffee table. Hugo would like to use the clips and write another book. Maybe Johnnie will file the clippings soon.

"I'm still mad at him," she says, and Hugo is quiet. "I think I'm braver than him."

Right after he returned from his voyage, Hugo told her he would never sail the ocean again. And he meant it when he told her. But now, as time has gone by, he just doesn't know.

Earlier, when Johnnie wasn't in the room, Hugo had said: "Anybody who tries to beat my record had better stand by. If they beat me, I'll try again. I got to."

The Conch reunion

Ocala
September 1990

The smell of conch fritters, frying in deep fat, wafts through the oak trees. Grace Fallon breathes deeply, looks at me and smiles. Wonderful food smells, and the people collecting around her, stir sweet memories.

"It's almost like home," she says.

Home, for Grace Fallon, once was Key West. A few years ago, she grew tired of it. There were too many people to suit her, the cost of living on the tourist-drenched island was higher than her bank account could bear, and the small-town Latin atmosphere she remembered from childhood was gone. Like a lot of disgruntled Conchs, the nickname for native old-time Key Westers, she and her husband moved away to find a new paradise.

But in Ocala, her new residence, homesickness set in. Mrs. Fallon, 64, fretted awhile. Then, in what she admits was the best idea of her life, she organized a reunion for Conchs and held it in Ocala.

About 20 people came to her first reunion 1983. Last year's attracted 400 people. They included former Conchs from Tennessee and a busload of elderly Conchs from Key West. When the reunion was over, and it was time to board the bus, many of the old Key Westers cried.

Today when I visit the pavilion at the Ocala boat basin, nearly 300 former Conchs have gathered even though thunderstorms threaten. I'm glad to be here. When I was a boy, my family lived, briefly, in Key West. I have many warm memories.

"There aren't very many real Conchs left in Key West," Mrs. Fallon, a third-generation Conch, tells me. "Most of us see more people we know at the reunions than we do when we visit Key West."

A colorful working-class town for most of the century, famous for the Caribbean culture, sponge diving, fishing, cigars and well-known authors, Key West began changing dramatically about two decades ago. Some of those changes, Conchs will tell you, were unwelcome.

Drug-smuggling brought crime and corruption to their island, they lament, while uninhibited young people, collectively known as hippies, stayed to watch the sunsets, smoke pot and hang out. In the 1970s, Key West was discovered by the nation's gay community, who liked the town's tolerance of non-traditional lifestyles well enough to buy homes and start businesses. Developers, realtors and land speculators also found reasons to appreciate Key West. They could make a lot of money.

Today, the three- by five-mile island attracts about 1.5 million tourists a year. Young people who sport the latest hairstyles, clothing and attitudes vacation at pricey hotels, spend small fortunes at art galleries, drink pina coladas at fancy nightclubs that hold Hemingway lookalike contests, and devour gourmet meals at restaurants that accept all manner of credit cards. Key West and the rest of Monroe County have the highest cost of living in the state.

Disgruntled Conchs began migrating in significant numbers to Central Florida in the early 1970s. Some chose Tampa, with its Latin population and its ties to the cigar industry. Ocala, a former cigar mecca and at the time a small conservative town, also attracted old-fashioned Conchs. Central Florida was less costly than Key West, too.

"Many of us just couldn't afford to live there anymore," says 70-year-old Mario Blanco, who moved to Orlando two decades ago and who recently put his house up for sale. Orlando has gotten too big for him. He won't resettle in Key West.

"I miss Key West," he says. "I miss it a lot. When I visit the island, I'm always disappointed. Now it's a crowded place just for tourists. Outsiders have taken over. The town's not run by Key Westers any more."

At the Conch reunion, two hours from the nearest salt water—under oaks and pines instead of mangroves and gumbo limbos—Conchs rule. They dance the rhumba and mamba. At the reunion, good talk is as important as music. Ex-Conchs tell about the good old days, when they could leave doors unlocked and forget about wearing shoes and catch snapper on cane poles and never have to worry about their children snorting cocaine.

"When I started out there was hardly any crime to speak of," says Harry Sawyer Sr., born 64 years ago in Key West, where he was sheriff for three decades. "Now there's drugs, murders, just about any crime you could think of. Hell, I started bein' a sheriff in the early 1950s and it was in the 1960s before I think I investigated a homicide."

Sawyer, who has yet to move from Key West, speaks with a Conch accent, a delightful bouillabaisse of Cuban, Cracker, British and Creole pronunciations and made-up words. In pure Conch, "work" may sound like "woyk." The oldest Conchs, whose parents and grandparents came to Key West more than a century ago from the Bahamas, may substitute "gritsbox" for stove and "locker" for closet.

"These reunions keep Key West alive," says Ocala's Delores Drudge, who spent most of her 54 years in Key West. "We always hope that something will happen and we'll be able to go back and reclaim our city."

She sighs. When she drives around Key West on yearly visits, and sees the new condominiums and restaurants and streets packed with moneyed tourists, she knows her Key West is gone.

"It's still got lovely water," she says to me. "But it's not the real Key West to me. A lot of the people who go there now, they walk around and buy things and eat in air-conditioned restaurants and they think they're experiencing Key West. But they're not. The Key West culture is gone. You don't hear the music. You don't hear the stories and the accents. And you're lucky to find any real Key West food."

At Conch reunions, Conch food is plentiful. Under the pavilion, we wolf down black beans and rice, fried plantains, fritters and bollos—deep-fried black-eyed peas mashed and mixed with garlic, onions, salt, pepper and hot sauce.

We eat Cuban sandwiches lovingly assembled with ham, pork, cheese, lettuce and tomato, and sample Key lime pies made with real Key limes. Like native Conchs, Key lime groves have disappeared from the Keys in recent decades, the land considered too valuable to waste on fruit. Many ex-Conchs manage to grow limes in Central Florida back yards even if the climate is less than sub-tropical.

Between bites, and gulps of eye-opening Cuban coffee, Conchs renew acquaintances. Standing next to a table covered by pies, reunion organizer Grace Fallon suddenly recognizes her long-lost friend, Dottie Garcia, now 73. "When we were girls, we used to work at the Kress five-and-ten over on Duval Street!" Mrs. Fallon cries.

"Yes," says Mrs. Garcia, who now lives in Key Largo, two hours away from her old hometown. "We both sold candy, and we ate more candy than we sold."

Tampa truck driver Gilbert Allen, 49, who grew up in Key West, has been eavesdropping. "I used to steal candy from them when candy only cost a nickel!" he says. "I think they let me do it. It was so different. People knew each other. People had nicknames. See that old guy over there? I don't know his real name. But everybody called him 'Rubber Man.'"

Rubber Man turns out to be Gabriel Garcia, lithe and graceful, even at age 81. He was born in Key West but lives in Orlando today. Rubber Man explains, "I was a good baseball player when I was young. There was this old lady, my biggest fan, who loved to watch me play. One day, there were three men on base with two outs and somebody hit a flyball to left field. I jumped and caught the ball to end the rally. The old lady yelled so everybody could hear. 'That's my boy! He stretches like rubber.' After that, nobody knew me as Gabriel. I was the Rubber Man."

When Rubber Man visits Key West now, nobody calls him by his nickname. Few people know him at all. If he reads the *Key West Citizen*, he recognizes few names, except in the obituary column. "I'm a stranger in my own hometown," he says. "It's enough to make you cry."

Johnny Blackwell, who was born in Key West 76 years ago but lives in Ocala now, understands Rubber Man's emotions.

"I think John Milton must have written that book about Key West," he says. "Called it *Paradise Lost*."

Sponge-O-Rama

Tarpon Springs
November 1995

Living in urban Florida sometimes gets me down.

New houses start to look to me as if they were designed by wicked architects who would never live in them. Developers forever are removing perfectly good native shade trees and replacing them with anemic plants from strange lands. Downtown buildings, glassy and impersonal, seem at a glance hostile to anyone who possesses a soul.

Have I mentioned our roads?

Six-laned highways are clogged with speeding vehicles, windows rolled up even in pleasant weather, drivers speaking intensely on cellular phones, no doubt doing business, business, business on the run, the modern Florida way.

Well, as I told you, sometimes it gets to me. On those days when I'm poised to give up, on those afternoons when I'm about to let loose with a cry of anguish, what I do instead is drive over to Tarpon Springs and visit the Sponge-O-Rama.

At the Sponge-O-Rama, life slows down, appropriately, to a sponge-like crawl. Nothing is modern. Nothing is hurried. The Sponge-O-Rama is good for the low-tech soul.

Nothing about a sponge, or a museum that celebrates the sponge, is very contemporary. There is no talk of the Internet over by the manual cash-register, nobody communicating big deals by E-Mail with Wall Street. Instead you stand in air-conditionless splendor, chew the fat with flesh-and-blood humans, hear pretty good stories, and always learn something, usually about the Greek sponge fishing tradition in Tarpon Springs.

Also—and this can be important on those days when you are disgusted with only-money-is-important modern Florida—the Sponge-O-Rama is free.

Oh, you can spend a few bucks if you want in the Sponge-O-Rama store, and you probably will want a couple of sponges, a postcard or two, and a bottle of Greek spaghetti sauce—but you will be challenged to spend very much. The Sponge-O-Rama is not Disney World, it is not Busch Gardens. The Sponge-O-Rama is a relic of Real Florida, when tourist attractions were little Mom-and-Pop joints propped on the side of quiet magnolia-shaded two-lanes.

•   •   •

The Sponge-O-Rama looks as if it must have been built in Tarpon Springs just about when the Greeks began diving for sponges, about a century ago. But it was created three decades ago by a New York couple who liked history and wanted to operate a museum to celebrate the romance of sponge diving.

The museum exhibits they hand-built must have been considered old-fashioned even in the 1960s. They lovingly painted black hair and black mustaches on department-store mannequins and dressed them as Greek divers, captains, deckhands, cooks and sponge-handlers. The mannequins were nothing fancy. They weren't robots—Disney is good at robots—and they couldn't speak. Still aren't robots and still can't speak. At the Sponge-O-Rama, mannequins wait eternally behind dusty glass, like figures in a 19th-century wax museum.

The Sponge-O-Rama reminds me of those wonderful places my folks took me when I was a boy, inexpensive places now gone, places that evoked history and wonder and sometimes even fear. Strolling through the Sponge-O-Rama displays, I begin to feel like a 12-year-old, rambunctious, hoping to encounter something a little gross.

The Sponge-O-Rama doesn't disappoint. Down a spooky corridor, illuminated by a light so dim it deserves to be called a dark, I encounter the dead mannequin sponge diver. He lies in the bottom of a wood skiff with blood pouring from his nose and ears. A sad-eyed mannequin deckhand looks on helplessly. Says the sign: "Greatest fear is a severed air hose which is his life line, for that means instant death. This diver's greatest fear came true."

Other educational displays at the museum show the different ways fishermen harvested sponges, and how they shared in profits, and what they ate when they were at sea, and how they had fun when they came home. The Sponge-O-Rama leaves no stone, or sponge, unturned. Sponge-O-Rama even knows, intuitively, that visitors must have dozens of questions they've always wanted to ask, about sponges.

"How many different species of sponges are known?" asks a hand-painted question. The answer is provided: 5,000 species!

"What is a Sponge?" Answer: A skeleton of a one-celled animal.

"What is Known as the Sponge-Diving Birthplace of America?"

If you guessed Tarpon Springs, you qualify as a genius.

Sponge-O-Rama is currently owned by Theo Koulianos. His family has worked in the sponge business here, and in Greece, for seven generations. He is 49, robust, fast-talking. And busy! Right now, he is so busy with visitors that he can't talk to me. He points in the direction of his father, Mike.

Mike, who is 80, fills me in about the family history. Mike's grandfather was a sponge-diver in Greece. Mike's father captained a sponge-boat in Greece and in Tarpon Springs. Mike was born in Tarpon, raised in Greece, but worked on the docks in Tarpon. By now my mind is spinning trying to keep up. Mike marches on: he got married, moved to Indiana, worked in the steel mills, joined the military, was wounded in battle, became a certified public accountant, moved back to Tarpon, had a curio shop, sold sponges, raised five fine children, and saw that they got college educations.

"The old spongemen," Mike says, "did not want their children to work in the sponge business. We wanted them to go to college, to become professionals."

So where does the Sponge-O-Rama come into the story?

Now Theo is free to gab and I'll find out. Theo tells me he never thought he would work in the sponge business. Theo was a physical education major at Indiana State, but he never taught a class; instead, he moved to Orlando, just about when Disney was picking up steam, and opened a series of golf pro shops.

The golf shops failed big-time. Theo and his wife limped back to Tarpon with only $135 in their bank account. They invested their $135 in sponges and sold them at a nice profit. They reinvested in more sponges, and more sponges after that. Soon they were able to rent a shop, in which they sold—you guessed it—sponges.

About this time, Theo decided to go to law school.

"But I had made only C's as a phys-ed major," he will tell you with humility. "No school would accept me." Finally, he found one, the Atlanta Law School, that would. Theo attended law school part-time, driving 1,000 miles round-trip each week to Atlanta. Weekends, he sold sponges in Tarpon Springs.

He graduated from law school, but, no surprise, decided to stick to the sponge business. He purchased a sponge boat that had belonged to his wife's grandfather. Then two more. Sometimes he went out on the boats and watched the divers. Sometimes he handled the sponges as they came aboard.

In 1982, his left knee began to swell. Soon he was crippled. Nobody knew what was wrong. Four years passed. At Mayo Clinic, he was diagnosed with a rare disease, *Myco Bacterium Marinum*, which he had gotten from handling wet sponges. Friends prayed over him, and he was healed.

Now he is big and strong again. He no longer goes out on boats to handle wet sponges that could make him ill, yet the sponge business remains powerful in his blood. Onshore, he is never far from them, buying and selling, or talking about them at the business he bought, the Sponge-O-Rama. He and his wife have even founded a private school, and sponge profits are funding it.

Sometimes Theo wonders about the future of an old-fashioned place like Sponge-O-Rama in this modern, hectic world. Looking around, he sees that even parts of Tarpon Springs, a town that respects the past, is changing to reflect the new Florida. There are shops that sell trendy frozen yogurt instead of the Greek yogurt, shops that no longer sell Greek fishing caps but will sell you new-age sandals for $100 a pair.

The Sponge-O-Rama, looming on the Anclote River waterfront like a ghost, is old and dilapidated. But last year, Theo says with pride, nearly a quarter-million people passed through the museum.

And they bought 50,000 sponges in the gift shop.

For me, no Sponge-O-Rama adventure is complete without a visit to the absolutely free sponge theater. At the box office, Theo picks up a microphone and invites everyone inside. It is a little warehouse of a building, with 16 metal benches lined up in front of a small screen. Then the movie flickers on.

The movie, a documentary, is ancient, perhaps a half-century old. It is in color, but so grainy and out-of-focus that I'm tempted to rub my eyes.

But it doesn't matter whether it is in focus or not. It casts a spell. It is a romantic documentary, about men vs. the sea, men vs. the elements. Brave divers, menaced by sharks, harvest spongy gold!

"Sponge fishing," barks the narrator, "can be happy work when the fishing is good." Sitting in the dark audience, I don't doubt it for an instant.

And then, on the soundtrack, the narrator starts reeling off the importance of sponges, explaining the proper use of a good sponge, telling just how a clever person can use a sponge to clean a car, or a boat, or a wall, or a dish, or just about anything else in this world. And while he is talking so persuasively, so passionately about proper sponge-use, a choir of voices in the movie background is chanting, hauntingly, prayerfully, subliminally:

"REAL sponges. NATURAL sponges. REAL sponges. NATURAL sponges."

The movie is over. Limp as a noodle, I resolve never to buy a shameful synthetic sponge again. I am funneled helplessly through the gift shop, where of course I purchase a very fine wool sponge, a wool sponge plucked from the Gulf of Mexico by a brave Greek diver, a wool sponge that Theo Koulianos calls "The Cadillac of Sponges."

Long Live Sponge-O-Rama!

Cross Creek oranges

Cross Creek
October 1994

Horace Drew Jr. believes he probably first set eyes on the orange grove while lying on a pillow on his mother's lap, in his daddy's Buick Roadster. He does not remember the exact moment so many decades ago—he was six months old at the time—but he has heard the family history, a family history whose roots go deep into the soil of a special place.

The place is North Florida's Cross Creek, where Horace grows oranges as his kinfolk did before. For more than a century, Drew blood, sweat and tears have nourished the tender trees against the harsh elements here. Now Horace is 77, and Florida is modern, and almost all of the old citrus growers who farmed at the Creek are dead or gone.

Sometimes, at night, when he walks through his grove, he can hear them, their voices, their sighs, their stories. "This place hasn't changed much, like the rest of the state has," he says. "It's old country. I think the old spirits are just comfortable here."

As another winter approaches, the Drew Grove is in good shape. Horace has tried to make sure. He practiced law in Jacksonville for more than five decades, but in his heart, and on weekends, he was a citrus farmer. Now he lives at the Creek for half the week, to better keep his eyes on his fine trees. He walks among them, shirt plastered to his back by sweat, talking about them as much to himself as to visitors. Look here. This is a good tree: See the green? Green tells you a tree is healthy. But look at this! Leaf curl!

He hunkers, takes out the worn pocketknife and cuts away a dead leaf.

"I know every one of these trees," he says, waving freckled arms.

He planted them. He watched over them. He has loved them. Too often he has watched them wither and die from the cold. Virtually all the other citrus growers at the Creek and elsewhere in North Florida have gone out of business, headed south or passed away.

Horace Drew Jr.'s roots go too deep to abandon the Creek. His trees, about 750 of them, are heavy with fruit. Fall is here, the air seems dryer by the day, and soon the oranges will be ripe and marketable. Yet looking north, anticipating winter, he has to wonder. Will he lose everything again?

Three times during the last decade he lost everything.

In 1983, a once-in-a-century arctic cold front dropped grove temperatures to 14 degrees. Onto whatever survived he grafted new buds and began again. In 1985, still another couldn't-happen-again cold front barreled through the Creek, and again, he had to start from scratch.

By 1989, he had a promising crop and allowed himself some optimism. A few days before Christmas, it snowed. Ice covered the roads and hung from the trees and wires. Electricity went off, and he couldn't pump water to insulate his orange trees against the chill. In the grove, temperatures never had fallen so low. "Eight degrees," he wrote into his diary.

"Lost everything we had," he'll tell you now with dignity. "There is nothing as demoralizing as dead orange trees."

He and his caretaker, Leo North, tore the dead trees from the earth with bulldozers, formed great piles and ignited them. Everything he loved—the trees, his little business, his family's history—seemed to disappear in the black smoke.

A government grant, designed to assist farmers after catastrophes, helped put him back on his feet. He planted some cold-hardy persimmon trees as a hedge against winter, but, of course, being a Drew, he had to put new orange trees into the ground.

Drews do not know when to quit.

The Spaniards brought oranges to what they called the Land of the Flowers in 1565. Indian people ate the oranges, spitting seeds as they moved inland. When William Bartram, the famous botanist, explored the territory in the late 1700s, he found orange trees scattered about interior North Florida.

George Rainsford Fairbanks, Horace Drew's great grandfather, acquired the family land in about 1855. He was a historian and attorney who lived most of the time in St. Augustine, but his love was farming oranges at the Creek. Anyone with good land seemed to farm them in those days. The body of water nearest the Creek was called Orange Lake, and the two nearest towns were named Island Grove and Citra. Oranges were a cash crop, as good as gold.

Horace's daddy, who acquired the family grove in 1919, was a doctor in Jacksonville. Like Drews before him, he loved oranges, and the grove became his refuge from his big-city patients and urban life.

Horace got to spend boyhood weekends at the Creek, hunting and fishing. He caught black bass by the bucketful. Some mornings, his mother sent him out with his gun, and he'd bring back a squirrel for breakfast. He'd hike to the lake, hide in the grass and wait with his shotgun for the dawn. As the sun came up, ducks blotted out the sky.

"We never killed more than we'd eat," he says now.

He'd haul his ducks back to the farm and, under the oak tree near the spring-fed pond, pluck the feathers. When panthers smelled the fresh duck meat, they would caterwaul from the nearby woods, sounding to him like a woman screaming. Horace would listen to the ungodly racket while his eyes bored into the darkness of the trees, then he'd grab his ducks and sprint for the house.

As Horace matured, he helped in the grove. His father's farm, known as the Drew Orange and Fruit Company, produced the famous "Floridian Brand." Horace has the old labels that were pasted onto crates shipped north. The trademark was an alligator basking on an orange.

Horace graduated from the University of Florida's law school, got married and experienced combat during World War II. In 1951, after his father's death, Horace took over the farm at Cross Creek.

The nearest paved road, a country mile away, is across a hayfield and through a deep oak hammock. Bald eagles patrol his sky. As he works in his grove, deer watch from beneath a cathedral of pines.

The air smells sweet, and his ponds are filled with gin-clear water. Over in his house, his wife, Shelley—he calls her "Momma"—assembles her book of citrus recipes, compiled during their last half century together at the Creek.

"I love this land," Horace says. "I truly love this land."

Over decades many people have fallen in love with the Creek. Among them was a struggling writer named Marjorie Kinnan Rawlings. She arrived in 1928, wrote stories on her front porch, drank moonshine and learned to shoot, cuss and grow oranges. She lived three miles down a dirt road from the Drews.

"I was a boy," Horace will tell you, "but I remember Miz Rawlings. She was a good neighbor, a nice woman. She helped another woman, Zelma Cason, conduct the census. They'd come on horseback. Miz Rawlings liked the coffee and the company."

A movie, *Cross Creek*, was made of Mrs. Rawlings' life some years ago. It was filmed on Horace Drew's land.

Horace no longer owns that part of the Creek. He sold more than 200 acres last year, including some prime orange groves, after he suffered a minor stroke. He has recovered, but his doctors advise him to spend less than his usual 12 hours a day tending trees. Now he owns about eight acres.

"It about killed me to sell any of my grove," he says. He sold it to a man who used to help him in the grove decades ago. That man is married now to a doctor, and they say they want to farm oranges too, and keep the orange business going at the Creek, the Lord and winter willing.

When Horace passes from this world and joins his kin in the next, the Drew family's tradition in the orange business is likely to end. His children, successful in life and in commerce, have wandered far away from the Creek, and have no interest in growing oranges, at least for now, in a place that most modern farmers say is too cold.

"You feel the history here," Horace Drew says. At noon he sits on a bench near a pond and looks at his groves and beyond them to the oak hammocks where Indians hunted in the last century and where he hunted in this one.

"You feel the spiritual ties to the land and the people who were here. I don't talk about this much. It's hard to. It's more like a religious feeling than something you can explain with your mind."

As he awaits another winter, Horace Drew may be the last of his kind.

A haunted house, with egg salad

St. Petersburg
October 1993

This is a story about a haunted house and a killing. Well, the house may be haunted, and if it's not, it should be. Hauntings are notoriously hard to prove, but Rocky and Jan, who have been around the block a time or two, swear their story is God's honest truth.

"I could tell you stories that would curl your hair," Rocky says ominously.

Perhaps this is one of them.

Rocky, who has passed his 70th birthday, is Rocky DeSimone. Jan, a few years younger, is married to Rocky. They have owned a St. Petersburg delicatessen, Jan's Heros Sub Shop, for nearly 30 years. Before that they owned a bunch of delis, all called Rocky's, in New York City, mostly Brooklyn, where they are from.

There is Flatbush Avenue in the way they talk, the way they interrupt each other, and the way they tell a story, which is pretty spectacular. You get good meals at Jan's Heros, but you get even better stories.

The stories are about baseball players and Mafia bad boys Rocky knew back in New York. Or about the weird half-rabbit, half-cat Jan says she feeds behind their restaurant on Fourth Street N. One story is about how they met in a New York luncheonette, where Jan was watching a horse race on TV, and Rocky came in flushed with drink and waving a *Racing Form*, which he refused to loan her, a selfish act that somehow led to their 40-year-plus marriage.

But back to the haunted house.

It was 1955 when Jan's parents retired to St. Petersburg. They bought a two-story home on 22nd Avenue N and lived there peacefully for years. When the old folks passed away, Rocky and Jan inherited the property and moved down in 1964. They liked the barn-like house and the neat yard shaded by a huge oak and a prolific mango tree. It was a fine place to live. Only one thing:

"I always had strange feelings in that house," Rocky says.

Rocky, see, has ESP. He's had it since he was a boy and his grandmother's ghost watched over him. "The house I grew up in, it was all spooked up," he says, sitting at the counter in his undershirt. Jan puts down her crossword puzzle and listens so she can correct Rocky if he strays from the facts.

"My mother's mother was murdered in that house," Rocky says. "My grandfather hit her, and she fell and hit her head on the stove and died."

Jan sniffs. "They didn't call it murder."

"Hell, no," Rocky says. "My grandfather put her in bed and called the doctor. The doctor called it a heart attack."

The kitchen door swings open and Rocky and Jan's 33-year-old daughter, Cyndy, hears about this incompetent doctor and declares:

"He was a schmuck."

Patient reader, you are probably wondering when you will get to hear about the haunted house. But not so fast. This is not television, and Rocky and Jan are old-fashioned. They have to warm up by telling the old stories about New York.

"My grandmother's ghost was in the house I grew up in," Rocky says. "I could feel her there."

"He was used to ghosts," Jan admits. "I grew up different."

Anyway, Rocky's ghostly experience in New York prepared him for the house he and Jan inherited in St. Petersburg. Right away Rocky could feel the presence of spirits, even if Jan couldn't. Yet even she noticed some peculiar things.

"Big horseflies on the windows," Jan says, as a customer walks in to collect a meatball sandwich.

"The biggest damn horseflies you ever saw!" Rocky shouts. "Hell, you don't see horseflies like those in Florida!"

"It was like the Amityville Horror," Jan says, and the story takes an unexpected diversion into a book review. It's a struggle steering them back to the St. Petersburg Horror.

"I'd be rockin' Cyndy, sitting on the porch beneath the bedroom," Rocky says.

"And I'd hear footsteps upstairs," Cyndy interrupts. "I'd say, 'Momma's home!'"

"I wasn't home," Jan says, her eyes zeroing in on yours. "I was drivin' a cab back then. I wasn't home!"

"Nobody was upstairs," Rocky says significantly. "Ya know what I mean?"

At noon, business picks up in the little sandwich joint. One customer is so charmed by the haunted house tale that he drags a chair to the counter to hear better. "One night, we hear a crash in Cyndy's room," Jan says gravely. "We go in there and she's in bed, but it looks like something has her pushed out of the way and pinned her against the wall."

"The lamp fell on the bed, right where my head would have been," Cyndy says.

"Something moved her out of the way," Rocky explains, raising his caterpillar eyebrows.

"That's when I knew there were two ghosts," Jan says.

"A bad ghost, and the ghost of Jan's mother," Rocky says.

"My grandmother was protecting me, her only grandchild," Cyndy says pleasantly.

Rocky and Jan admit their story sounds whacko. But hey, strange things happen in this world, and as evidence they offer the tale about the old friend who had a haunted television in her living room. After gentle prodding they return to their own haunting.

"How do you explain the pennies on the windowsills?" Cyndy asks triumphantly. Nobody in the sandwich ship has an explanation for the ghosts who leave pennies on the windowsills. Cyndy would put them in a bank. The next day, new pennies would appear, and the damn horseflies would be back.

Sometimes, drinking coffee at the dining room table, Rocky would feel Jan walk up behind him. Only it wasn't Jan. It was a cold breeze.

"I feel things," Rocky says, and a new customer nods, as if hearing a ghost story at a deli is the most normal thing in the world. "When Jan is playin' solitaire, I can tell what card she's gonna turn over next. Am I right or wrong?"

"Well," Cyndy points out, "your feelings have never helped you pick the dogs at the track."

"Or jai alai," Jan says.

This forces Rocky to brag for a few minutes about his gambling prowess. Eventually, the room settles down, and we finally get to the meat and potatoes about The Haunting.

One day in 1971, or maybe it was 1972, Rocky, Jan and Cyndy were walking up their sidewalk when Rocky had the most powerful feeling of his life, so powerful he refused to enter the house.

"I knew a man was going to die in that house, and because I was the only man livin' there, I was gonna be the dead man."

"My husband is a kook," Jan says. "But I love him, and I trust his feelings."

As Rocky waited in the yard, Jan went inside and calmly packed their suitcases. They checked into a motel. After two weeks, they rented another house. Their old house lay vacant and waiting. Several months went by, and a friend called. A couple of pals, new in town, needed a place to stay. Could they stay in the old house? Rocky and Jan said yes.

"What a deal they got!" Rocky erupts. "The house was furnished. We didn't even go back for the furniture."

The new tenants moved in on a Friday. On Sunday morning, Rocky's telephone rang. A cop wanted to know if Rocky owned the house at such and such address. Said there's been a stabbing.

So they drove over, right? There were cop cars in the yard. And an ambulance. The man had been beating his wife. She let him have it with a nine-inch kitchen knife.

"I was raised in an Italian family," Rocky says. "We know that when a man dies, he don't leave the Earth right away. He goes searchin' for another body. There was SOMETHING IN THAT HOUSE that made it happen!"

"The cops ruled it a justifiable homicide," Jan says calmly.

"The bastard bled all over my house," fumes Rocky, his boiling point low. "It was everywhere. Even on a light bulb on the ceiling."

"She killed him in self-defense," Jan says.

"He couldn't just lay down and die," Rocky mutters. "He had to walk around and bleed. You couldn't get the blood out of the tiles."

So that's the story of the haunted house, which Rocky and Jan eventually sold to a doctor, who enjoyed carpentry even though he was a lousy carpenter, which sounds like it might be a story worth hearing next time. You finish your sandwich, say your good-byes, and then take a drive.

You stop at the two-story home on 22nd Avenue. From the sidewalk, it no longer resembles the handsome snapshots Jan showed you back at the restaurant. It needed a ton of paint 10 years ago. The yard is overgrown. You look up at the bedroom, the bedroom where Rocky says something invisible once walked, and count windows. Thirteen.

Nobody answers your knock and you leave a note on the door. Climbing into your vehicle, you hear a strange noise, something like horseflies, insane, horrible horse-flies.

But the troubling buzzing is just your stomach, digesting a fine lunch.

Or maybe the noise was the plot thickening.

Back at the office, the phone rings. Bill Bocik, the 29-year-old carpenter who bought the house a year ago, has found the note you left in his door. You ask if anything, er, unusual has happened in his new home. He pauses and says, "You should talk to my wife."

"That house," says Christine Bocik in a husky voice. "There's something wrong with it.

"When it's quiet, you can hear people walking around upstairs," she goes on. "And like the only one home is me. Couple times, I'm sure I've seen somebody, out of the corner of my eye moving past the doorway, but when I get up to look, nobody's there. The house gives me the creeps."

You can understand that. Ever notice any pennies?

She pauses a long time. "They're everywhere. I find them on the floor and pick them up and put them in an ashtray. A couple days later, I find the pennies scattered on the floor."

And flies? Please, don't say you've noticed flies.

"By the hundreds sometimes. Fat ones. I don't know where they come from."

She sounds deliciously scared as you tell her the stories you've heard. "I don't like the house," she says. "I never liked it."

Bill and Christine, who are ending their two-year marriage, have been living apart and away from their house for several months. Christine has no plans to go back and recover what belongings she left when she moved out. "I'm never going in again."

Bill agrees to show you around.

Old clothes are scattered across a carpet that smells of mildew. The broken living room window is boarded up. You see no ghosts and hear no tap-dancing spirits in the bedroom above. When the divorce is final, Bill says, he's moving back and will begin the repairs and clean up. He's not afraid. He says he kind of likes the idea of owning a haunted house.

"But I don't really believe it," he says. "It would be a lot of fun, though, if it was. I've always wanted to see a ghost. Maybe I could even have a seance."

He bends to pick up something on the kitchen floor.

He hands you a penny.

Miss Olive

Miami
Halloween 1991

All the kids on my block knew Miss Olive. She was crabby and old and so stooped she needed a cane. Hobbling down the street, she talked to herself. At night, candles flickered in her otherwise dark house. She was probably the only person in steamy Miami who had a black roof. We all swore she was a witch.

Miss Olive scared us. She lived in the house next to the field where we played baseball. A foul ball into her yard enraged her. She'd burst through the back door waving her cane and screaming. She called us dirty SOBs, except she didn't use the initials. She'd take our ball into the house.

Game over.

Everyone on the block had Miss Olive stories. My mother had two. Miss Olive was one of the first people my family met when we moved to Miami in 1952. Mother was weeding in the front yard the day Miss Olive stopped on her way from the bus stop. Miss Olive tapped the cracked sidewalk with her cane and spoke in a manner my mother found threatening.

"Somebody could trip on this," Miss Olive grumbled. "Somebody could get sued."

My mother, warm and friendly, introduced herself to Miss Olive. She told Miss Olive how we had just moved from Chicago, how my dad hoped to make a living playing the piano, how musician jobs were scarce and how my dad was out of work temporarily. For the moment we were poor. We couldn't afford a law suit.

Miss Olive surprised my mother by offering the loan of lawn equipment. She said we could borrow her edger if my dad would edge her sidewalk when he was finished with our own. We took Miss Olive up on what seemed to be a kind offer.

Within minutes the ancient, rusty edger broke down. Miss Olive expected us to fix it, or replace it, and we did. Our already strained budget was strained even tighter. My dad worked in her yard to help make things right.

My mother's second story is about Miss Olive's heater.

Our small house lacked heat. Miami, fortunately, seldom gets more than a taste of winter. But one day a strong front blew in from the north. Miss Olive offered the loan of an old kerosene heater. My parents were grateful. I was three and sickly.

My dad had a temporary job at an all-night Miami Beach restaurant. So only my mother and I were home. Mother woke at dawn, wheezing and coughing and hallucinating about spider webs. No hallucination, the spider webs on the ceiling turned out to be soot. During the night the heater had malfunctioned. We were probably lucky to be alive.

We decided to stop borrowing from Miss Olive. It was too expensive, too dangerous.

Miss Olive, we began to realize, was a lonely woman. She had been married but nobody knew what became of her husband. She had a grown daughter who never visited. Miss Olive was a hairdresser in downtown Miami, but she bragged about a more glamorous career. She told people she had once been an opera singer.

Nobody, adults or children, knew what to make of Miss Olive's opera story. But Miss Olive said she had scrapbooks to prove it. Nobody wanted to see them because it would involve going into her house, which smelled of urine. Sometimes she forgot or neglected to take her dog out for walks.

Miss Olive did look like a cartoon version of an opera singer, though. She was a robust woman with huge breasts and hips. You could almost imagine her wearing Viking horns and singing Wagner at the Met.

There was something else that gave credence to her claim. At night, from our front porch, two doors down from hers, we could hear her playing the piano and singing. She had a glorious, powerful, soprano voice.

What a mysterious, complex, cantankerous woman she was.

I suppose everyone has known a Miss Olive, the neighborhood grouch. She was ours, and she had complaints about everything and everybody, so many complaints that after a while people laughed instead of taking her seriously.

After she retired, Miss Olive's behavior grew more and more bizarre. She picked big fat ants off her fence with tissue paper. She took to walking into homes uninvited. Miami in the 1950s was the kind of place where people seldom locked their doors at night. But people who lived near Miss Olive locked theirs during the day. I remember my mother holding a finger to her lips to warn me to be quiet one morning: Miss Olive was trying our doorknob.

We pretended not to be home. We could hear Miss Olive muttering.

We kids decided we didn't have to take Miss Olive seriously, either. When we fouled a ball into her yard, and she rushed out, we hopped her fence and raced her across the lawn. It became a game. She'd scream, swing her cane and reach for the ball. Most of the time we got to the ball first, danced around her and laughed.

Cruelty could be fun.

Sometimes our foul balls missed her yard and landed on her roof or aluminum bedroom awning with a loud bang. We could hear her cursing inside the house and blundering into furniture in her eagerness to come out and get us. Sometimes she'd babble incoherently from the porch. Sometimes she'd weep with rage. Then she would call the police.

The police were regulars at Miss Olive's house. Two, three, often four times a week someone from the sheriff's office arrived during our games. At first, we'd scatter at the sight of the patrol car. After a while, we stopped running, because the police didn't take Miss Olive seriously either.

"Look," an officer told us one day, "you kids should be nicer. We don't like to come here. We flip a coin to see who has to come here. Give her a break."

We cut her no slack, though. Our games, our foul balls, our taunting continued. So did police visits. They'd park along what was our right field line, walk in resignation into her house, hear her complaints, listen to her play the piano and sing, probably look at her scrapbooks, and then come out to lecture us.

Miss Olive was right to be angry. Nobody wants to be laughed at. Nor did she deserve the baseballs bouncing on her roof. But she was her own worst enemy.

She developed a new strategy for dealing with obnoxious children. When our ball games began, she'd stand near first base with her garden hose. Nobody wanted to hit a single because she'd manage to water you along with her grass. One day, a friend of mine, David, tired of being watered, shouted at her. A moment later, when somebody bounced a high foul off her roof, David raced Miss Olive for the ball. They arrived in a dead heat. Miss Olive rapped him on the forehead with the nozzle of the hose hard enough to draw blood.

David told his parents. They called the police on her.

Miss Olive disappeared. We heard she was taken to a rest home. When she returned, subdued, a few weeks later, we had no pity. On Halloween night we egged her house.

She was the witch.

Strangely enough, she kind of liked me. I didn't sass her, she knew my mother and when she asked me a question I answered politely. I was also her paper boy. Sometimes she tipped me a quarter on a 45-cent bill. A 25-cent tip should have bought Miss Olive compassion.

I dreaded entering Miss Olive's spooky home to collect my money. Her living room was dark and dusty and filled with newspapers, junk and horrible smells. She always wanted me to stay and talk. She wanted me to look at her scrapbooks. She wanted me to listen to her sing and play the piano. I could only hold my breath for so long. Then the stench of her house, and her dog, would overwhelm me. I'd fight my stomach for control.

When I was 12, and my little brother was about five, I took him to the field for a game of catch. Miss Olive was standing in her yard next to first base. I brought my brother over to meet Miss Olive, the neighborhood celebrity, the witch about whom he had already heard so many stories.

Miss Olive obliged with her most outrageous behavior yet.

She said she had something to show us. Something she might use on bad boys. Want to see it? Yes! We sure did. She tugged on her cane. . . . My eyes almost popped.

My brother and I raced home, excited and happy about the story we could tell. Guess what, Mom? Guess what Miss Olive has? Miss Olive has a sword cane!

Adults were less thrilled than children about Miss Olive and her sword cane. This time, when she went away, she never returned. Somebody bought and repaired her house. The new owners, who had children, were too good to be true. They didn't care when the ball dropped on the roof or on the awning. Baseball continued.

I don't remember ever reading Miss Olive's obituary. I seldom get to Miami these days. To tell the truth, I don't like Miami, which is too big and crowded for my taste. But when I have to go, I always find myself driving through my old neighborhood and thinking about my childhood.

On my last visit I took a snapshot of my old house for my scrapbook. Then I walked to the field where I spent so many happy hours playing baseball. I stood on the dirt worn away by generations of feet running the base paths. I shut my eyes and let my old friends come to life: Dennis, Billy, Manuel, Andy, Bert, Jesus, Anthony, David, Timmy. I wondered where they were now and what they were doing.

I thought about Miss Olive, too. Who had she been, really? What was she like as a young woman? Was she ever happy? What happened to her husband? Why didn't her daughter visit? Had she really been an opera singer? Or was she a witch?

Why was she reduced to playing her piano and singing so beautifully for a paper boy who couldn't wait to escape her company?

Miss Olive, what went wrong?

Winter

Orange Blossom

Starry, starry night

Lake Kissimmee
January 1994

After sunset, in the woods, screech owls trill. As I hunker next to the beginnings of the campfire, something moves behind me, a gray-brown bird. When I turn, the whippoorwill hops across the pine needles and disappears into shadows. I drop a pine cone onto burning newspaper. The cone flares.

Here comes the night.

We are camping at a place called Lake Kissimmee State Park, in the middle of the state, 20 miles from the nearest town, Lake Wales. It is a fine place to see wildlife but perhaps even a better place to experience a spectacular winter night.

During the day my wife and I hiked the eight-mile Buster Island Hammock loop through oaks and pines and flat scrub. Black vultures and bald eagles rode the thermals. We found tracks of a wild turkey next to fallen acorns. A six-point buck moved slowly across a prairie into the bright sunlight and failed to see us. Only at the last did it sense our presence. As we stood, unmoving, it instinctively veered around the path, stopping to look back. When we resumed our hike it jumped and ran, terrified, tail twitching like a white flag of surrender.

Now, after sundown, come the other wonders, the other rewards, of a winter night in the woods. One is building a fire. An obsolete skill in the city, it is useful here where there is no other heat. A cold front pushed through this morning, and temperatures now dip toward freezing. I start with newspaper scraps, dead twigs and pine cones. Over them I construct a kind of pyramid from small pine and oak logs I brought from home. When match touches paper the pine cones catch and explode with violent flame, as if doused with gasoline. Glowing ashes drift lazily skyward for the forest canopy. Watching them I catch glimpses of stars that shine like lasers through the trees.

No longer do we have skies like this in the city. In my youth, in Miami, sometimes you could see the Milky Way. Children who grew up in Tampa Bay could see the glory of night, too. All of our city children have lost the privilege. The night sky has been blotted out by high-intensity crime lamps and brightly lit outdoor billboards.

There is no crime here to speak of, except for the occasional poacher who sneaks into the 10,000-acre park under the cover of darkness and uses bright lights to find the glow of a deer's shining eyes. There is no commerce to wash out the sky either: The concessionaire who rented canoes went out of business last year. The only lights in the park are from scattered campfires, lanterns and teenagers with flashlights.

A bear crashes through the saw palmetto. At least that is what it sounds like. I move away from the fire and point my light. The beam reveals an armadillo, near-sighted, full of purpose. It pushes its snout deep into the sand, smelling for ants, oblivious to every thing else. I move closer. The armadillo continues hunting. I move so close I am sure it can smell my boots. Kneeling, I attempt to touch it. The terrified armadillo leaps, changes direction in midair and rushes headlong into the underbrush.

An alligator will eat an armadillo that ventures too close to the water, though not on a chilly night. Reptiles, their blood cold, slink into the mud, into holes, and wait for a warmer dawn. A bear would take an armadillo, if there were bears in this park, and a bobcat might attack a small one. At dusk yesterday, a bobcat trotted across the road as my son rode his bicycle. "They have longer legs than I thought," he announced. Earlier we had seen tracks in the sand. They are night creatures.

Raccoons come with dark as well. As in the cities, people here feed them out of what they feel is compassion and create domestic, obnoxious pests. A raccoon steps tentatively into light cast by the fire. I stamp my feet until it retreats. A moment later I hear it trying to pry open the ice chest I jammed tightly beneath a picnic bench. Raccoons chew through ice chests in this park; I get up and store mine in the car.

Away from the fire, away from the light, the sky overwhelms everything else. This is a good time to visit the field near the creek. My children ask if they can stay by the fire and roast marshmallows. Their mother and I shake our heads no. We'll roast marshmallows later. Right now it's important that they look at stars with us. The memory of seeing this sky with their parents might be important to them one day. For now, we want them to remember there are things grander than human beings, technology and marshmallows. All they have to do is look up.

We drive toward the field using only parking lights to preserve our night vision. We get out and walk tentatively through the woods without turning on our flashlights. We bump into each other and limbo under a gate. Our puny eyes aren't very good at this, though once I am sure I see my daughter's thin shadow in the starlight.

Soon, we hear voices. Other people have had the same idea. Ahead is the silhouette of what appears to be a cannon. No weapon, it is a large telescope tended by a young man who identifies himself as Kenneth Webb. He invites us to look through his telescope at the Owl Nebula, below the bowl of the Big Dipper. Using our imaginations we see wings.

Webb is from Lakeland. So are his two companions, Tim Tippery and Wade Young, who have brought their own telescope and cameras to record the night. When the moon is absent from the sky, they are drawn to this park like moths to flame. "In Lakeland, sometimes we set up our telescopes," Webb says. "You can see the moon okay and Saturn and some of the other planets, but everything else is washed out."

"This is one of the darkest spots in the state."

The voice belongs to George Aycrigg, who stands at his telescope next to his pickup truck. Aycrigg is the assistant park manager and an avid stargazer. In November, during the new moon, he and the park sponsored a "star party." Three hundred amateur and professional astronomers, and their telescopes, showed up. George let them camp in a field ablaze with goldenrod. When the sun went down, the night sky seemed to be on fire, too.

We inspect Orion, the constellation of the Hunter, and admire Betelgeuse, Bellatrix, Rigel and Saiph—and a thousand stars I can't name or make out from home. Gemini, the twins, rise next, with Castor and Pollux brighter than I have ever seen them from my city back yard.

One of my astronomers, I'm unsure just who in the dark, finds the Crab Nebula in the Constellation Taurus. I look through his telescope. His voice says, "You can't see the Crab if you look directly at it. You have to look away from it."

I look away, and the faint gas cloud becomes visible in peripheral vision. On July 14, 1054, it was a star. Then it exploded and became visible in broad daylight, according to the Chinese astronomers who recorded the event. Standing in this cold and windy field, I wonder if we are the only human beings in the world watching the faded supernova at this moment.

I would like to think so.

Winter cranes
on the prairie

Micanopy
February 1993

You hear them before you see them, as the sun rises and the wind rushes over the prairie. "Gar-oo-oo. Gar-oo-oo," they cry, trumpeting and rattling, sounding like rusty gates, only amplified a hundred times.

It is winter, and here come the sandhill cranes. They're flying in a deep-V formation above the tall grass, looking down at the ducks and the herons and the alligators and the human beings gazing at them in wonder. Sandhill cranes by the dozens, hundreds, maybe thousands are putting on a show at Paynes Prairie State Preserve.

The migrants from the Great Lakes region claim as their winter home the 19,000-acre preserve and pastures near Gainesville. From late October to early March they're rearing last year's young, feeding on insects, flying, dancing and singing those sandhill crane songs.

Gar-oo-oo. Gar-oo-oo.

"It gets noisy," says Jim Weimer, preserve biologist. "If you're here when they are, it can almost be deafening."

It can be thrilling to nature lovers who flock to the preserve with binoculars, cameras and bird books. The presence of so many sandhill cranes lets us know at least part of the natural world is all right. Despite pollution, despite endless development, despite all the efforts to civilize the Florida landscape, the natural world, at least for now, is hanging on.

"When you see all these cranes," Weimer says, "you're getting a glimpse of what Florida was like thousands of years ago."

Watching cranes is a gift.

There are two kinds of sandhill cranes in Florida. The most plentiful are the greater sandhills from the Midwest and Canada. The rarer kind is the Florida sandhill crane, a threatened species. Only an expert can tell them apart. They're both gray and four feet high. They both have a dull red patch on their heads. In flight, both have a six-foot wingspread.

If you see a crane during summer, you're looking at the Florida sandhill, the uncommon year-round resident. In the fall and winter, you could be seeing either, but you're probably watching the tourist birds that have flown south to enjoy our weather.

Paynes Prairie, with a crane population that may exceed 2,500 birds, is probably the best place in the state to watch cranes. The prairie and nearby ranches and farms offer splendid crane accommodations.

Sandhill cranes, which feed on insects, seeds, small snakes and lizards, like to hunt in pastures, recently mowed meadows and open prairies where they can see danger approaching. At night, they almost always return to the shallow marshes of Paynes Prairie State Preserve. They roost standing up, asleep in the water, trying to feel safe from predators.

Many things, of course, would like to eat them. Bobcats and raccoons take some. So do coyotes. Paynes Prairie boasts alligators, which have survived millions of years because they avoid going hungry. When you visit Paynes Prairie, studying the sky for cranes, it's also fun to pay attention to the marshes around you.

Alligators may look slow and lumbering, but they attack prey with a sprinter's speed. The preserve biologist has seen supposedly slow alligators ambush, catch and devour streamlined otters. He once saw an alligator launch itself like a missile from a lake and grab an egret from a tree branch. He once saw an alligator with a coyote in its mouth.

Sandhill cranes are hunted and eaten in some areas of the country, though no longer in Florida, where once they were considered a delicacy. When botanist William Bartram visited the prairie in 1774 to describe its flora and fauna, he was fed sandhill crane by his Seminole hosts. He ate it without joy, feeling he was devouring one of God's musical instruments.

"As long as I can get any other necessary food, I shall prefer their seraphic music in the ethereal skies," he wrote in the book known today as *Bartram's Travels*.

With predators about, sandhill cranes take nothing for granted. They're wary. As a dozen cranes feed, one studies possible sources of danger. When it feeds, another crane instinctively becomes the sentinel.

The best time to see cranes in large numbers is at dawn or dusk. From the U.S. 441 preserve overlook south of Gainesville, you sometimes can see them flying toward distant pastures within an hour or two of sunrise. Sometimes they pass overhead in flocks of up to 50. Sometimes there is wave after wave of sandhill cranes. In the late afternoon, when they return to the prairie, you can watch it all once more.

A more reliable place to watch cranes is probably the La Chua Trail, near Gainesville. On the La Chua Trail, you'll have to walk two miles down a levee to a wooden platform overlooking the marsh. You will see alligators and northern harriers, the hawks of the marsh, looking for something to eat, perhaps a careless green-winged teal. Through binoculars you may see bald eagles sitting atop trees rimming the prairie. You may even see a bison. Hunters shot the last native bison in Florida in 1821; they were reintroduced to the preserve in 1980.

Listen for cranes. They cry when they take flight and when they are nervous. Your presence in the marsh no doubt disturbs them. Stay quiet, though if you bring a tape recorder—and some people do—this is the place to turn it on. Later, you can play crane music on your car stereo while stuck in insterstate traffic and you need a reminder of more mysterious worlds.

As morning goes on, many cranes take flight and leave the prairie for the day. Look for them in pastures outside the preserve. Wacoota Road (County Road 18), near the south preserve entrance, offers fine vantage points at pasture fences. Another good spot is County Road 346 north of Micanopy, where last month I saw 400 cranes in a single pasture. There was a half-mile of cranes, on hill after hill. They were feeding. They were singing. They were dancing. It is one of the wonderful things about cranes —they dance. They dance when they are courting and when they are frisky and when they are nervous. They hop straight up in the air and kick both legs forward. It can be folly to attribute human values to animals, but they look like they are having fun.

The absolute best time for crane watching happens in late February or early March. That is when the sandhill cranes of Paynes Prairie feel something in the air, something instinctively that tells them it is time to head north. According to Darwin, the instinct to migrate takes precedent over all other avian drives. The cranes, like other birds, must obey that urge.

They like a southeast wind on a clear morning. Migration begins two to six hours after sunrise (they wait until the wing-saving thermals start to build). They take to the air and cry their trumpeting gar-oo-oo cries. They circle, glide, climb, circle, glide, climb, cry and then head north in a straight line.

Sometimes the migration lasts a few days. Sometimes it goes on for a week. People walking the streets of busy Gainesville hear the strange cries, look up, and see hundreds of sandhill cranes in the air at once.

It's a gift from winter.

Glory and obsession
of a bird man

Tallahassee
January 1995

> *The intellect of man is forced to choose*
> *Perfection of the life, or of the work,*
> *And if it take the second must refuse*
> *A heavenly mansion, raging in the dark.*
> *—The Choice*
> W.B. Yeats

Nobody knows, for sure, when Henry M. Stevenson began thinking about writing an epic book about birds. It could have been as long as four decades ago. It was only in 1974, when Henry was poised to retire from his teaching position at Florida State University, when he actually broke the news to his wife, RosaBelle, about his intention to pursue his dream full-time.

RosaBelle—the perfect name for a steel magnolia—understood exactly what that would mean to her 61-year-old husband. Henry, the most intensely focused man she ever knew, would work on his book day and night, except on Sundays, the Lord's day, when he attended church, sang in the choir and read his Bible.

"Henry," she says firmly, "was going to carry on."

RosaBelle knew her Henry's habits. The other six days he surely would work on his own Creation, spend hours in the field doing research, or in his favorite living room chair, writing up his notes. Then he'd be gone for days or weeks at a time, visiting museums and libraries, tracking down old bird skins and old records. And when he got home, he would not take her out to renew acquaintances over a meal or a movie, but shut his office door and pound the old Underwood like a man possessed.

He'd obsess about the book, gulp Rolaids at bedtime, ignore her pleas to relax. He'd ignore her, his children, the grandkids. He would ignore the house and chores and social obligations—all for an academic, scientific bird book that likely would have a minuscule audience and add little to family wealth.

But that was Henry. Birds—Florida's birds—were what seemed to matter most to him in the world, not money, not glory. Not even his wife and children, who wanted a full-time husband and full-time daddy, were sure of where they stood. If Henry worried about the price of his obsession on them, he never said.

Henry Stevenson chose perfection in his work over perfection in his life.

He would write his book—or die trying.

He succeeded.

Nineteen years after he officially began, *The Birdlife of Florida* became one of the University Press of Florida's most expensive volumes ever, at $120. But when his life's work came off the presses, as hard-core birders signed up for the privilege of buying the 907-page tome before the official publication date, as the praise started rolling in from scientists and reviewers across the country, Henry had to miss the celebration.

RosaBelle would like to believe—feels compelled to believe—that her husband was in a heavenly mansion that looked out on blue skies, lush trees and impossibly beautiful birds, maybe some real rarities, like Carolina parakeets or passenger pigeons. Henry would like that.

She's 77 now, but you'd never guess. Not with her dark hair, good looks and enthusiasm for life. RosaBelle Stevenson, who still substitute-teaches in public schools, steps lightly across the wide lawn in front of her Tallahassee home, then stops to turn over a dead mouse with her shoe. "Wonder what killed him?" she says in a drawl like warm cane syrup.

Henry, she says, would have known. He was so brilliant. So good at analyzing things. She met him at the University of Alabama, when she was studying to be a teacher, and he was working on his master's in ornithology, and they both sang in a Methodist club choir. She was an alto and Henry sang bass. People who sometimes found Henry's personality a bit frosty might be shocked, but one day, in the middle of choir practice, he reached up and gave RosaBelle Ard's beautiful curly hair a sharp tug.

They had their first date on October 7, 1938. He borrowed his daddy's Ford and bought RosaBelle a nickel cup of hot chocolate. Then they drove over to the old mill stream—not to neck but to listen to the birds. They listened to birds on other dates too, and read the Bible together.

Henry's father was a Methodist minister, like his grandfather, great-grandfather, great-great grandfather and great-great-great grandfather. But Henry's calling was birds. He knew when he was a child studying for a Boy Scout merit badge. By the time he was 18 he had already published a paper on a Bell's Vireo in an important science publication.

Then he met RosaBelle.

On November 11, 1939, Henry wrote into his journal: "Got married." His wedding present to RosaBelle was a hard-bound collection of his favorite bird articles from *National Geographic*.

So RosaBelle knew what kind of life she was getting into. She knew that if she wanted to be a part of his life, she would have to accept that studying birds was Henry's one great passion. She followed him to Cornell where he got his doctorate under the great ornithologist Arthur Allen. She followed him to poorly paying jobs throughout the South. In 1946, she settled into Tallahassee with him, watched him daily go off to teach his Florida State classes and then into the field to study birds.

"He was a perfectionist," RosaBelle says. "I knew nothing would take second place to his work. And birds were his life."

•   •   •

He was tall, slim, and craggy like so many rural men. He wore glasses with thick, dark frames and liked basketball sneakers for walking in swamps. He spoke with a soft Southern accent and favored straw hats to protect his neck from getting too red under Florida's broiling sun. RosaBelle says: "He could look like a hick."

He felt uncomfortable in neckties, though he always wore a suit to church. He had an amazing bass singing voice, a fact that many colleagues and friends never knew. It never would have occurred to Henry Stevenson to tell them, not because he was embarrassed, but because he valued modesty in all things. He loved sacred music. At St. Paul's United Methodist in Tallahassee, his favorites included *Oh, Savior, Hear Me* and *The Lord's Prayer*. Yet his voice was powerful enough to sing a solo in Handel's *Messiah* or Verdi's *Requiem*. At home, he listened to the classics. His son Ernie says, "If it was written in the last hundred and fifty years or so my dad didn't like it."

Henry and RosaBelle had four children, all successful adults. Ernie, 50, taught high school biology 20 years and then became the North Florida director for the Fellowship of Christian Athletes. Nell, 52, is a middle-school principal in New Jersey. Henry Jr., 48, is an electronics technician in Houston. Jim, 41, has taught honors biology at Tallahassee Leon High for 15 years.

Their dad quoted Shakespeare to them. He read them the Bible, though he seldom explained the scripture—the children were expected to figure out meaning for themselves. And if he disapproved of their behavior, he straightened them out, sometimes spanking them with a belt.

Ernie says, "The one thing you never told my dad is, 'Everybody is doing it!' He didn't care what everybody else was doing."

Henry never smoked. He didn't fudge the truth. At tax time, he drove RosaBelle mad, making sure their return was 150 percent accurate. The strongest beverage he was known to consume was Mountain Dew.

He never swore, not even to say "damn" or "hell."

One of his children once complained about an acquaintance who was "a brown-noser." Henry Stevenson, expert on the animal kingdom, hated the connotations of that common phrase. "Brown-noser" was deemed too vulgar for his household.

For the most part, he was too busy with his work to pay much attention to the children. RosaBelle was what people today call a "Supermom." She taught full-time and then came home and cut the grass. If the children needed homework help, she gave it. If they hurt, she applied the bandage. When they ran into the house asking to see daddy, she'd say, "Don't disturb him. He's working." Or "Daddy's not home."

Henry might be in his office, tending to his notes, or teaching at school. More likely he was in the field. People who worked with him call him "a classic ornithologist." They mean he spent his time outside watching birds rather than inside a building reading about them or teaching.

He was the last person to ever see the nest of a Bachman's warbler—now thought to be extinct. He was among the few people remaining on the planet who could describe the appearance of an ivory-billed woodpecker flying across the Chipola River.

The ivory-bill, like classic ornithologists, is from a bygone era too. If it's not extinct, it soon will be.

Henry M. Stevenson put 30,000 miles a year on his truck, driving with his head out the window to look for birds. "We were always sure he was going to die in a car wreck," RosaBelle says. "He always had his eyes on the heavens."

Seeing an interesting bird, he'd slam on the brakes and skid off the road. "My father was the reason they put seat belts in cars," says his son Ernie with a laugh.

Henry carried a canoe on his vehicle in case he had to pursue a bird across a lake or a river. He took meticulous notes on bird migration and bird distribution. He compiled data for the *Florida Field Naturalist*, *Florida Naturalist* and *Audubon Field Notes*. He ran Christmas bird counts for *Audubon*, splitting up groups of birders to cover more territory, even if two of those birders were just-marrieds on their honeymoon and dying to stay together.

"My husband wasn't a people-person," RosaBelle explains. He was impatient with small talk. He disliked obligatory gatherings. Once the subjects of birds and possibly baseball—he religiously followed the Atlanta Braves—were exhausted he was stumped for a topic. When the granddaughter of a colleague died, he asked RosaBelle to accompany him to the service.

"Why?" she asked.

"You'll know what to say."

Sometimes, during important birding expeditions, he irritated volunteers who helped him by questioning—often brutally—their credentials.

"What did it look like?" he'd ask, suspicious. "What was its song like?" They'd stutter and he'd wave his arms in frustration. He had taken the time and effort to recognize the songs and habits of hundreds of bird species. Why hadn't they?

"He could be cantankerous," says Herb Kale, an old friend and ornithologist for *Florida Audubon*. "Sometimes he shouted at me, and I'd shout back at him."

He trusted the eyewitness accounts of few experts. And sometimes he distrusted even them. Once, suspicious of people who were feeding him what he considered outlandish data, he laid out 70 bird skins and invited them to take a test. Only three passed, two graduate students and his son Jim, who was 10.

What Henry trusted, most of all, was a dead bird in his hand. It was another way he was a classic ornithologist. Like John James Audubon and Charles J. Maynard before him, he believed in shooting birds for no-doubt-about-it identification.

He shot them with a 410-gauge shotgun. Oh, he had federal and state collection permits, though that seldom prevented irate nature lovers from calling the game commission when they saw him blasting away. But Henry knew scientists needed these birds for study and ignored complaints. After all, he also collected road-kill birds and birds that struck radio towers at night and fell to earth.

He'd bring them home, skin them, store them in the freezer for a while. He'd store other interesting road kills too. "I was always getting a surprise opening the freezer," RosaBelle says. "We ate all kinds of strange things."

"Mom!" protests her son Ernie.

"Ernie, it's true. Do you remember that beaver? I'd never eat beaver again."

Of all his children, Jim was closest to his dad. Jim was an outstanding baseball player—Henry had once been a flashy centerfielder in a church league—and driven to be the best at whatever he tried, including birding. For the most part, it never occurred to Henry to praise his son. He never attended even one of Jim's baseball games. If Jim wanted to spend time with his dad, Jim had to go birding.

"He taught me every twit in the swamp, every song in the field, and almost every shorebird," Jim once wrote into his own journal. Eventually, the boy tired of trying to please his dad. As a teen-ager he rebelled by doing something almost unforgivable: He studied reptiles instead. Years passed before he rediscovered birding. He and his dad had an on-again off-again relationship.

"My greatest dread was I'd die before Henry," RosaBelle says. "He couldn't have cared for the children by himself. He couldn't have found somebody to cook or do his clothes. Henry would have had a real hard time coping without me."

In 1975, he officially began his book, patterning it after Arthur Howell's 1932 opus, *Florida Bird Life*, a work of rich scholarship that collected everything known about Southern birds to that time. In 1954, Alexander Sprunt revised the book, though Henry and other experts thought the new edition was light on original research and careless with the facts. Soon after Sprunt's book, friends began encouraging Henry to write a book someday as definitive, or better, than Howell's.

RosaBelle expressed doubt about Henry's dream.

Years before, when he had written a college textbook, *Vertebrates of Florida*, the Stevensons ended up paying some publication costs. Never again, RosaBelle declared, and Henry agreed. But when he began the new work, he had no contract, no agreement, no guarantee that anybody would publish it.

Tall Timbers, a non-profit research facility near the Georgia border, gave him a small grant and an office in which to work. One year of research turned into two, and two into four, and four into eight.

Henry believed in being thorough. He criss-crossed the state gathering data. A 500-mile drive to Miami sometimes turned into a 2,000-mile birding expedition. He visited every museum in the nation that had skins from Florida birds, including the Smithsonian, where he spent two weeks picking through its collection. He flew to London to visit museums where skins from Florida birds were stored. He tried to read every scientific paper about Florida birds ever written.

"Whatsoever you do," Henry told his children, quoting Colossians 3:23 from his Bible, "do it heartily, as unto the Lord."

When he focused on birding, the rest of the world went away.

On one field trip, as he drove 55 mph on I-10, he failed to notice the ominous rattle coming from the rear. Suddenly, the camper top and the canoe blew off the Isuzu pickup truck. He didn't stop because he didn't know how to fix it. A son came back later to recover the lost items.

His disinterest in anything lacking feathers, and his reputation for being the absent-minded professor, were well known. When he was still teaching, he took students on field trips in an FSU van. On one trip, he stopped for fuel. He was so eager to get to the birding that he forgot to remove the fuel hose from the van. When he drove away, he pulled down the gas pump.

In 1985, when Henry was 71, RosaBelle began worrying about him. Maybe he was getting too old for the field trips, for the stress he put on himself. If Henry had any doubts, he kept them to himself, except to quote *Macbeth*:

I am now stept in so far, that, should I wade no more, returning were as tedious as go o'ever.

• • •

Henry recruited an old friend, one of South Florida's finest birders, to help. But after a year, the man, in his mid-60s, began to doubt his commitment to Henry Stevenson's vision. He asked out of the project.

Henry began looking around for another aide, somebody willing to sacrifice everything for The Book, somebody younger. He remembered Bruce Anderson.

Born in 1948, Anderson was something of a child prodigy when it came to birding. He had memorized Arthur Howell's 579-page *Florida Bird Life* as a boy. Like Henry Stevenson, he was writing scientific papers for prestigious journals as a teenager. An Orlando resident, he studied biological sciences at the University of Central Florida and then started graduate school in Oklahoma. But he lost his enthusiasm for his studies, quit school and went to work for the state's labor department.

Henry had met Bruce a few times and been impressed by the young man. Among other things, he liked the fact that Bruce had gathered hundreds of bird skins for UCF's collection. Bruce had no qualms about shooting a bird or two in the name of science.

On August 17, 1986, Henry offered Bruce the job.

"It never occurred to me to say no," says Bruce, whose name follows Henry's on the cover of *The Birdlife of Florida*. "It was the greatest honor of my life. I'd always admired the classic ornithologists, and Dr. Stevenson was the last of his kind."

Bruce had no intentions of quitting his job with the state, but he told Dr. Stevenson—he never called him "Henry" and it never occurred to Henry to tell the younger man to call him by his first name—that he could contribute to the book after work and on weekends. A few weeks later, the state promoted Bruce to special deputy. In his new job, more demanding than the old, he'd have to travel the state as an administrative hearing officer, settling unemployment compensation claims.

He had less time to give to the project than he thought. But he didn't want to disappoint Dr. Stevenson. He'd given his word. Anyway, Dr. Stevenson was getting old and needed help.

"If, for whatever reason," Dr. Stevenson wrote him in 1986, "I am unable to complete this book, the project should fall into your hands . . . I have absolutely no reason to expect this to happen, but life is full of unexpected events."

But Dr. Stevenson felt fine. Medicine kept his high blood pressure in check. And his cholesterol was a healthy 170. Every morning, before breakfast, he did sit-ups. Remaining physically fit was something else he had in common with Bruce, who ran 40 miles a week. But they also were very different. Bruce had a rich social life and Dr. Stevenson had none. Bruce was a flashy dresser—even wore a lot of jewelry—and Dr. Stevenson was oblivious to fashion. Bruce could become excited enough to swear.

"But only once in his presence," he says. "I slipped and a four-letter word came out. An immense silence fell upon the world."

Some weekends they'd go on field trips together, their expenses paid by a small grant from the game commission. They drove, usually in silence, with windows open. Over the hum of tires, over the howl of the wind, Dr. Stevenson could hear birds twittering. When he heard an interesting one, they'd stop the truck and walk into the woods for two hours. If they stopped at water, they'd canoe for two hours. They'd record every bird they saw and heard. Six months later, they'd return to the same spot and gather data again. Then they'd spend hours in museums, studying bird skins.

Only one photograph was taken of them together, which Bruce keeps on the bookcase in his bedroom. In the photo, Dr. Stevenson holds the skin of a Carolina parakeet and Bruce holds the skin of a passenger pigeon, two extinct birds, the last of their kinds.

After researching together Bruce would go home to work on his part of the book and Dr. Stevenson would drive home or to his office at Tall Timbers and work on his. Bruce would mail his part to Dr. Stevenson, who often rewrote it so it would sound like his voice, a scientist's voice, precise and emotionless.

"A rare to uncommon summer resident across n Florida," went one of Dr. Stevenson's passages about the Swainson's warbler. ". . . an occasional to rare transient throughout; a few may winter in s Florida (ca: 4 reports through 1992). Fifty or more museum specimens known, of which 2 suggest winter: Lake "Jessop" (Jessup? Seminole Co.), "winter of 1869,' R. Thaxter (MCZ 47270) and n Key Largo, 1 DOR 6 Dec, 1971 (L Brown GEW 4561)."

To most people, Dr. Stevenson's prose probably sounds like utter gobbledygook. But the above passage offers precise, authoritative directions to readers who may want to check the facts for themselves by visiting MCZ, the Museum for Comparative Zoology at Harvard, and asking for Specimen No. 47270. A DOR is a dead on the road; future researchers can find that specimen, No. 4561, in the collection of GEW, or Glen E. Woolfenden, stored at Archbold Biological Station at Lake Placid.

Bruce usually took no offense in the editing. He just worked harder, sometimes until 4 a.m. Bruce had no wife who would complain about his late hours, but his romantic life screeched to a halt. His friends eventually stopped asking if he wanted to go out because they knew he wouldn't. By project's end he had stopped eating right, stopped exercising, gained 40 pounds, suddenly noticed he was middle aged and getting older. He tells people his life was postponed for a few years.

"I was there to serve Dr. Stevenson's vision. This was his book."

By 1990, Dr. Stevenson had been working on his book full-time for 16 years. The game commission, which had been funding the research, wanted it finished. But Dr. Stevenson kept discovering new data. And he'd type it into his manuscript and hand it to a secretary, who would dutifully type it into the computer manuscript, as Dr. Stevenson hovered nervously. He distrusted computers as he distrusted most technology.

Dr. Stevenson's manuscript provided detailed accounts of more than 500 bird species. It was 2,998 pages long. Finally, it seemed to be done.

A book like this isn't published overnight. Months went by. A year went by. Bruce and Dr. Stevenson fretted. Then Dr. Stevenson began researching a new scientific paper on Carolina birds. Now it was RosaBelle's turn to fret. So much for Henry's retirement.

"It was so Henry!"

On November 1, 1991, he visited his back yard and wrote his last field note:
For the first time in memory, a Carolina wren came to my feeder that contained nothing but seeds. Wood thrush still in the yard.

On November 4, he drove to Tall Timbers for his last day of work.

He wrote a letter to a *Tallahassee Democrat* writer about her column on Daylight Saving Time. He opposed DST because it complicated his bird data collections.

Noon in the summer was different from noon in the winter.

Next he read with pleasure a letter from Walter Taylor, an ornithologist at the University of Central Florida. Taylor had read Henry's and Bruce's manuscript and considered it a brilliant work. Henry typed out a thank you note.

Then he got a phone call from an editor at University Press of Florida. Everything was going smoothly. The book was moving ahead.

Henry Stevenson left his office and walked across a wide green lawn to a small red brick building where he could share his news with Dana Strickland, the young secretary who had typed most of his manuscript into the computer. Henry could intimidate other scientists, and his presence could fluster amateur birders, but she found him endearing, from the Bermuda shorts he wore with blue socks to his mechanical ineptitude. "Mr. Henry," as she called him, didn't even know how to work a copy machine.

Mr. Henry bumped into Dana in the hall and told her his good news about the book. She hadn't seen him in a while, so she invited him into her office to sit and talk a spell. "Let's catch up," she said.

Mr. Henry, who liked her Georgia accent, who had taken to calling her "my Southern girl," sat for a talk.

Suddenly, he clutched his chest.

It was his 77-year-old heart failing.

Dana quickly dialed another secretary, who knew she was serious and called 911. Two scientists—one, fittingly, an ornithologist—heard the commotion, ran into Dana's office, laid Mr. Henry on the floor and tried to revive him.

At 3:50 p.m., medics arrived by ambulance and by helicopter. But they couldn't revive him either. Henry Stevenson, the last of his kind, was officially extinct.

He left the world like Moses, without seeing the Promised Land. But those who knew him wonder if it mattered that he never saw his book, birding's own Bible, in print. For this unusual man—the strangest of birds—the long journey to get there may have been enough.

"My dad was a goal-oriented person," says Jim Stevenson, the son who probably knew him best. "Within an hour of finding out his book is going to be published, he drops dead. His goal is met and now he can die. It's so typical of him."

"He died fulfilled," RosaBelle Stevenson says. "But I wish he could have at least seen the book."

RosaBelle has been gratified by the outpouring of emotion about her husband from Henry's old colleagues. She had no idea they thought so highly of him. He never told her, never uttered anything that sounded like a boast.

She has been thrilled by rave views for *The Birdlife of Florida.*

"It is the most accurate, most comprehensive review of the birdlife in Florida since 1932," says Noel Wamer, who is writing a story about the book for *American Birding* magazine.

"It is truly monumental," says the *Smithsonian's* Storrs Olson in his review. ". . . a heroic effort that cannot be duplicated."

"I think Henry would have been pleased," RosaBelle says. But she can't be sure what Henry would think. Henry mystified her, and sometimes she walks around their home, visits his cluttered office, looks at his musty science books, sits in his worn chair, gazes at his old sneakers, picks up his cracked old Bible, goes into his back yard to pick figs from his beloved tree, comes back into the house, plays tapes of Henry singing religious hymns, goes to the living room, stops at his photograph on the fireplace mantle, and scolds him.

For leaving.

For being the way he was.

For being Henry.

Yet even in old age she's not a person to dwell on the unpleasant for long. She walks outside and—despite pleadings from her children—climbs the stepladder and shakes pears off the trees. "Who'll do it if I don't?" she asks. Or she pulls on her husband's old rubber boots, picks up a shovel and scoops muck out of their pond. Henry would have approved. Sometimes he made her bristle by giving her lists of things he wanted done around the house.

His life's work, his grand book, has one picture, a modest sketch of a wading bird, a limpkin, that Bruce Anderson drew for the cover and title page. Otherwise, there are no illustrations except for maps. The audience for this book—professional ornithologists and the most expert, fanatical of amateur birders—are people who know what birds look like. So far, 330 of them have paid $120 to buy the 4 1/2-pound book.

RosaBelle's favorite part is the "In Memoriam" section written by her son Jim, who praises his father for his dedication, expertise and integrity. It is the only real emotion overtly expressed in 907 pages.

"I don't know that I really knew him," Jim says, driving his dad's pickup truck through the dark streets of Tallahassee one rainy night. "He kept a lot of things to himself. Sometimes I thought my dad was playing roles, doing what was expected of him, teaching, the family, the church.

"But this brilliant, analytical man could become a child in front of a bird. They brought out the joy of life for him like nothing else."

Four days after his father died, Jim saw sandhill cranes in the marsh by his house. Old habits die hard; automatically he dialed his father's phone number.

Who else would he have called?

Henry, wherever he was—raging in oblivion's dark or smiling in a heavenly mansion—would have wanted to know about the cranes.

Miami Beach cheesecake

St. Petersburg
March 1993

Suzanne and I finish supper at a nice downtown restaurant. Of course I order cheesecake. It's my habit. It's good cheesecake, perfectly respectable cheesecake, but I'm still let down. I have impossible cheesecake standards.

It is my dad's fault. He worked half his life at the biggest hotel on Miami Beach. As chief steward at the Fontainebleau, he carried out the head chef's orders at the hotel's half dozen restaurants, from dawn until long after dusk, six days a week. The pay was lousy, the benefits lousier, and he never got holidays off.

However, he did smuggle home the world's greatest cheesecakes. They were an honest foot across and about six inches high—wonderful, mountainous cheesecakes. They were moist, and they were rich, and they usually were topped with fresh strawberries.

When we ate like the rich folks we felt like royalty.

We were a blue-collar family. Children of the Depression, my parents scrimped and saved and did without. When I wanted a new Nellie Fox baseball mitt, or a six-transistor radio to listen to White Sox games, I saved my paper-route money and bought them myself. We weren't poor, though sometimes we felt that way.

On the other hand, we ate the secret cheesecake of kings. As *Gunsmoke* played on the black-and-white television, as my dad lay on the couch in his undershorts and my mom finished bobby-pinning her hair, we sat in the living room and ate illicit cheesecake, the same cheesecake that Frank Sinatra might be ordering across Biscayne Bay on Miami Beach.

My dad, a Sinatra fan, was once a professional musician himself. Calling himself "Ernie Bergen," he played the music of the Big Band era. In 1952, hoping to cash in on Florida's tourist boom, he was optimistic enough to move his family from Chicago to Miami. There were fewer musician jobs than he hoped, it turned out, and after struggling as a nightclub pianist for two years he shelved the music dream and went to work at the Fontainebleau.

For my dad, free cheesecake was just one of the perks. All the big acts played the Fontainebleau. Martin and Lewis. Henny Youngman. Red Skelton. Frank Sinatra.

Sinatra was my dad's favorite. Late at night, he'd slip into the back of the Poodle Room and catch part of Frank's act. My dad was a pretty good saloon singer, too. Playing the piano, he'd lean back from the keyboards and croon "The Lady Is A Tramp," copying Sinatra's phrasing in our living room. One time he saw his hero up close. My dad was there when Sinatra came into the hotel kitchen to praise the chef's chicken cacciatore.

I was more impressed by my dad's ability to score cheesecake than I was with his "I saw Sinatra" stories. I looked forward to the nights he would come home carrying the plain white box tied with string. "Look what I have, Bea," he'd say. My mom would take the first heavenly bite, shut her eyes and sigh.

It is funny thinking about it now. My dad, infamous cheesecake smuggler, was a straight arrow, the most scrupulously honest person I've known. He always drove just under the speed limit. He was the kind of man who would alert the sales clerk who gave too much change. But as those cheesecakes proved, he wasn't a goody-two-shoes.

My dad was the Robin Hood of cheesecakes.

"How do you get the cheesecakes?" I asked him once. He looked me in the eyes and said his friend the baker gave the cheesecakes to him. His answer was enough for me then, though I'd like more detail now. Did the baker have permission to hand out expensive cheesecakes to employees? Did Dad put the cheesecake box under his coat when he strolled past the security guard?

Was cheesecake smuggling part of a guerrilla war against the notoriously skin-flint hotel owner?

I'll never know the answer to those questions. Dad died in 1982, not long after the hotel fired him, not for years of cheesecake pilfering, but for a more serious crime. He got old and the new hotel management wanted younger blood.

It may sound strange, but all these things run through my mind when I order cheesecake at restaurants now. I think about growing up, and my dad, and how you never know someone as well as you think. Then my wife leans over the table, touches my hand and says, "I married you for the cheesecake, you know."

We met at college in 1969. On our second date, I invited her over for a cheesecake my dad had brought home. She was very impressed, and a week later we became engaged. We married the following summer. We have three children. We're still in love.

Thanks for the cheesecake, Dad. Thanks for everything.

Sweet potato pie

St. Petersburg
January 1994

The grand sweet potato pie idea did not come all at once. Thunderbolts of inspiration happen in the movies and in fictional books but seldom in real life. Doretha Bacon's pie plan evolved over several years, calorie by calorie, crumb by crumb.

"I always knew my sweet potato pie was special," she'll tell you. "And I knew I wanted to do something special with it. It took awhile to figure what."

Mrs. Bacon grew up eating sweet potato pie, a traditional dessert among African-Americans in the South. Her mother made a fine sweet potato pie, and that talent came naturally to Doretha, too. When she opened the first of her Doe-Al's Country Cooking restaurants in St. Petersburg a quarter century ago, sweet potato pie had a prominent place on the menu. Wise diners always leave room for a slice.

"It's popular with my customers," she says modestly.

A few years ago, Mrs. Bacon was walking down a Publix aisle when she happened upon the crowded dessert freezer. There were the usual apple, cherry, coconut and lemon meringue pies offered by those successful corporate pie women, Sara Lee, Marie Callender and Mrs. Smith.

Conspicuously absent were sweet potato pies. Mrs. Bacon started thinking. Mrs. Bacon believed her sweet potato pies were as good as any pie on the $279-million pie market. One of these days, she thought to herself, I'm going to sell sweet potato pies in a big way. Closing her eyes, she could almost imagine it: A sweet potato pie factory, conveyer belts humming with sweet potato pies, supermarket freezers bursting with sweet potato pies, Americans making Mrs. B's Sweet Potato Pie a household name.

People who know her well say that when Mrs. Bacon latches onto an idea, they start rolling up their sleeves. Hard work lies ahead.

"When my aunt says she's going to do something," says Steve Cruz, "she's going to do it."

Mrs. Bacon is a robust woman with short gray hair, large round glasses and dangling, silver earrings. Wearing the white uniform of a cook, she spends most of the day on her feet, walking around her restaurant, working with food and issuing orders. Her husband Eddie—they married 30 years ago after meeting on a blind date—often advises her to rest.

"I'm not ready to rest," she says firmly. "You can say I'm sixty-five but no-body will believe it. I run right by them."

Mrs. Bacon started running the moment she graduated from St. Petersburg's Gibbs High School near the end of World War II. Right away she opened her first business, a beauty shop. When it failed, she moved to New York and worked as a waitress.

She got a job in Manhattan as a live-in babysitter, continued saving money and eventually graduated from the New York Institute of Dietetics. That led to a food career that has included stints at nursing homes, hospitals, bowling alleys and finally her own restaurants.

The Bacons moved to St. Petersburg after Eddie's 27-year military career came to an end. Doretha had no plans for retirement, though. She wanted to start the kind of restaurant that always has been popular in the Deep South, a restaurant that served lots of family-style food in big bowls placed on groaning tables.

The odds were stacked against her. Only three percent of American compa-nies are owned by black people, according to U.S. Census figures, for reasons that include racism, low-income communities, poor credit, a lack of business experience and education. In 1969, no bank would loan the Bacons money for their restaurant.

Doretha, though, saw no racial slight in the rejection.

"We didn't have any credit here," she says.

When they had saved money, they rented a place and opened a restaurant. "Nobody can tell me I can't do something for such and such a reason," she says. "I've never let anything get in the way of anything I've really wanted to do. I wanted a restaurant, so I got the license and opened the doors."

Doretha and her sister Alice were partners. They called their place Doe-Al's. The menu was written on brown paper bags. They served fried chicken, barbecue, mullet, collard greens, okra, and blackeyed peas. Dessert was her delicious sweet po-tato pie.

The recipe is no secret, though proportions are. Her pie contains sweet pota-toes, flour, shortening, non-fat dry milk, whole milk, cane sugar, eggs, flavorings, spices, salt and butter.

"If there's a key, it's butter," she admits. "If people think they're not going to get butter in a Doe-Al's pie, they've got another think coming."

Alice eventually left Doe-Al's to start her own day-care business. But Doretha and her husband, and a scattering of relatives and friends, carried on in a series of restaurants in black and white neighborhoods throughout the city.

Several times she has closed her doors for lack of business. But her loyal customers, who include diners of all races, have always encouraged her to start over again. She launched her latest Doe-Al in the fall, Mrs. B's Doe-Al's, in downtown St. Petersburg's Huntington Hotel. She has been working 12-hour days to make it work.

But she confesses to some distractions.

Now in a supermarket freezer near you:

Mrs. B's Original Recipe Southern Heritage Sweet Potato Pie.

In an industrial neighborhood near the Thunderdome, Doretha Bacon has her own modest sweet potato pie factory. It has been humming rather steadily for five months. Mrs. Bacon has been an even busier woman than usual.

She has had a sweet potato pie box designed. She has made many pies. And like a missionary preaching the gospel, she has zealously visited the corporate headquarters of supermarket chains to spread the word about them. When she visits, she has a hot sweet potato pie in hand.

Last summer, she headed for Atlanta and Kroger's regional office. She stopped first at a friend's kitchen and baked a pie. Then she picked up some whipped cream and pecans, the *piece de resistance*.

"I set that man up," she declares.

The Kroger buyer picked up his fork, worked some pie around his mouth and inhaled the rest.

"He almost drank my pie!" Doretha Bacon says with delight. "He said, 'I'll take five hundred!'"

The pies have found homes in freezers belonging to Kroger, Publix, U-Save, Kash n' Karry and selected Winn-Dixie stores throughout the South. "It's not in all stores," Mrs. Bacon says. Some supermarket managers in white neighborhoods have been reluctant to stock the pie, wondering if it would appeal to their customers.

Mrs. Bacon patiently explains to them her experience in the restaurant business: People of all races enjoy sweet potato pie, anytime, anyplace. Once they have sampled it, they will want more. Just give it a chance.

Still, Mrs. Bacon wishes to be known for more than just one pie. She is laying plans to market her apple and coconut cream pies, in regular and diabetic editions. And maybe sometime down the line, America will be ready for her home-made salad dressing and famous barbecue sauce.

In the meantime, sweet potato pies are keeping Mrs. Bacon and her 21 employees busy enough.

"I knew this idea was going to take off," she says. "Everything else these days seems to be cut out of a pattern, stamped out. If my pie ain't country, I don't know what is."

Recently, the supermarket chain Publix placed an order for more than 4,000 pies, which presented a series of logistical problems.

Mrs. Bacon stores her recipes in her head. Like any experienced cook, she adds things and tastes things as she goes along. That kind of cooking works fine at a small restaurant. To make 4,000 pies, she had to write down the sweet potato pie recipe and convert it into mass-market proportions. If that wasn't a challenge, Mrs. Bacon's 5,000-square foot factory, which she leases from a frozen-food storage company, is not equipped to burp out thousands of pies.

"Oh, we worked so hard filling that order," says Juanita Thompson, who has helped Mrs. Bacon, a distant relative, since 1969. "Pies, pies, pies. When I finally went to bed, I didn't count sheep. I counted sweet potato pies."

Mrs. Bacon and associates stayed awake for 72 hours making pies by hand, placing them into boxes by hand, then carrying them into a huge freezer. They delivered some pies in Mrs. Bacon's station wagon.

"We were ready to kill each other by the end," Steve Cruz says, "but we finished the job. I was so hyper and full of coffee I couldn't go to sleep."

Cruz, 39, takes after his aunt. He was 14 when he started washing dishes at her restaurant. Except for a stint in the military, he has never left her. When he is not managing her restaurant, he is the vice president of the pie company. He is lining up investors to help finance additional equipment for the factory. He spends most of his time looking for new accounts and heeding his aunt's orders, which are legion.

"Our restaurants have been successful," he says, "but I think the future is in pies."

Mrs. Bacon agrees.

"I'm not ready for my restaurant to die, but pies are going to take up all of my time," she says. She looks across the kitchen and sighs.

"I wish I started on pies twenty years ago."

Today the South.

Tomorrow the World!

At the manatee necropsy

St. Petersburg
April 1993

A manatee, the number 9302 written in chalk on its side, lies waiting on a stainless steel table, stone-cold dead. A wildlife officer discovered it floating in the St. Johns River yesterday and sent it immediately to Dr. Scott Wright at the state's Marine Mammal Pathobiology Laboratory in St. Petersburg. Finding out what kills manatees is his line of work.

"If we don't know what's killing them, we don't know the problems they face in the environment," Wright tells me, brandishing a large knife with a white handle and a flashing blade.

The manatee is a young male, seven feet long and 700 pounds. A living manatee is generally gray, the color of an African elephant, but 9302 is dark brown, with black patches, and bloated with gas.

"I don't know how much we'll be able to get from this one—it's too rotten," laments Wright, who has necropsied everything from tiny bats to mammoth sperm whales. Wright's lab, on a corner of the Eckerd College campus, is no place to visit after a pancake breakfast. When he does a necropsy on a manatee, a manatee that may have been dead for days, the room is filled with unspeakable odors. I don't know if I'll make it. My stomach has climbed to my throat.

"You get used to it," says Wright, who grew up hunting and fishing in Florida and trained at the University of Connecticut for his life's work. "But I wouldn't want to do this with a hangover."

Dressed in a blue jump suit, yellow apron and brown rubberboots and gloves, he examines the skin of manatee 9302 for abrasions. Nothing there. Then, with his knife, he begins his first incision. His two assistants automatically step back. They know a decomposing manatee, filled with gas, can explode like a balloon when pierced.

Manatees, an endangered species that number fewer than 2,000 animals, face many perils in Florida waters. Boats plow into them, breaking bones and rupturing internal organs. Water management floodgates crush, trap and drown them. A cold snap can stress manatees enough to lower their defenses against infections from which they might otherwise recover. Although manatees are vegetarians, they sometimes accidentally consume fishing line, which can fatally block their digestive systems. Immune disorders and pollution also play a poorly understood role in manatee deaths.

In 1992, the state opened a $300,000 St. Petersburg laboratory designed to collect reliable mortality information under strict scientific conditions. Wright supervises the facility. At 43, he has been examining dead animals for various state and university institutions for nearly a decade, working on endangered species from bald eagles to Florida panthers.

"We don't do surgery here," says Wright, who once necropsied 11 deer in a single night on behalf of the Florida Game and Fresh Water Fish Commission. "We're sort of highly educated butchers who have to work quickly. The longer we take, the faster decomposition can alter tissue. Decomposition is the enemy."

Dead manatees, like the one Wright is about to cut open, have been studied by state and federal wildlife specialists since 1974. But research until recently was hampered by crude equipment, inadequate facilities, inconsistent standards and not enough people to collect dead manatees and work on them. Years ago, biologists often necropsied decomposing manatees on river banks as the sun beat down and vultures watched from the nearest palm tree. In 1989, when Wright joined the state's manatee team, his equipment consisted of a box that contained two knives.

Now dead manatees throughout the state are trucked to the Eckerd College lab in specially designed refrigerator trailers that slow decomposition. The facility, a plain white building surrounded by a tall fence, contains two offices and four computers, dressing rooms and showers, a laundry for washing contaminated clothing, a walk-in refrigerator for storing dead manatees, and a sterile lab for tissue analysis.

The necropsy room where Wright stands poised over the bloated manatee has sinks, hoists, scales, hoses, drains, collection jars, buckets, sharp knives and electric saws. It has, thankfully, a powerful exhaust system that at least mitigates odors by sending them outside, where they are absorbed by Boca Ciega Bay breezes, auto exhaust from the nearby Pinellas Bayway and the already pungent sewage-treatment center next door.

The decomposing manatee does not explode.

I hang on to my breakfast.

Wright and his assistants go about their work. One aide painstakingly removes a fin and then a bone from the ear for posterity. An ear bone, like a tree, has growth rings. Finished, the aide cuts off the manatee's head, for future study. If the manatee were fresh, the brain would be saved for additional research.

"No point on this one," Wright mutters. "The brain is soup."

I look gingerly over his shoulder as he examines internal organs, takes samples and dictates his findings to another aide. He also thinks aloud. What killed this manatee? He is unsure. Yet there are signs of illness. A healthy manatee that died suddenly often has a full stomach. This manatee's stomach is virtually empty. Why did it stop eating? Wright finds a small section of fishing line in the stomach. Last year he necropsied a manatee that had swallowed a fishing line and hook. The hook tore up 25 feet of intestine, causing a fatal infection.

"But I don't think this line is the culprit."

Wright weighs the 100-foot intestine, which looks like a fire hose. It's only 60 pounds. This manatee should have a 120-pound intestine. The featherweight intestine is additional evidence of something amiss. Now Wright feels the colon for feces. Normal manatee feces are soft. This colon is clogged by hard feces. What caused the digestive breakdown? Wright has no idea and he fears that further lab tests on the badly decomposed organs will turn up nothing. Still he continues.

"A carcass, as bad as this one is, provides the last chance to collect information. So you take advantage."

Some biologists think toxins and heavy metals depress manatee immune systems, opening the door for fatal illnesses. Wright takes liver and kidney samples for their studies. As he cuts, fluid squirts onto his face and eyeglasses. He grins, walks to the sink and washes.

"Manatees carry pathogens that could make humans sick," he says. But it's never happened in the 19 years that even inexperienced biologists have been performing manatee necropsies in Florida.

"We're careful," he says.

At the Eckerd College lab, business stays brisk during the winter and early spring. Cold months are the most perilous for manatees. If a ferocious front catches them in unsheltered waters, they can die outright of hypothermia or become weakened and die of a variety of diseases. During winter, they instinctively gravitate to springs and power plant outfalls where water stays consistently warm. Concentrated in relatively small areas, manatees are vulnerable to speeding boats and premature death.

Outside, on a trailer, covered by ice, is today's second manatee. "I think it's pretty fresh," says a biologist who collected the dead manatee from the other coast this morning and brought it to Wright. The manatee does seem in better condition than the last. It's gray and streamlined instead of brown and bloated. The overwhelming odor of decay is missing, thank heavens. The dead animal weighs 478 pounds.

"We should get more information from this one," Wright says with the unmistakable enthusiasm of a person who loves his work.

Born in St. Louis, he grew up in Tampa, where his father introduced him to the outdoors at an early age. Later, he lived on a Pasco County ranch, and worked with horses and cattle and hunted and fished at every opportunity. After St. Petersburg Junior College, he studied zoology at Florida State, the University of South Florida and the University of Florida but settled for a job with Pinellas County parks as a maintenance worker, a ranger and finally a supervisor.

He wanted something more for himself: In Wisconsin and Connecticut, for a fatter paycheck, he designed sewage systems. "But one night I was watching poop fly off this piece of equipment and I thought 'This is crazy.'" He entered the University of Connecticut's pathobiology program and emerged five years later with a doctoral degree and the opportunity to get his hands on interesting animals that happened to be dead.

For the game commission he necropsied the last two alligators to fatally attack human beings in Florida, hoping to find a pathological reason for abnormal behavior. "But they turned out to be beautiful, healthy animals," he says. "We concluded that the people in the water simply represented a suitable prey package and were taken."

He has necropsied a sperm whale that expired on the beach in Fort Pierce. The trick when working on huge animals, he says with a straight face, is avoiding falling into the body cavity. "Nobody would give you a ride home," says Wright, who will soon marry a biologist who studies manatees—live ones.

Using a hoist, Wright and his assistants swing the dead manatee onto the examining table. An aide writes "MSE9305" on the body. Wright points out symmetrical markings on both flanks. They aren't from boat propellers, he says, and they weren't made by boat hulls. They are the kinds of marks one sees on manatees crushed in floodgates.

He slices open the manatee. Inside, it has decomposed more than he hoped. Still, he notes the healthy layers of blubber. A diseased animal that stops eating would have begun to deplete its surplus of fat. This manatee has large fat stores and a belly full of grass. Death may have been sudden.

"Some ribs are dislocated," he adds. It's like a great weight pushed down so hard on the manatee that something had to give. Wright's floodgate theory is looking good.

Then he notices the lungs. They look sickly. He takes a tissue sample for later study. "It could be pneumonia," he says. Injured badly in the floodgate, perhaps the ailing animal got sick and developed a fatal pneumonia. But maybe the manatee became ill first—and then blundered, weak and helpless, into the fatal floodgate. (Later, he would learn the pulmonary infection was caused by an organism ordinarily found in the digestive track. He still was unsure how the manatee died).

"It's detective work," Wright says. "Sometimes you never find out."

Outside, the sun is shining through the deep blue skies. Inside the necropsy lab, amid the horrible smells, Scott Wright has been working on dead manatees for nearly five hours. "I'm tired," he says. Tired and something else.

His stomach is growling.

"You know you've been in this business a long time when you still get hungry," he says, looking into my very wide eyes. "Right now I'm thinking about a meat loaf sandwich on home-baked bread."

Looking for the right whales

Fernandina Beach
March 1994

> *Now small fowls flew screaming over the yet yawning*
> *gulf; a sullen white surf beat against its steep sides;*
> *then all collapsed, and the great shroud of the sea*
> *rolled on as it rolled five thousand years ago.*
> —Herman Melville, 1851

Call him Chris Slay, the Ahab of a New Age. Like the obsessed captain of an artist's grand fiction, he too is passionate about his whales. Slay—what a name for a whale man—even hunts them. Yet his intention is not to strike them dead with Ahab's harpoon. With all his might he tries to protect the world's rarest large whales from mortal harm.

"Inbound tanker, this is survey plane Seven-Two Seven."

Every day, weather permitting, he boards a small Cessna and flies along the Atlantic Ocean near the Florida-Georgia border and patrols the only known northern right whale calving grounds on Earth. From a bird's eye view 750 feet above the white-caps, he tries to direct ships away from the whales and their young.

Black and shiny, blowing steamy geysers of hot breath, right whales during the winter show up in the busy shipping channels, or in front of the ever-present dredg-ing barges, or just off the island where nuclear submarines are armed for doomsday. True leviathans, right whales grow to about 50 feet and 70 tons. They move slowly, swim at the surface, and seem oblivious to danger.

"Please be advised," Slay broadcasts over his VHS radio. "There are two right whales at the entrance of the St. Johns River shipping channel two nautical miles ahead. Over."

When Slay radios, most captains respond immediately. They know he works for the New England Aquarium helping the federal government in a new comprehen-sive program designed to keep ships away from whales. Yet some have no idea who he is or what he is doing. Some have no idea that large whales—much less the world's rarest—are found in the shipping channels of a land better known for palm trees and alligators.

Sometimes a language barrier adds unbearable tension to an already dramatic situation.

There is the ship, pushing a wake, steaming ahead, bearing down, a captain with a thick European accent at the helm.

There is the right whale mother, innocently tending her calf, the way millions of years of evolution prepared her, but in the worst possible place.

Slay tries to remain calm as disaster looms in the shipping channel.

"Right ahead of you," Slay says in a gentle southern twang. "Right whales. Just ahead. Please be advised."

As he holds his breath, the ship eventually slows.

Then it changes course. His lungs start working again. In the channel, the right whale continues to suckle her calf. They're safe—at least until next time.

"Every whale is precious," Slay later explains in an airport waiting room. "You lose one right whale, and you've lost too many."

Northern right whales once were among the planet's most common large whales. Literally and figuratively they were the "right whales" to exploit. They swam sluggishly near shore, showed little fear of men with harpoons, and conveniently floated after death while bones and blubber were extracted. Even so, they numbered in the thousands and thousands and were hunted for 800 years. In *Moby Dick*, Melville was sure that whales were so many, and the sea so vast, that whalers could never kill them all.

"He swam the seas before the continents broke water; he once swam over the site of the Tuileries, and Windsor Castle, and the Kremlin," he wrote. "In Noah's flood he despised Noah's Ark; and if ever the world is to be again flooded, like the Netherlands, to kill off its rats, then the eternal whale will still survive, and rearing upon the topmost crest of the equatorial flood, spout his frothed defiance to the skies."

Melville was all wet.

"Whalers put the hurtin' on 'em," Slay explains.

He and Melville—and Ahab too—would have much to discuss.

Right whales were nearly extinct by 1930. In 1937, the League of Nations persuaded most whaling countries to leave them alone, and in 1949 the International Whaling Commission granted them complete protection. Today, only about 300 northern right whales survive in the Pacific and about that many in the Atlantic. They are considered the rarest of the great whales.

As an endangered species, the right whale is protected from intentional killing and harassment, and the federal government is poised to name several coastal areas as "critical habitat," including a 200-mile stretch from the Altamaha River in South Georgia to Sebastian Inlet in East Central Florida.

The ominous-sounding designation primarily will give the whales, and the places they are most exposed to harm, a higher public profile. Other possible measures, including restricting shipping traffic, have been rejected, for now, by federal officials. The National Marine Fisheries Service, which oversees the program, is waiting to see how the shipping industry complies with voluntary measures to protect whales.

The Atlantic right whale, which hugs the congested coast from Nova Scotia to Florida, is especially vulnerable to shipping traffic. In the winter, pregnant whales migrate south to have their young in an area that boasts five commercial shipping ports, two Navy bases and a large armada of pleasure and work boats. Only seven to 12 calves are born in a good year; last winter, two calves were found dead in Florida waters. One was too decomposed to determine how it died. About the other there was no doubt: A Coast Guard cutter captain reported running it over.

"Two calves," sighs Chris Slay. "Right there we might have lost twenty percent of the new population for the year. We have to do something."

At 32, Slay is both delicate and athletic. He has light brown hair, wears metal-framed glasses and speaks quietly in bursts. Every day, after work, he goes for a long run or throws his kayak into the surf, paddles out and rides the waves to shore. Then he returns to his rented waterfront condo and listens to rock music—the Clash or the Velvet Underground—or curls up with his battered copy of *Contemporary American Poetry* or *Moby Dick*.

Papers, relating to his work, are piled on tables, stacked on the floor or taped to walls. A fax machine hums frantically. Old clothes and foul shoes are scattered about the living room, which seems to be filling slowly with beach sand. Sometimes Slay is so busy with whale work that he forgets housework. He forgets to eat breakfast, or eats breakfast at lunch. He's out of dishes, so he spoons his raisin bran from a huge wooden bowl that most people would use to toss a salad.

He grew up hundreds of miles from the nearest whales, on a family farm in southwest Georgia, where his father had a liquor distribution business and his mother was a schoolteacher. Slay's passion was literature and poetry. He wanted to be a poet, perhaps the next Yeats or Dylan Thomas.

The sea beckoned. After high school, he fled to the coast to work on a shrimp boat. He eventually enrolled at the University of Georgia as an English major, but every summer he returned to the sea, and to the shrimp, to make money. After graduating, he considered teaching or writing as a career. After all, he had friends in the college town of Athens who were making a living following their muse. Four people he knew had even started a band. They called themselves R.E.M., and they were selling their dreamy records by the millions.

Instead Slay found a position, funded by the federal government, on a dredge deepening shipping channels for Navy submarines at King's Bay, Ga. His job was watching to see if endangered sea turtles turned up dead in the dredge pipes.

In 1988, he was working on a dredge when what he took to be black plastic pipe—two enormous pipes—surfaced. It was his first look at right whales. He took a photograph and gave it to New England Aquarium researchers who were trying to document the presence of right whales and their calves off Jacksonville.

The New England Aquarium, a non-profit Boston-based conservation organization, had been studying right whales since 1981. That summer, when the researchers followed the whales north to Canadian waters, Slay went along as a volunteer. Later they offered him a paying job. Protecting living things who have no voice can be an art too.

"I've seen wonderful things," he likes to tell people now.

On a single amazing day off Nova Scotia, he saw the world's largest mammal, a 100-foot long blue whale. He also watched a humpback, sei, minke, fin and a sperm whale, the focus of Melville's prose. He saw orcas—killer whales. They are the only known natural predator of right whales.

Right whales are special to him. During summer, the normally sluggish animals put on one of nature's most spectacular shows. "Imagine, a full city block of seething, tumultuous whale sex," Slay tells wide-eyed people, keeping their attention. For most of the year, right whales are slow-moving, bovine, content to spend their days straining thousands of pounds of microscopic plankton through their baleen and into their bellies.

Then amore.

When a female is ready to mate, she puts out a signal—probably an audible signal—that draws males from miles around. A female often is surrounded by 30 amorous males or more. Intimidated by the attention, or waiting for an especially attractive male, the female swims belly up. Males, shoving each other, jockeying for position, try to stay close enough to control her with their flippers. When the female has to turn to take a breath, the best-positioned male enters her with a maneuverable, prehensile penis that some times stretches nine feet.

Mating may take no more than 30 seconds. When one male finishes, another is waiting. And another and another and another. Right whales practice a natural phenomenon known as "sperm competition." Males instinctively try to wash out a competitor's sperm with quarts of their own and thereby ensure that their genes will continue.

Right whales are especially suited for the task. A blue whale, the largest animal to ever draw breath, has internal testes that weigh about 150 pounds. A right whale, half the blue whale's size, has testes that weigh about a ton.

"The largest ever to grace the planet," Chris Slay says.

When mating, right whales pay no attention to what is going on around them. Slay sometimes pulls up in a boat, takes out a compound bow, and fires a special arrow into a whale. Then he retrieves the arrow and the tiny piece of skin it has captured for a biopsy. The whales never even flinch.

"If you were making love to a beautiful woman," Slay explains patiently, "would you notice if a mosquito bit you on your back?"

In the fall, close to 10 percent of the northern right whale population heads south. This includes about a dozen pregnant females and perhaps two dozen juvenile whales. The remaining right whales vanish into the sea's great void. Researchers have no idea where.

The winter waters of South Georgia and North Florida seem to be perfect for pregnant right whales, neither too warm or cool, about 55 degrees. The water is relatively shallow, which means a mother whale can better watch her calf. Orcas seldom bother right whales so far south.

A calf is 12 to 18 feet when born. It feeds on its mother's milk, as much as 100 gallons in a day, exclusively. The mother converts energy from her blubber and eats nothing during her southern stay. When a mother feeds her calf she floats unmoving at the surface, both especially vulnerable to ship strikes.

Not that ship strikes are the only problem. In Canada, commercial fishers sometimes accidentally catch whales in huge gill nets anchored to the bottom. The whales usually break free. But in the summer of 1990, Slay saw a right whale in the Bay of Fundy dragging part of a gill net. Researchers were unable to cut the net loose.

The whale migrated south with other whales, getting weaker as it swam along. In the winter of 1991, it washed up dead near Slay's Fernandina Beach condo. Slay helped with the necropsy, a grisly, odoriferous affair. When the pathologist plunged the knife, the decomposing, gas-filled animal exploded, routing shrieking researchers and spectators. Undaunted, Slay and the pathologist returned. The whale, probably weakened by the net, had been killed by a ship.

"In that whale," Slay says, "was the embodiment of all their troubles."

Although few people associate whales with Florida, right whales have been migrating into southern waters for eons. The Spaniards called Jekyll Island, off South Georgia, the Isle of Whales. Fernandina Beach had a small whaling operation in the last century. But few people know about that aspect of their area's history.

Most Floridians, including some born here, have no idea that large whales— much less whales so rare—even visit. Slay tells them to keep their eyes open. Walking along Jacksonville Beach he has seen them cavorting less than a quarter-mile from shore.

Of course, it's unusual to spot them while beachcombing. Most of the time, the whales are well offshore, out of sight, seen by only a scattered number of mariners, who may or may not understand that seeing whales in winter is no coincidence but a natural, North Florida phenomenon.

Bill Kavanaugh is an exception. For two decades he has brought ships in and out of Port of Fernandina and made note of winter whales. "You don't see them very often," he says, "but you do see them."

But it never has been common knowledge along the waterfront. New England Aquarium researchers only knew, for sure, that right whales were having young in the South Atlantic about a decade ago. That's when an off-duty Delta pilot reported seeing a lot of whales heading south. Since then researchers have been gathering information and documenting ship strikes and mortality. They have found eight dead whales, mostly calves, in South Georgia and North Florida waters since 1988.

In an average month, more than 430 commercial ships come and go through the area used by whales. Citing national security, the military doesn't release shipping figures. But aircraft carriers, destroyers and submarines travel through in significant numbers.

"The whales have to pass through an amazing gauntlet," Slay says. At least they try. Last winter, an 82-foot Coast Guard cutter from Connecticut was cruising south past St. Augustine when it hit a 15-foot calf. Nobody had told the captain that right whales and their calves were in the area. The cutter had not reduced speed or posted a watch. The whale was cut almost in half.

"The whales can be difficult to see," Slay says. "They're black. They don't have a dorsal fin. They sort of sleep at the surface. But if you're watching for them, you're way ahead of the game."

Everybody seems to be watching now. Slay—and marine biologists from Florida, Georgia and the federal government—are making sure of it.

About twice a month, one or all of them calls on a port and conducts a whale seminar. They put on videos, a slide show, talk about the importance of whales, and explain why captains should treat whales like other ships. They hand out "Yield Right

Whale Habitat" warning stickers and ask captains or pilots who take ships in and out of the ports to attach the stickers to their charts.

"We don't threaten anybody," Slay says. No reason to, he adds. Intelligent people in the shipping industry understand that the federal government could take stronger measures than asking captains to voluntarily be careful when whales are around December through March. Stronger measures—rerouting or closing ports—might cost millions. Running a big ship today is a $1,000 an hour business.

On his official visits to the ports, Slay is always polite and neatly dressed. Although he is uncomfortable wearing a necktie, and never will be mistaken for a fashion model, he often wears a tie and laundered shirt and pants to these meetings.

"I come on like a young ensign," he says with a grin.

Anything to avoid looking like an "environmentalist" to the mostly conservative captains. In the firm voice he once used for reading his free-verse poetry in public, he tells them how important they are to the future of the rarest whale on the planet, and tells them he will be up in the airplane every day doing everything he can to keep them informed about where the whales are.

There have been no ship strikes this winter.

"So far," Slay says, "everything has been working like a dream. We're getting astounding cooperation."

"We don't want to be regulated," explains Lorraine Guise of the Canaveral Port Authority. "We're happy to take every precaution."

In January, a whale seminar was held in North Florida. Captain Drew Orton, of the Canaveral Pilots Association, attended. Four days later he took a large ship out the main channel. The first right whale he had ever seen surfaced in front of him. Orton immediately reduced speed. Then he figured out which way the whale was pointing, and turned the other way.

Sometimes it is boring to look for whales from the airplane. Sometimes it is exciting indeed. On one recent glorious day, Slay and his assistants counted 15 whales.

But that was unusual. Most days, if they see one or two, they are impressed. They call in the information to the ports, which are supposed to relay the news to incoming and outgoing ships. Or if a collision is imminent, Slay calls the ship.

Some days, he and his assistants see dolphins, leatherback sea turtles, and the gigantic ocean sunfish known as mola mola. Every once in a while, they fly over a hammerhead shark, or a tiger shark. Manta rays are common. But mostly they look down on an endless, empty sea.

"You really have to concentrate," Slay says. The trips, one in the morning and one in afternoon, last five and a half hours total. It helps that the whale researchers enjoy each other's company.

They share a commitment to the natural world, a passion for adventure and modest salaries. None of them receives medical or insurance benefits. None gets a pension. Nobody in Slay's crew is married. Sustaining a romantic relationship is difficult. Slay has tried.

"We're a nomadic tribe," he says finally. "We're always ready to pick up and move if it means a chance to look at a different ecosystem or experience the forces of the ocean in another part of the world."

They get together after work for sushi and sake at their favorite Japanese restaurant. They discuss life and they discuss whales. "Sometimes you get a sense that the whales know you're up there," says Marilyn Marx at supper. "They roll on their sides so their eye can look straight up at the plane."

"Maybe they're looking at us," Slay agrees. "Maybe they swim on their sides all the time. The thing about whales is how little we know."

At the little Fernandina Beach Airport, a 58-year-old pilot named Billy Foster is waiting next to his four-seat Cessna. He was an air-traffic controller in Jacksonville before he retired. Now he works for the New England Aquarium during the winter, and on his own time practices upside down flying and loops.

Nobody on Slay's crew suffers from motion sickness. It's a good thing. When they spot a whale, Foster banks the airplane and flies in increasingly tight circles for minutes while the researchers record the longitude and latitude. The inner ear—and the stomach it controls—can beg for mercy. Slay advises newcomers to whale work to stow a vomit bag and Dramamine in their gear.

"If you feel sick," he says cheerfully, "don't be self-conscious."

On a windy Tuesday, Billy Foster's Cessna 180 Skylane roars to life. The plane lifts over the oaks and pines and sand dunes and golf courses and shopping centers of Fernandina Beach and Amelia Island. The wind rattles the small plane. It drops, climbs, drops again.

"We haven't seen anything for days," Slay has to shout to be heard over the engine's whine.

The plane flies low over the beach. Walkers in sweatshirts hunt for fossilized shark's teeth. Teenagers toss plastic disks. Traffic moves smoothly down A1A.

The plane heads offshore.

There are sailboats, shrimp trawls, and fishing skiffs. A helicopter whirls by. Seabirds skim the whitecaps. "A dolphin," Slay shouts. In the shipping channel, out of the St. Johns River, a Texaco oil tanker pushes a wake. Beyond is a Toyota carrier ship, bright, immense, powerful.

Somewhere swim the leviathan whales, relics of an age before internal combustion engines and fossil fuel, hidden by the great shroud of Melville's merciless sea.

"Nothin'," Slay shouts. "Not a damn thing."

Captain Mills
and the ferry

Mayport
March 1994

The dark moon lifts the water, lifts it like a magnet, and pulls a current down the St. Johns River so hard that captain C. M. "Clayton" Mills shakes his head and says he is in for some real problems. Even before he takes the ferry boat out into the river he can tell. The current works the wobbly pilings over like a prizefighter.

"The tide gonna be pickin' up even stronger soon," he says. "My goodness. Crossin' the river today gonna be a challenge."

Mills, 59, lights a cigarette. He is standing in the wheelhouse and waiting for cars to board the last public ferry in Florida. The ferry, the Blackbeard, runs from early morning until late at night every day. It has connected Duval County's Fort George Island with the working class Navy town of Mayport since 1950. It takes a ferry about five minutes to make the short river crossing when the tide is slack and about nine minutes when it is gushing.

In 1993, the ferry transported 264,696 vehicles and their passengers across the 0.8-mile-wide river. If you ride the ferry instead of taking the nearest bridge, you save 28 miles and get to be part of history.

"This is the last of the Mohicans, I swear," is what Mills has to say about it. "Florida is runnin' out of ferries."

Once there were a bunch, in the Florida Keys, the Panhandle and at Tampa Bay. Tampa Bay's service, born in 1926, was called the Beeline Ferry. The trip from Pinellas Point in St. Petersburg to Piney Point in Manatee County lasted 45 minutes. Dolphins sometimes rode the bow wakes. In 1954 the Sunshine Skyway opened and the ferry was no more.

As the years passed, other ferries went out of business when replaced with bridges. But the Mayport Ferry, like old man river, rolled on. Then, in 1989, the Dames Point Bridge was built near Jacksonville and the ferry lost half its business.

This is no story about politics, understand—it's a story about Capt. Mills and his ferry. But you should know that politics almost did in the ferry, and that politics saved it.

In 1991, the Florida Legislature, faced with a $1-billion budget shortfall, took dead aim at the Mayport Ferry, which was losing $600,000 a year. Most roads and bridges generate no income, of course, but the governor wondered if a ferry was obsolete.

Lots of people objected, including some who lived hundreds of miles away and never rode the ferry. To them the ferry—even the thought of a ferry—was a charming and romantic relic of an older, more innocent Florida. Maybe they would never visit. Still, it was nice to know it was there in case they did, and that an old man of the sea like Capt. Mills would take them across the river even when the tide was ripping. There were Save-the-Ferry barbecues, petitions, newspaper editorials, and letters directed to the guilty politicians.

The people saved their ferry.

For now, it is the only floating road in the state system and makes it possible to drive Highway A1A, without detour, from the Georgia border to Key West. The price is right too: a couple bucks for a two-axle vehicle and a little more for the biggest trucks. Pedestrians and cyclists can ride for a couple of quarters.

The Blackbeard, built in 1956, is 170 feet long and can carry 50 vehicles. The Buccaneer, a smaller ferry built in 1949, is used in summer when beach traffic increases and can carry 35 vehicles.

Up in one of two wheelhouses—there is a wheelhouse on both ends of the ferry—Mills balances a Salem on his lower lip and watches the cars load.

There are Fords and Chevies and Cadillacs. There is a big panel truck with "Fish Company" written on the side. There is a Toyota four-wheel drive pickup with jacked up wheels and a surfboard in the bed and a 16-year-old boy behind the wheel eating boiled peanuts and looking guilty because it is mid-morning and a schoolday.

Joe Jack Caldwell, 65, sits in his Dodge pickup, headed across the river for a game of blackjack on the gambling ship that goes far enough into the Atlantic Ocean to satisfy government bureaucrats. Fisherman Jimmy Busbee, 30, looking dashing in a humongous hippie wool cap under which he could have been hiding a tackle box, leans against his Datsun rust-bucket and brags: "I been killing the sheepshead over at Little Talbot."

Upstairs, a minute or so later, Mills snuffs out his third cigarette. He says what he always says when ready to go. "It's time to change penthouses." He walks across a deck to the other wheelhouse, the one that faces the river. Then he revs the engine and takes out the Blackbeard.

Mills looks the way sea captains do in the movies. He has a short Hemingway beard, and hides his completely bald head under one of those New York cabdriver caps Papa favored in his later years. He also talks a blue streak about his life. He was born in Lake City but ran away to sea when he was 20, operated tugboats all over the tropics, then moved to Jacksonville where he ended up running the ferry.

The captain has to stop talking.

He has a wild river on his hands.

He is right to worry. When the moon is new, the outgoing tide is the strongest of the month. A heavy rain the night before has swollen the river. A lot of water strains to reach the ocean. The current swirls at the maximum, 3.8 knots.

Mills, who has operated the ferry for six years, has a strategy. For a moment though, it looks as if he is kidnapping the ferry and taking us to the Dames Point Bridge 10 miles upriver. He heads away from our destination, the 600-horse engine moans, and we barely make progress against the current.

Soon the captain's wisdom becomes clear.

Halfway across, he cuts the wheel, and the ferry slowly turns downriver, toward our destination. Now he lets the current work for him. He more or less aims at the dock.

Docking the Mayport Ferry is no delicate matter. We smash into it. Parked vehicles buck against their emergency brakes. Mills is not being sloppy—a dock sometimes works as good as throwing the engine in reverse. He tattoos the dock a few more times for good measure. Splinters fly.

"Dry wood," the captain hisses. "Environmentalists won't let us use creosote on the pilings anymore."

The dock gives off a sweet stink of boats, diesel, rust, fish and pelican guano. That's how a river should smell—that's how an old bridge smells too. But most of us, stuck in our air-conditioned cars, speeding along at 55 mph, are deprived of a Real Florida experience. We are fortunate to have a ferry.

Mills ignites still another cigarette—the surgeon general has yet to worry him—and watches the vehicles unload and a new group of vehicles come aboard. He says it makes him feel good, seeing those vehicles and those passengers, on his ferry. "People know they can depend on us," he says. "Only thing that can slow a ferry is a little fog."

The ferry runs in thundershowers and in hot weather and in cold weather too. In 1989, a vicious winter storm dumped snow and sleet on North Florida. All the bridges in Jacksonville closed because of ice.

Do you think the rotten weather stopped the Mayport Ferry? Not likely. That day Mills lipped another cancer stick and took the ferry across the river, the way he always does.

"I had a schedule to keep," he says.

The Cast Net King

Clearwater
February 1995

It is a winter afternoon, in the middle of the week, at the West Central Florida workplace of Mister Mutt Gilliam, the Cast Net King. Mutt is trying to work—he has every intention of building some new nets—but folks driving along Douglas Avenue see him toiling in his garage, and naturally they want to talk, and you know how Mutt is about talking. Mutt is a champion talker. He also excels at listening to other champion talkers.

"Some of these hard-core fishermen are great storytellers," he explains, glancing at his wife Pat to see if she is listening. She isn't, so Mutt feels free to whisper: "Hard to stay interested in my work when I'm hearing a good story."

Mutt, who has an untamable riot of brown hair and a beard that longs to be gray, is only living in his fourth decade. But he started working on nets when Eisenhower was president, which means he was four when he first laid hands on his stepdad's tools and materials. His stepdad was the original Cast Net King, Glenn Whitaker, who was building cast nets in the Tampa Bay area when Herbert Hoover was in office.

Building and selling cast nets—they're the small ones you see folks throwing by hand over schools of fish—forever has been a way of life for males in Mutt's family. So has catching fish in those cast nets, and, even more, telling fishing stories.

"My older brother, his name is Jeff. . .yeah, see, that's how I got the nickname Mutt. . .my real name is Garth—hell, nobody know me as Garth—but dad couldn't resist having a Mutt and Jeff. . .well, Jeff, see, he's a welder by a profession, but listen: He knows how to make a good net. . .He learned it when he was a boy. He's a good fisherman, a real good fisherman. We like to throw our nets on mullet. So one night we went up by Dunedin to get us some."

Mutt, at this point, fails to mention exactly where he and Jeff were fishing in Dunedin. Even master storytellers are obligated, by the angling code of silence, to keep secret their fishing holes.

"Okay, we're wadin'. Now when we catch mullet, we take them out of the nets right off and break their necks, to bleed them out, so they'll taste better, and then we stuff them into a sack. We had about 80 pounds of mullet in the sack. Jeff, he had the sack tied to his belt. Sudden, he hollers and gets knocked down."

As Mutt tells this, he does not get excited. But listeners do. What happened? they cry. What knocked Jeff down?

Mutt, carefully adjusting a net that is hanging by a hook from the ceiling rafters, seems to have gone deaf.

"Something got aholt of his leg," he finally allows.

A shark! his audience yelps. Heaven help him! What happened? Did the shark let go? Is Jeff all right?

Mutt suddenly goes mute as he checks and doublechecks a knot on an old net.

"Oh, it had to a been a shark," he says eventually. "Jeff got cut up some is all. Cut him from behind the knee all the way to his butt. He was all right."

In the fall of 1994, voters amended the state constitution and banned the use of gill nets in state waters. Soon, the 1200-foot gill nets used by commercial fisherman will be illegal. Cast nets, which usually are 25 feet across or less, will continue to be allowed. Commercial anglers who hope to catch fish in quantity may start using cast nets.

It will create an interesting problem for Mutt Gilliam, the Cast Net King. His business, already good, likely will get even better. Mutt can picture himself working around the clock sewing net panels together, making lead lines, adjusting rails. In other words, working like a man possessed.

Which is fine—he always has worked hard. But he also subscribes to the all-work-makes-a-dull-boy philosophy. He likes to play hard. At the drop of a hint he likes to go fishing. And in the fall, no matter what, he goes hunting. When he returns to work, just in time for the Christmas rush, he has a bunch of new experiences to weave into his tapestry of stories.

Working non-stop might put a crimp in the tall tales department.

"Sometimes I think the key to selling cast nets," says Mutt's wife Pat, "is telling hunting and fishing stories."

She knows her husband well. She met him when they both were second graders in Clearwater. They went their separate ways, growing up and marrying different people. But six years ago they came to their senses and hooked up for good. Pat works on nets with her husband in the garage, listens to his stories, corrects him when he exaggerates, greets customers, endures their stories and rolls her eyes at the appropriate moments.

Mutt is telling a couple of customers, anglers, a hunting tale: He was sitting in a tree stand at dawn, understand, waiting patiently for a deer to come along, and Pat was in a distant tree stand, when, suddenly, Mutt heard a shot coming from Pat's direction. Maybe she'd killed a deer. But Mutt didn't want to risk climbing out of his tree to find out; he was hoping he might ambush a deer of his own. He never saw a deer of his own, so three hours later he went to see why Pat had fired her gun. A dead buck lay below her tree.

"She tells me, "when you hear me shoot, don't you DARE waste time getting here. You COME QUICK!""

"I never said that!" Pat protests, laughing. "What a lie."

The day starts early. Sometimes Mutt begins working on his nets at 3 a.m. It is quiet then, and nobody stops to visit and talk, which can break a man's concentration, especially when he's counting net meshes. By 6 a.m., however, his shop starts to get popular, as people stop on their way to work to chat or to order nets.

He builds nets of different sizes, for different purposes. Some nets have heavy mesh to catch sizable fish with sharp fins and scales. Others are designed to catch minnows. Some are designed to sink slowly; some to sink like stones. Some cost less than a hundred dollars. The best nets cost hundreds.

He also repairs nets, including some he didn't build. Like any self-respecting net-builder, he believes his own nets are the best. But he tries to be civil when potential customers who have purchased inferior nets from other net-makers ask him to repair their mistakes.

A white Ford pickup truck squeals to the curb. Two husky young men, in their late twenties, leap out, carrying an inferior net. Yes, Mutt will fix it—he'll have it by Saturday. One young man, David Graham, admires a new Mutt net hanging from the rafters. Mutt says shrewdly: "I'll make you a good deal."

Graham is accompanied by his boyhood friend, Joey Reis. They're both fishing guides from Tarpon Springs. On their days off from guiding, they fish commercially with cast nets. They had a great day yesterday, Joey says: They caught 1,100 pounds of Nile perch, better known as tilapia, in a top-secret lake in Hillsborough County.

Nile perch sometimes weigh ten pounds or more. They have sharp scales and sharp fins which are hard on nets. Joey and David sometimes caught 200 pounds at a time. Muscles straining, breathing hard, they hauled the net and heard the mesh popping.

"If I could figure a way to make a net out of a chain-link fence, I'd do it," Mutt says, looking at the holes he's going to repair. "A Nile perch flat tears up a net."

They trade hunting and fishing stories. There's one about the deer of the Florida Panhandle. Another is about an unscrupulous hook-and-liner who bragged to Mutt about catching 45 redfish to sell illegally. Other stories are about alligator poachers, game wardens and honesty.

"People ain't honest anymore," Mutt declares, shaking his head. "Where does it all end?"

In the afternoon, on a good day, Mutt has time for some fishing. Usually he catches mullet, though once he netted a leopard ray by accident and another time he netted a nurse shark by mistake. "A ray won't ever hurt you on purpose," he says. "This guy I was with, he sees the ray and says to me, 'Give up your net!' But no way am I gonna give up a good net. It took a while, but I worked that ray out of there and let him go. He was probably more scared than me."

Ditto for the shark. He relaxed the net and the shark swam off. He doesn't like mullet to get away. On a good day, he catches enough to sell, and enough to keep for a fish fry. He comes home, and Pat calls the neighbors, who fix tossed salads, cole slaw, fried potatoes and maybe baked beans. Mutt fries mullet, and people crack open beers, and everybody goes home well fed and happy.

Then Mutt goes back to work. People driving by see him, and naturally they stop, perhaps to buy nets, but most often just to talk about fishing and hunting, which is okay with Mutt. He listens to the stories, and tells a few himself, until, way after dark, Pat finally walks over from the house and makes the announcement: "Closing time!"

which means Mutt, reluctantly, has to call it a day.

"But you know something?" Mutt says. "I'll turn out the lights and shut the garage and go in the house, but sometimes the fishermen, they just stand in the yard and keep talkin'. I guess they like their stories."

Harold's wonderful museum

Intercession City
February 1995

Last thing in the world I need is another lawnmower. But I stop at Harold Staie's warehouse anyway.

Mowers are lined neatly in front near the banana trees and pineapple plants that grow ramrod straight in huge black pots. Harold sells them too, at his warehouse on U.S. 17/92 near Kissimmee, the biggest of nearby towns. His business, which sits in the middle of a cypress swamp—I'm tempted to say in the middle of nowhere—is an eclectic place.

What intrigues me more than banana trees and mowing machines is the sign at the front window. It says *Harold Staie Presents Yesterday In Review—Player Piano Headquarters*. Drive the backroads of Real Florida long enough and you can find anything, even the headquarters for player pianos in a cypress swamp. The front door is locked, so I walk to the back.

He's home. And Harold Staie—pronounced STAY—could hardly be busier. But not with player pianos. A couple of fellows need a part for their mower, and when they came to fetch him, naturally they saw his orange and grapefruit trees, and he took them out into his groves for a tour, and then gave them, free, all the fruit they could carry. Time flew, and he still hadn't found them the part they wanted.

"They took apart a Briggs & Stratton engine trying to fix it," he whispers. He whispers because he does not want to offend the old gentlemen with his knowledge about their mechanical ineptitude.

Harold, a man with white bristly hair and hands accustomed to hard work, can restore anything. When he was a boy—we're going back 70 years now—chums called him Buster, because he busted things and then fixed them. He took courses in refrigeration repair, welding, electronics and printing. He worked as a plumber and as an electrician. He was an auto mechanic. He was a washing machine repairman—even had his own coin-laundry business. But mostly, he liked restoring old player pianos.

They're back in the dark warehouse, among his lawnmowers, tools, pipes, boxes, tins, his old photographs and his collection of *Popular Mechanics* magazines going back to 1905. "I wasn't born then," says Harold, who arrived on the scene in 1918. He looks at his vast warehouse and says, "I do a little of everything," and digs out a cupped washer for the would-be mower repairmen.

But those two gentlemen aren't looking at the cupped washer. How could they? In front of them is Harold's 1929 Model-A ice truck, which he got for a song years ago. One of his lawnmower customers jokingly offers Harold $100 for the truck, and Harold says, quite politely, that he can't do it, the truck, you know, has been perfectly restored: The truck runs! It's worth lots more than $100.

But forget about the truck. Harold has a lawmower problem in front of him. These guys need more than a washer. They need a pull starter, for crying out loud, and they need a blower housing. Harold's got them—he's got hundreds—but where in the world are they? Harold disappears, muttering, into the bowels of his warehouse, all 7,200 square feet of it, and he says, "What I like to do is restore pianos, but I wasn't making it, so I got into lawnmowers, and lawnmowers, I'll tell you, are drudgery."

Lawnmowers. Player pianos. Banana trees. The man's got everything there in Intercession City.

"I'll tell you," Harold says, "I got too many irons in the fire."

Harold's story is this. His father died young and his mother lost her job during the Depression and put him into a Wisconsin orphanage. Eventually, he ran away to work on a 22-acre tomato farm for room and board and 50 cents a day. His room was next to the attic. Inside the attic was an Edison phonograph that worked.

He never forgot the phonograph. After he grew up and joined the Navy, and after he established his own business and started making money, he began collecting old broken phonographs and old broken player pianos, and fixing and selling all but the collector's items. In 1967, after an especially harsh Chicago winter, Harold and his wife Ione, like so many northerners before and after them, decided Florida was the place to be.

They ended up with the warehouse. But they had paid scant attention to zoning laws, and their Osceola County property was zoned only for agriculture. So he couldn't use the warehouse as a true museum as he wanted. Instead, he had to sell fruit trees and fix lawnmowers and give private tours of his musical instruments by appointment for a buck a head.

But these old fellows who have come for a lawnmower part look all right and he gives them a player piano tour for free. I go along. Here's a 1920 Seabird. Here's a 1919 lamp phonograph that once entertained waiting guests in a brothel. Here's a 1915 Wurlitzer. He drops in a nickel and the player piano roars to life.

Harold loves the music but can't play a note. Says he's got two left hands. Can't carry a tune. Says he can't even dance, not with those two left feet of his. But he can fix music machines and he likes to hear them play.

He cranks up a 1915 Edison phonograph and puts on an old 78 record called *Don't Bite the Hand That's Feeding You*, which came out during World War I. The singer suggests that if you don't like America, go back to your own country. Harold says those sentiments are as true today as they were back when Woodrow Wilson was president. He is proud to be a member of the America-Love-It-or-Leave-It generation.

He tells us a story that at first sounds like American-as-apple-pie capitalism. One time this fellow wanted to buy Harold's warehouse and everything in it. Harold agreed to sell it for $250,000. The guy said wait a minute and hired property appraisers to make sure Harold wasn't trying to pull the old wool over his eyes. A little man with a Hitler moustache and a briefcase knocked on the door. He was from Christie's, the famous auction house. He appraised Harold's collection for $500,000. But Harold never received as much as a wooden nickel. Before the sale could be consummated, the buyer suffered a stroke.

"You never know when you're going to go," Harold says philosophically.

Oh, he's had close calls—even the lawnmower-player piano business has its hazards. One night, he heard a noise in his warehouse, and investigated, and a voice came out of the dark and said a gun was aimed his way, and if he wanted to live, he'd better lie down. So he lay down on his belly, but he could not resist asking the robbers for progress reports, and one of them finally said, "Shut him up." As $5,000 worth of inventory rolled out the front door, Harold at that point agreed to pipe down.

"I like to talk," he confesses.

He has a lot of energy. In fact, he couldn't be healthier, except for his back, which he hurt trying to move an 800-pound printing press by himself, which has left him a little stooped. Otherwise, he almost runs, never slows down, never sits, because he says when he sits he's apt to go to sleep, and he can't afford to sleep, what with all the pianos and fruit trees and lawnmowers needing his attention.

The fellows who needed a lawnmower part leave.

Now Harold has only me to show around. Which he does cheerfully. Here's his 1837 Melodeon. Here's his 1904 Band Organ once used on a merry-go-round. Here's a 1922 pipe organ. He worked on it three years without fixing it and paid somebody $2,500 to finish the job, only he didn't, he took off and opened a bar instead. Harold Staie shakes his head. You just can't find good help these days.

I say goodbye and we end up in the back yard again, and Harold walks me into his groves, and I end up eating kumquats off the tree and he picks some lemons and oranges for me to take home.

Then, before I know it, we're back in the warehouse, and next thing I know, I'm looking at his drills and lathes and saws again. I admire his old 78 rpm records and his collection of 50,000 steel phonograph needles. I gaze in wonder at his old cigar boxes and his collection of old cans of Prince Albert. When he was an orphan, he reveals, he and his chums used to call the neighborhood druggist and insist that Prince Albert be let out of the can!

"We horsed around a lot," he says.

At last, the huge dried-up ear of corn on a table catches my eye.

"Oh a friend of mine brought that," he explains. "She grew it in her garden in Indiana. She wanted to show me the kind of corn they grow in Indiana. Pretty nice corn. I just couldn't throw it away."

Harold Staie turns out the lights.

Randy White's excellent adventures

Pineland
January 1994

I wish Randy Wayne White and I were looking for the swamp ape, the legendary Bigfoot-like creature said to haunt the Everglades, but sometimes you settle for less. As he is wont to say, "Life is unfair." He points his boat into tranquil Pine Island Sound and we go looking instead for some pretty fish.

White, a 43-year-old Fort Myers resident, has looked for the swamp ape before. He has done many exciting things, in Florida and other exotic locales. He has searched for crocodiles, poked through jungles for tigers, jumped unclothed into an Alaskan bay in January, trained with Navy underwater demolition experts and been stabbed on a sidewalk in Peru.

He is a tough guy, all right, and the author of *Batfishing in the Rainforest*, a collection of his real-life adventure stories and philosophic musings from *Outside* magazine. He also has written three successful mystery novels, including a new one, *The Man Who Invented Florida*, featuring the marine biologist Doc Ford, no stranger to violence and intrigue.

I live a dull life in the suburbs except for the possums that sometimes need chasing when they visit the back yard to eat the cat's food. Some real excitement would be nice for a change. I stand in White's boat—only daredevils stand in moving boats—so I can better keep my eyes peeled for menacing sharks.

He stands too, and looks spectacularly unimpressed. That's probably because we're cruising at three knots and White, for heaven's sake, belongs to something he calls the "Jumping Out Of The Boat At Night Club."

"It's a small, twisted membership," he explains. "When the moon is dark, there's this bioluminescence glowing in the water that's rather hypnotic. It's fun to just jump into it."

From a moving boat? At night? In shark-infested waters? Suddenly I long for my own comfortable bed and the kind of pajamas that come with feet.

"Oh, we stopped doing it," he says, noticing my pallor. "It got to where when you jumped in the water the guys wouldn't come back to get you."

Mark Twain.

That's how a life of wandering and adventure and writing began for White. When he was a boy, his mother took him to the Pioneer, Ohio, library where he discovered the book *Huckleberry Finn*. From then on he wanted to be a writer.

There was a slight problem. White had no idea how. He liked his teachers, and they liked him, but he had a hard time keeping up in class. After high school, he was offered scholarships based on his baseball and diving prowess, though he felt he was poor college material.

Instead, at the height of the Vietnam War, he tried to enlist in the Navy. Bad knees disqualified him, so he hitchhiked back and forth across the country, several times, for the adventure. Eventually he settled into a life of installing telephones.

He liked installing phones. It was hard and physical. Also, the phone company had a fast-pitch softball team, and he was an able player. But even fast-pitch softball, and telephone lines, lost their appeal. During an Ohio snowstorm, as he hung from a telephone pole, he tapped into the lines and began calling newspaper editors whom he hoped might want to hire a man without a shred of writing experience.

The *Fort Myers News Press* said yes, and a few years later he was a star columnist, and a few years after that he quit the staff, became a fishing guide and started freelancing for *Outside* magazine. Sometimes, editors from New York would call the marina where he kept his boat and ask for him. "Randy's not going to cover the America's Cup for you or anybody else," the marina owner would bark, "until he gets these godamn mullet gutted."

White managed to fish, cut bait and write. Paul Theroux, the author of *The Mosquito Coast* and a travel writer of note, once called White "a fishing guide of genius" though he was probably advertising White's ability to spin an outdoors yarn as much as his talent for reeling in the big ones.

We have brought no fish poles to Pine Island Sound, and as the schools of yardstick-sized redfish materialize in the shallow water I long for a light plug rod and a Baby Zara Spook lure—white with a red head. I'd wiggle that baby across the water like a wounded finger mullet and wait for one of the heavy reds to pounce. I'd show Randy White a thing or two about macho. No, it would never happen—here's how fishing works for me: If I've got my rod, I never see fish. So I relax with White and watch 10-pound reds cavort across the flats.

White hardly takes people fishing for pay anymore. After guiding more than 4,000 anglers over the years, he tired of it. Also, he got busy traveling and writing. He just returned from Borneo. He just returned from Vietnam. He just finished writing a story for *Outside* magazine about attending the CIA Terrorist Driving School. All White will say about it: "You have to drive very fast. It's scary."

Doc Ford, the protagonist of his novels, seems to be his alter ego. Doc doesn't reveal much either, though he is a terrific listener, a "private person, a man who attracts people and valued his friends yet went his own way." So we keep our mouths shut and our eyes open. We watch the fish of Pine Island Sound. It's a peaceful pursuit.

We see small grouper and a number of docile nurse sharks, stuck to the bottom like cabbages. Every once in a while the shadow of the boat startles your basic, piano-sized stingray out of the mud. Peaceful, my eye. The tails of those rays have barbs like quill pens. This is no place to tumble overboard.

"My sons and I swim here all the time," White says. Their names are Lee Wayne and Rogan, and they are 13 and 10. They share some of their dad's adventures, at least a few of the domestic ones.

Every once in awhile, near the cottage White uses on Pine Island, they pick up their CO°-powered pistols and shoot their dad with gobs of paint. "Hurts like hell," White says. During the war games dad and boys have worn paths between the poincianas and gumbo limbos that cover the ancient Indian mounds dotting the island.

They also fish, play ball and hug. White seldom passes his sons, or his wife, without hugging them. "When I travel, I get very homesick," he says. "When I'm traveling in Florida, sometimes I'll cut a trip short and come back early. But when you travel halfway around the world, and there's no easy way back, it's much easier to be away from your family."

His wife, Deb, is a triathlete. White has run marathons, though he says he got heavy when he gave up snuff. He recently started jogging again—and dipping Skoal. You want to be upwind when he is at it. He spits into the water, onto the sidewalk or into a Coca-Cola can, and things get messy.

The people who come close to knowing him best are used to it. They include other snuff dippers, tobacco chewers, fishing guides, mullet netters, marine biologists, bartenders, dock workers, baseball players, commercial crabbers, crabby writers, beer-drinking buddies, slack-jawed country fiddlers, retired alligator poachers, Seminole Indians, cowhunters, and the guy who stopped his boat on Pine Island Sound when he saw White's the other day, grinned and called out:

"When I was driving on the mainland today I saw some tourist throw trash out the window! I chased him down and said, 'Is this what you do back in Michigan?'"

"Good for you!" White boomed back.

White is an environmentalist, though not the fire-breathing variety. He thinks some environmentalists go too far, or not far enough, and he remembers the time he stood and left a national Greenpeace convention in disgust. He thought there was something hypocritical about Greenpeacers who were wringing their hands about polluted oceans while they were polluting the air with their cigarette smoke. Anyway, Greenpeace sends no Christmas cards his way, and White loses no sleep about it.

"I'm not a politically correct person," he says.

He has a biography of John Wayne on his shelf, near books by John Steinbeck and John D. MacDonald, and he has a picture of the Duke waiting to hang on the wall behind his office television. He is in favor of capital punishment. "We don't have real capital punishment in Florida," he says. "What do we have, two thousand murders a year? And maybe one or two executions?"

At the same time one of his best friends is the gentle Buddhist teacher Peter Matthiessen, the author who won a National Book Award. White is interested in Buddhism, interested enough to read books about it, and once tried sitting and meditating with the patient Matthiessen. "But we can't get together without giggling," White says. "Peter said, 'Now, this is very serious', but we sat and giggled."

They met some two decades ago in the Everglades when White mounted the only known swamp ape expedition in history. This was during a period when swamp apes, also called skunk apes because of their strong odor, seemed to be constantly in the Florida news, peering into windows, molesting cattle, crossing roads and shaking up motorists who claimed they had not been drinking.

White sent swamp ape expedition invitations to famous people across the land. "Mostly I saw the expedition as a chance to chew tobacco and drink beer with buddies in the Everglades," he says. President Jimmy Carter was a no-show, but Matthiessen, the author of *The Snow Leopard*, *At Play in the Fields of the Lord* and *Killing Mister Watson*, was an enthusiastic participant.

The swamp ape eluded them.

"I don't believe in the swamp ape," White says. Only innocent places can have monsters, and Florida has lost its innocence. "There are far more troubling things roaming this state," he says darkly.

He's talking about more than criminals armed to the teeth. He means lawyers who steal with fountain pens, and the kinds of business people who would sell the last piney woods of the last panther to make two bits.

The old Florida that nourished the dreams of crusty cowhunters and gave birth to the fiddle classic *Orange Blossom Special*—the old Florida that had more rough edges than a sandspur—is in danger of disappearing beneath the glitter of the new. White believes his job is preserving those endangered Florida voices. In his new Doc Ford novel, set in modern times, a crafty old cowhunter discovers in the Everglades what seems to be the Fountain of Youth. It's a lovely book.

White—former telephone installer, now world traveler and novelist—counts his blessings these days. "I've been so lucky," he says.

Only once has he felt that somebody truly meant him harm. That was during a trip to Peru, where, for a magazine story, he took a ride on the highest standard-gauge railroad in the world. At 16,000 feet, a body can suffer from altitude sickness, and White's body did. But even worse was what happened when he arrived in the city of Huancayo below. The Shining Path, murderous revolutionaries, were on the prowl.

As he walked a sidewalk, two men attacked from behind, smashing him in the back so hard he almost fell. He fought them off, and, shaken, returned to his hotel. There he discovered the long slice in the back pocket of his vest. The thick notebook he kept in the pocket was sliced open too. The knife blade had penetrated a quarter inch into its pages.

"The bastards had just walked up and stabbed me," he later wrote. "Just walked up and stabbed me without a word of warning."

I spend the night at White's house after our quiet afternoon on the water. When he leaves for his weekly meeting of the Masons— "It's so secret I can't even tell my wife what happens"—I visit the nearest mall for some uninspired shopping. Later, we go out for a couple of drinks, and nothing happens, not even a good bar fight. Before sleep, I find myself watching a James Bond movie; 007 would be inspired by Randy White. I know I am.

I leave early the next morning after a great big bowl of Raisin Bran; for breakfast, White takes his coffee, black. On the way home, I drive over the speed limit.

Not once, but two, three maybe five damn times.

Stalking the
ghost orchid

Fakahatchee Strand
March 1995

Florida has no mountains, no canyons, not even a good redwood tree. What it has is amazing swamps. The most amazing swamp of all is in a place near Naples called the Fakahatchee Strand. Driving my truck or riding my bike along its only dirt road, I've seen bear tracks and always expect to encounter a panther.

Slapping at mosquitoes, looking into the deep, dark tangle of vegetation and black water, I never think about stepping off the road. The Fakahatchee is too aggressively wild. I love wilderness, and probably take some risks now and then, but I'm no hero.

Given a choice, I always pick dry feet over wet ones. I always calculate the chances of getting lost. I'm anxious when visiting the lair of water moccasins, the husky swamp snakes known for opening their cotton-colored maws wide just before striking.

Then I hear about the wonder of the Fakahatchee, the mysterious ghost orchid. I hear the plant poachers have been at it again.

Maybe it is time for a swamp walk.

A cold front blew through at dawn. At 11 a.m. gray clouds are scudding across the sky like migrating geese as a howling wind batters the tops of the largest collection of royal palms north of Cuba. The water in the swamp looks like iced tea, and probably will feel that way. Perhaps Mike Owen, the Fakahatchee Strand State Preserve biologist, will call off our expedition.

He's waiting.

"The good news is that it's cold enough today that we shouldn't be bothered by mosquitoes," he says cheerfully.

"The bad news is that the cottonmouths might very well be out. Look for them high, out of the water, in the sun, maybe on a stump, trying to stay warm. Whatever you do, be careful where you put your hands."

My group, which includes two dozen members of the Native Plant Society, mills about on the dirt road, looking into the very heart of wildness, all the while thinking about poisonous serpents with dripping fangs.

"The water looks pretty deep," somebody says, breaking the silence. Only one of us is wearing waders. The rest are in jeans and light slacks, sneakers and hiking boots.

"We may find some waist-deep water," Owen answers. "It's going be an adventure."

From the back of the crowd, a man carrying an expensive camera asks the question on every mind:

"We're going to *walk* in that?"

Not walk. Wade. The ghost orchid is back there. The ghost orchid, among the rarest of endangered species, lives back in the swamp, back in the wet forest, back in the deep sloughs, entwined around the slender limbs of pond apple trees and pop ashes. When in bloom, the ghost is supposed to look like a pale ballet dancer, long-limbed and delicate: a true swamp fairy.

The ghost orchid may be gone everywhere but the Fakahatchee, which contains among the most diverse and rare plant life in the United States. More than 100 species alone are listed as threatened or endangered. Thirty-three kinds of ferns, some 10 feet high, grow here, the most on the continent. There are 16 species of bromeliads, air plants resembling pineapples, including some found only here. But the Fakahatchee is an orchid paradise, a perfect swamp for them, shaded, humid and usually warm enough to sustain tropical life. Forty-four kinds, all listed as threatened or endangered, are hidden in the dense tangle of jungle.

We would like to see them while we still can.

The ghost, and other orchids here, in the Big Cypress National Preserve and in Everglades National Park, long have been preyed upon by unscrupulous and ignorant people. Before the state bought the Fakahatchee in 1974, the swamp in fact was known as a supermarket where orchid lovers could easily harvest rarities for their own collections or to sell to other unethical people at a handsome profit.

At 74,000 acres, the strand—a strand is a narrow swamp—is the largest park in the state system. The Fakahatchee, 20 miles long and about five miles wide, is the largest strand in the ecosystem known as the Big Cypress Swamp. Much of it is under water, unsurveyed. The Fakahatchee has no facilities, not a public bathroom, or a campground, or even a paved road. It is among the least visited of Florida's parks.

The Fakahatchee is patrolled now, and the wide-scale poaching has all but stopped. National and state orchid societies discourage the harvest of native orchids of any kind. Still, the Fakahatchee's staff is small, the place is large and remote, and some poaching continues.

"You can tell some poaching is going on," Owen, the Fakahatchee biologist, says. "A tree that had orchids growing on it a few weeks ago might not have them next time you see it."

Most poaching is done innocently, out of ignorance. Occasionally, despite warning signs, a preserve visitor will be overwhelmed by a beautiful orchid on a roadside tree and simply pick it and possibly even show it off to a ranger. Rangers generally just warn the casual plant pickers; they don't make a big deal out of it. The serious poachers, they do. But serious poachers are smart, often know more about the orchids than preserve personnel do, know where the best plants are, and more often than not get away with their crimes.

In 1993, there was a spectacular exception. The preserve manager caught four men on the only road, in the middle of the afternoon, heading for their vehicles carrying pillowcases and plastic bags. They had three ghost orchids and more than 100 other rarities—plants worth more than $3,000 on the black market.

Owens promises to tell me later about the case, which was complicated and involved Indian rights. For the time being, I'm interested in knowing more about the amazing swamp. What is it about the Fakahatchee's plants that drive grown men and women to crime?

Like most people who love nature, I know more about animals than the plant kingdom. But plants interest me, especially the rare stuff, and this is the place for the rarest of rare. Yet seeing the holy grail—the ghost orchid—isn't going to come easy.

"I've never had any leeches on me," Owen is telling a man. "But they're here. I've seen them on snapping turtles. About an inch long."

Suddenly I'm thinking of Humphrey Bogart, covered with leeches in a favorite movie, *The African Queen.*

"The best way to do this," Owen says, "is to just plunge right in."

The water isn't waist-deep, but it does reach the thigh. We gasp, moan and laugh the laugh of civilized people who know they're doing something daft. We're 90 minutes west of Miami, and 45 minutes east of Naples. We're in the middle of 4.5-million people, in fact. Yet we are in what is probably the wildest stretch of territory east of the Mississippi River. And we're going in deeper.

I wonder if some of us might be getting in over our heads, literally and figuratively. One young woman has brought two children, including a three-year-old daughter. The woman picks up her child; she doesn't know it yet but she'll carry the child for the next five hours. Four people in our party are elderly. They look frail.

Soon we're climbing over downed trees, trying not to trip over cypress knees, kicking our way through vines, using our hands to fight the sharp branches that lunge for our eyes, stepping into holes, yelling "oops" and staying alert for alligators and cottonmouths.

None of us is new to nature. I doubt any one of us is particularly afraid of snakes. At the same time we want no surprises, not from a cottonmouth, of all snakes.

Cottonmouths are legendary for their aggression. People who know snakes often have a cottonmouth story. When I was a teen-ager who loved to bass fish in the Everglades, I feared no snakes or alligators; they always fled at my approach. Then I encountered a four-foot cottonmouth coiled on a big boulder. The cottonmouth held its ground. Thirty years have passed and the hair on my neck still stands up when I remember how the snake's jaws gaped open as it hissed.

This place might have more cottonmouths per acre than anywhere else on Earth, rangers claim. Two years ago, the Fakahatchee manager was riding an all-terrain vehicle, an ATV, down an old logging trail. He was driving close behind another ATV. Suddenly, the lead ATV ran over a cottonmouth. The ATV's large tires spun the furious snake high into the air. The preserve manager, coming up fast from behind, had to duck. He no longer tailgates in the Fakahatchee.

"Listen," Owen says. "I don't think it's like we're going to be stepping over cottonmouths. In the last fifteen months, I guess I've seen maybe four while I was wading. But I'll tell you: I hope we see one today! It would be wonderful, a real blessing!"

Owen is a University of South Florida graduate who did science for the state's marine research division in St. Petersburg. Then he went to work for the park service and found, as they say, his niche. He feels at home in the swamp. He is slender and prematurely gray. His enthusiastic voice makes him seem younger than 35 years.

"There's so much diversity here!" he says. "We're lucky to be here!"

At first, I have the feeling most of us in the swamp disbelieve him. We're attracted to the swamp—the abstract idea of swamps, anyway. At the same time we're repelled by the thought of actually wading through primordial ooze.

But after an hour or so most of us begin to relax. Cottonmouths haven't ambushed us. Alligators aren't creeping along the bottom toward our unprotected flesh. Leeches aren't sucking our vital juices. So far, bruised shins, poison ivy and the occasional spider web in the face have been the only surprises.

We're in a wonderland.

Amazing cypress, laurel oak and supplejack. We inch through wild coffee, cocoplum. We pass leather, birdnest and resurrection fern. Isn't that a fuzzy-wuzzy air plant? No, Owen says, but I wish it were. Lizard tail, another plant, is as fragrant as French perfume. Owen cups swamp water in his hands. That tiny plant is a bladderwort! he says. Endangered!

The Fakahatchee, Earth soup, is utterly alive.

Early afternoon. Two hours into the trip. We press on through Virginia creeper, cabbage palm and possum grape. We see Pickerel weed. Strangler fig. Lance-leafed arrowhead.

Owen stops, glances at the sun, wonders if we're going in the right direction. Who has a compass? he asks.

"Everybody," shouts a man behind him. I laugh, but mine is in my pack.

People get lost here. Last time was about a year ago. An overly confident man dropped by the office to tell rangers he planned to walk from one end of the Fakahatchee to the other. Rangers suggested he do something else. Only the most rugged outdoors people, with the most advanced survival skills, should even consider such a hike. They usually carry hammocks and mosquito netting and allow four or five days of travel. The confident man, clutching an out-of-date hiking guide, insisted he would be fine. He just needed a few directions.

He entered near Alligator Alley and found an old logging trail. After a mile or so, the logging trail disappeared into the dry brush. The brush soon turned into swamp. Now the man was in the water, picking his way through the densest vegetation he had ever seen. Hours passed. The sun got low. Panic set in. His heart thumping wildly, he reached into his pack and withdrew, of all things, a cellular telephone. He dialed up the preserve office and complained of heart palpitations.

Rangers sighed and grabbed their chain saws and leaped into their all-terrain vehicles. When the ATVs ran out of trail, the rangers walked, cutting their way toward the lost hiker. Then they slogged. They found him at 3:30 a.m. He was fine. Park rangers now joke that the cellular phone should be part of every Fakahatchee survival kit.

We carry no cellular phones.

The nearest civilization, if you can call it that, is Copeland, a near-abandoned logging town, whose handful of residents live mostly in dilapidated trailers without phones. At night, bears, including two weighing at least 400 pounds, roam the dusty streets, foraging for food among garbage cans.

On the far end of the Fakahatchee is a place infamous in the annals of Florida swamp peddling, the notorious Golden Gates Estates, where a developer once sold thousands of lots over the telephone to elderly Yankees who didn't know their retirement property was under water. The state is now in the process of buying back land. Still, about a hundred hardy souls live out there, without running water or electricity or telephones, in the boondocks of all boondocks.

Three hours into the trip. We begin to string out in the swamp. The vegetation is so thick you can lose sight of somebody 10 feet in front of you. An elderly woman calls, "Please slow down!" We do. We reach higher ground, a hammock, and stop for a break. Royal palms and oaks and gumbo limbos predominate. We sink into the mud beyond our ankles. The mud sucks at our boots.

We descend again into the swamp, deeper now. Men shout as icy water laps against their crotches. Women laugh at the men. Mike Owen is happy too, though not because he enjoys a frigid crotch.

We're in prime orchid territory.

"Here's one!" he yells.

We slog toward him. The orchid is wrapped around a pond apple limb. It's a clamshell orchid, a threatened species, in bloom, tiny and delicate, breathtaking. A woman describes the color as magenta. Another woman says, "No, not magenta . . . Well, it's a deep magenta, but more like velvet. It's a ruby."

Hikers carefully withdraw cameras from packs, step forward and photograph the living jewel. Somebody says, "I hope the poachers don't know about this place."

They struck the Fakahatchee on Dec. 21, 1993. It was a raw, overcast day. At 1 p.m., preserve manager Mike Petty was patrolling the Fakahatchee's only road. Two vehicles were parked next to the swamp. One was a special pickup truck, the kind often used by farmers. Suspicious, Petty drove past and turned around and waited. Within minutes four men crawled out of the water, carrying sacks.

Petty introduced himself. The men—three Seminole Indians and a well-known orchid expert—were calm and polite. They showed him the contents of their sacks and said they were collecting plants to stock the Seminole Indian Reservation nursery in Hollywood. Petty counted 136 plants, all but one either threatened or endangered. Petty called over the radio for law enforcement officers. The orchid expert, the leader of the party, showed him a piece of paper. It was the state law governing endangered and threatened plants. The law seemed to exempt Florida Indians from collecting protected species.

Officers arrested the men anyway.

Lawyers for the Seminoles in the celebrated case said that if there was a problem with the law, the Legislature should change it; otherwise, let the Seminoles collect plants. State attorneys said the law only seemed to exempt Florida Indians.

The orchid expert who accompanied the Indians into the swamp had owned a well-stocked Dade County nursery until Hurricane Andrew blew it away. Then he went to work for the Seminoles.

He told people the Fakahatchee—it's a Seminole word for "muddy water"—was one of his favorite places in the world. He knew it like the back of his hand. He also knew how to harvest orchids. He knew that plucking an orchid from its host tree would kill it. So he and the men were careful to saw off the limbs that held the precious orchids. They had limbs and orchids in their sacks, a fact that turned out to be important.

In the summer, the case went to court in Naples. Most everyone who attended the trial was interested in the issue of Indian rights. But that important issue was never resolved.

Maybe state law did allow Florida Indians to collect endangered plants. But there was another state law that prohibited the cutting, mutilation or harvesting of trees in state parks. That law did not exempt Florida Indians.

If the Seminoles had simply taken orchids, they arguably would have been exempt from the endangered species law—but their orchids would have almost certainly died. The moment they cut limbs from the host trees, which they needed to do to keep their orchids alive, they broke the other law and committed a second-degree misdemeanor.

The Seminole men pleaded no contest to the lesser charge of damaging trees owned by the state. The judge fined them each $100 and banned them from the Fakahatchee for a month. The orchid expert, a non-Indian, pleaded no contest, too. The judge fined him $500 and banned him from the preserve for six months.

The ban ended a few weeks ago.

Preserve law officers carry his picture in their trucks.

They haven't seen him.

Four hours in. We're running out of daylight. The chance of seeing a ghost orchid is vanishing along with the sun. We're also collectively tired, cold and cranky. Mike Owen shows no sign of turning back.

We stay. A woman trips over a submerged log and falls. Now she's soaked to her shoulders. Air temperature is dropping. Tonight it'll dip into the 30s. Owen is reluctant to go back—the slough is the best place to find interesting orchids—but he is merciful. We start back.

Wait a minute. What's this?

To me, the plant looks like a three-foot strand of spaghetti, wrapped around the limb of a pond apple.

This is an orchid?

"It's a ghost orchid!" Owen shouts.

It's not in bloom. It doesn't even have leaves. It is as bland as can be.

Moments later we find another. It's not blooming either. It's just as nondescript. But Owen says it is the most healthy, the most robust ghost orchid plant he has ever seen. When it blooms, it will be spectacular. Too bad it's not blooming now. Please come back some other time, he pleads.

The slog back goes faster than any of us expects. A few people, daydreaming about the dry road and their warm cars ahead, stop concentrating on the present moment's task of wading through a difficult swamp. They step into holes, they slip on algae-covered logs, they trip over vines. They topple into the water like dead trees. I meditate on each step like a Buddhist monk. I bark my shins on submerged roots and puncture my hands on a hog plum vine. But from the waist up I stay dry.

Three times the swamp vegetation is so impenetrable we change our route. The sun is lower.

Are we going to be stuck here in the dark?

Then, up ahead, somebody sees something white and comforting. Cheers echo through the swamp. It's the road.

Standing in the water, I take one last look around. With no cottonmouths in sight, I use a vine to haul myself out of the Fakahatchee Strand.

Despite the wet and the cold and the anxiety a swamp holds for completely civilized people, I'd like to go back. Not so I can make the useless boast that I wade in macho swamps. But to better understand the Fakahatchee's place, and perhaps my own, in the natural way of things—to be reminded forcefully about a real world beyond television and radio talk shows and what my computer magazines call the information superhighway.

I need to see to see that orchid in glorious bloom.

I follow Mike Owen back to the preserve office. He says he wants to show me something. He opens a huge, heavy book, the out-of-print *The Orchids of Florida*. He turns to the last entry in the old volume.

It's about ghost orchids. There's a color photograph of a ghost orchid. It is as beautiful as he described. I scan down to the last paragraph. It's even more lovely than the photographs.

I read it again and again.

I try to imagine the author, on the day he finished the book, and the moment he was writing the last paragraph, so many years ago. Perhaps he had a very good photograph in front of him to refer to, or copious notes he had scrawled while standing in the swamp as the mosquitoes hovered. Perhaps he was relying on his warm memories.

Encountering a ghost orchid—the bloom hanging under a pond-apple branch, fairy-like, a ghost in flight—clearly was an emotional moment for him.

"Should one be lucky enough to see a flower," he wrote, "all else will seem eclipsed."

High School memories

St. Petersburg
December 1991

I discovered the dusty briefcase while cleaning the garage on a Saturday afternoon. I'd forgotten I had it. I carried the case into the sunlight and shook it over the sidewalk just in case a mouse or a monster cockroach was in residence.

What tumbled out disgusted me more than rodents or palmetto bugs. Inside were the memorabilia of youth, saved by my mother and perversely brought to St. Petersburg when I moved from Miami. Kneeling on the sidewalk, I was confronted by old high school report cards.

Looking at them, I actually started sweating. All the shame and revulsion and regrets came back in a flash. It didn't matter that my last high school class ended 25 years ago, that I graduated from a fine university, that I'm married to a wonderful woman, that I have three terrific children, that I have been blessed with a rewarding career. I studied those report cards and felt once again like a miserable loser. I guess I felt like a typical high school student.

I hated high school. Yet I loved every moment—I think.

I never had so much fun in my life. I also am sure I was the world's most miserable teen. For most of my high school career, I was a classic underachiever. Not dumb—I read a lot, wrote well enough to be on the school paper and was uncommonly thoughtful—yet I seldom managed to connect with my studies. I must have been a good teacher's nightmare: The smart kid who will take an "F" rather than risk trying and actually failing.

Is there anything as terrifying as being a teen-ager in high school?

Or as wonderful?

My transistor radio was tuned to WQAM and filled with the glorious music of The Beatles, The Supremes, The Beach Boys, The Crystals, The Stones and James Brown. I fought constantly with my mother, who thought my glorious music was horrible. I had good friends to give me support except for when they hated me. But friendships are part of high school's wonderful dread, too.

I didn't have a car, good clothes, or a steady girlfriend. I had to take the bus, wore embarrassing Sears fashions and usually dated girls from other schools because they were less likely to realize I was a fink. Finky Klinky! In high school, you believe only the worst about yourself. At the same time, I considered myself pretty cool. Once, at a dance, I stood among the usual greasers and smoked a pipe.

I've actually had this nightmare: *i*'m still in high school. I'm still in Miss Alligood's English class. She wades into me, threatens to fail me, when I insist *Moby Dick* is a bore except for the neat ending. In another nightmare, I get a letter saying a clerical error shows I really didn't graduate from high school. I have to go back. I have to live through high school again.

For this graduate of Miami Edison, Class of '67, once was enough. Yet sometimes I wish I were back. Times were so innocent, so pregnant with potential. Anything could happen. Everything felt new and exciting. I can remember the first time I heard *She Loves You*. I can remember my first kiss under the stars on the 10th fairway of Miami Shores Country Club. What a wonderful world it could be.

Yet I felt like a brown shoe in a world of tuxedos. On weekends, when I was sure my classmates were living it up at parties, and drinking beer, and driving home in their convertibles, and making out with cheerleaders into whose Cokes they had dropped some aphrodisiac aspirin, I either worked at a number of horrible jobs or fished with my dad.

It's fun thinking about those jobs now. I toiled at a Miami Beach hotel, where I sifted through garbage cans for silverware thrown away by careless dishwashers. My other job was peeling onions. Before leaving the hotel I'd wash my hands a dozen times, and squeeze lemon juice on them, but as I rode the bus home I knew everybody was smelling me. I knew they were sitting there, thinking to themselves: "That poor boy stinks of onions. He'll never get a date! Why doesn't his father give him money for a nice Corvette?"

I loved fishing with my dad. On the water, as we reeled in snapper, he treated me like a buddy. At home, on school nights, he tugged at my ducktail and told me to get a haircut. Every time I asked when I could get a driver's license the answer was the same: Not until you improve those grades, not until you grow up.

Do all teen-agers love and hate their parents?

I was in love with a girl named Barbara. I was in love with a girl named Patti. I fell in love with a Georgia. I loved a Mary. I fell madly in love with Kathy. Kathy was the greatest slow dancer I ever knew, even if she was a younger woman. When I was 17 she was 14. Ashamed, I kept her a secret. I didn't want to be known as "a sophomore king," something my hateful friends would never let me forget.

When you're in high school, anti-social behavior is fun. My friends and I threw eggs at cars from alleys and then ran, giggling, from enraged drivers. A friend and I built a dummy and pushed it in front of a passing car, and the elderly driver almost skidded off the road. I felt guilty every moment I was in high school. I never missed Mass on Sunday.

I didn't know anybody at school who was gay. But any male who was the slightest bit sensitive, who maybe overpronounced his "S's", was a suspect. Mike, my best friend, asked if I could whistle. I couldn't whistle. Still can't. Mike said, "Queers can't whistle!" I shot him the bird.

I didn't know any boy who was actually having sex.

But we talked about sex all the time. We studied the *Playboys* my friend Domingo hid in the loose bricks of the barbecue pit in his back yard. We discussed the wonders of something called Spanish fly, said to drive women insane with desire. I pictured a winged insect, or maybe something tied with deer fur and a No. 2 Mustad hook. An innocent, I didn't even know what a condom was, though I had seen the machines in gas station restrooms. "Prophylactics," said the signs. "Not to be used for birth control." I knew it had to be something dirty and consulted Domingo, my most sophisticated friend.

"Oh," he said. "You mean rubbers. They're so you don't get a girl pregnant."

I didn't know any girls who were having sex. But there were rumors, always, about Bonnie, and we boys wanted to believe them. Bonnie was exotic. She wore tons of eye makeup. She piled her black hair high like the lead singer in the Ronettes. I liked watching her dance at sock hops. I admired her skin-tight, leather mini-dress. Once she asked me: "What are you leering at?" I tried to go to Confession every Saturday.

Like everyone else in high school, I hated how I looked. Every time I thought about a date pimples erupted on my chin like volcanoes. I put peroxide on my hair so I could look more blond like a surfer. Not even my mother noticed.

I had no fashion sense. I wore plaids with stripes. I wore cheap fake Weejuns called Weekenders that made me a laughing stock with the rich kids whose parents could afford the brand name Bass. When Madras shirts were the rage, I wore velour. Luckily, nobody asked me if I could whistle while I was in velour. My reputation, already shaky, would have been ruined.

There were 443 kids in my senior class. Only 22 were black. I knew none well. Yet because I felt like an outsider, because my family lacked money and community standing, I thought of them as allies. Among other things, I was a Catholic boy with a Jewish-sounding last name.

At my WASPY school, Jews and Catholics could be as unwelcome as kids with black skin. Miami still was the Old South. Some kids who knew I was Catholic were certain I worshiped statues or consulted with the Pope before making important decisions. One day, a rich kid, Chuck, drove me home after school. He looked at my house with distaste. Hurricane Betsy had blustered through South Florida the week before, and our windows were still covered by the masking tape we put up to prevent flying glass.

"What are those?" he asked. "Jew shutters?"

During my senior year, I tried to get into a journalism club called Quill and Scroll. I guess I was rejected because of my grades. Anyway, it hurt. I accepted an invitation to join Junior Exchange. On the night of my initiation, a car drove up full of boys from the club. They dragged me out of the house past my bewildered mother, pushed me into the trunk and sped away. At the initiation party, we pledges had to wander around with whole eggs inside our underwear. At the end of the evening, we were commanded to break the eggs. Our mothers must have wondered about the stains in our BVDs.

I was sports editor of the school newspaper during my senior year. Writing was my only talent. I worked at it and won awards. My column was called Klinky's Korner. I pestered a *Miami News* sportswriter into letting me help on weekends. I pestered him so much he hired me for a part-time job. Sometimes I got a byline, and $7.50 a story. My foot was in the door to a career.

I wasn't the best writer on the *Edison Herald*, though. The best was the news editor, Duka. Duka was an A-student, the wittiest person I knew and perhaps the sharpest dresser in school. I once irritated him by suggesting he write shorter paragraphs. He went on to journalism school at Northwestern. He got a job at New York, a trendy magazine, and then at the *New York Times*, where he was fashion editor.

He passed away a few years ago. Complications from AIDS, according to his obit. I got out my high school yearbook this morning and looked him up. In the picture, he's standing at the top of the stairs, grinning with what can only be teen-age delight: John Duka at 17. I'm sure he thought he'd live forever.

Spring

Magnolia

The sad poet of spring

Seminole
April 1995

Think of Wilburn Folsom as kind of a guardian angel. His job is helping take care of the lush grounds at War Veterans Memorial Park next to the VA Medical Center at Bay Pines.

Most days he's finished with work by mid-afternoon. Every once in a while he closes the park and stays later. A few weeks ago, that's what he was doing when he found the words that broke his heart.

Now he has more to worry about than keeping the Pinellas County park neat. Somewhere, he now knows, is a girl who may need an honest-to-goodness guardian angel.

Tell Wilburn Folsom how nice his park looks and he beams. At 47, he enjoys spending his day outdoors, pruning, mowing, picking up litter, doing whatever is needed to keep the park so special. It's good honest work, especially in the spring, when the breezes blow off Boca Ciega Bay and it feels wonderful to be alive.

"A real nice place," he says.

Don't try to pry too many words out of him. One of those taciturn Oklahomans, he doesn't talk any more than he has to.

If he were inclined to write poetry, he might have a lot to say about the arrival of spring. At his park, everything seems to be in bloom at once, from wildflowers to the trees, the slash pines and oaks. Always there seems to be a gentle breeze rustling the highest fronds of the sabal palms, the soundtrack to Florida's spring.

Spring is for picnics, and as Wilburn Folsom drives through his park, he can smell hamburgers grilling and baked beans bubbling. At the playground, a gray-haired woman rides a swing, kicking her legs high as if she were a child again; her husband stretches out in a lounge chair, sleeping like a baby. And over on the bay, a pair of anglers wade along the shoreline, hoping—spring is a hopeful time—for a bite.

Ospreys, the big fish hawks, hover over the water, screeching, until they dive on the skinny mullet that have returned to the bay after their winter trip into the gulf to spawn. Over in the palmettos, blue jays and cardinals go about the business of raising babies.

Yes, if Wilburn Folsom were inclined to write poetry, he might have a lot to say about the arrival of spring.

Instead, all he can show you is the poem he found.

He came upon it a few weeks back, after he had closed the park. He had left his truck and was taking a last look around. Near shelter No. 4, over by a thicket of palmettos, he saw a sheet of paper.

He had a mind to ball it up and throw it away, but something stopped him. He unfolded the paper—lined, torn from a loose-leaf binder—and discovered, printed neatly in pencil, the unsigned poem. When he was young, he always kind of liked poetry. He doesn't pretend to be an expert and didn't know if the poem is well-written. What he did know is that poem moved him.

The young girl sits alone
Frightened eyes
Timid heart
Hiding in a dark corner of her room
Praying for a happy home
Grasping for an unseen hope
Lost within confusion
Running from the world's insanity
Dead ends and steep cliffs block her path
Why must she live this way?
The love she desires is just a dream
A wish upon a star that hasn't been granted
Things aren't always what they seem
Or are they?
Torn between love and hate.
The mask she wears hides her pain.
No one cares.
It's not their problem.
Even after she is seen battered and bruised by
the people she has always loved
No one cares
The cruelty of the world is pictured through her
Her eyes show her pain
Her pleading heart begging desperately for love
For someone to care
She leaves this world with the scars of insanity
covering her wounded soul
and then she unwillingly becomes a useless statistic
for the world to look upon, shrug and carelessly say,
"What a shame."

Wilburn Folsom grew up loved. He comes from a close-knit family that always gets together on holidays and birthdays. He loves his adult children, his nephews, his nieces. He felt compassion for the young woman who came to his park, sat surrounded by its beauty, and saw only her sad predicament.

He took her poem to the maintenance shed and showed his friends.

"You picked it up off the ground," a co-worker told him. "You're her guardian angel now."

Every day now, when Wilburn Folsom drives through the park doing his work, he keeps his eyes peeled. When he walks through the picnic grounds, picking up litter, he looks for her. Maybe she'll be sitting on the wooden swing in the shade, in the alcove among the oaks, a pencil and notebook paper on her lap.

"Children today, they have so much to worry about, don't they?" he says. On a lovely afternoon, the kind that has inspired poets throughout the ages, he is staring at that empty swing.

"I keep looking for a young girl who looks lost," he finally says.

The ospreys screech, the palms rustle, the oaks drop their pollen. Along the roads, wildflowers bloom. The blue jays and the cardinals raise the next generation.

Life goes on.

One with nature

St. Petersburg
June 1993

Measure your health by your sympathy with morning and spring. If there is no response in you to the awakening of nature—if the prospect of an early morning walk does not banish sleep, if the warble of the first bluebird does not thrill you—know that the morning and spring of your life are past. Thus may you feel your pulse.
—Henry David Thoreau's journal, February 25, 1859

It has been a good spring for coral snakes. I see them on my morning runs in the nature park near my St. Petersburg home. They are highly venomous. As I jogged down the trail recently one slithered across the path. Jumping, I cried out my surprise. The snake coiled briefly in a defensive posture and then fled into the brush. As I rushed by, my heart pounding like an Indian's drum, I felt as if I were flying.

It was the kind of moment I treasure as I resist middle age and a much too civilized existence. For the rest of the day, as I sat at my computer terminal, thinking about running past that snake, I felt a connection to the wild Earth.

Computers, television, air conditioning, motor vehicles, fattening foods and other wonders that encourage sedentary behavior are the enemy of a natural life. A soft couch is comfortable, but it can also be poison to the body and the spirit. Running, walking or riding a bike is the antidote, a way to maintain an exterior and interior wilderness amid overwhelming technology.

"I never feel that I am inspired unless my body is also," Thoreau wrote in his June 21, 1840 journal. "They are fatally mistaken who think, while they strive with their minds, that they may suffer their bodies to stagnate in luxury or sloth. The body is the first proselyte the Soul makes. . . . The whole duty of man may be expressed in one line—Make to yourself a perfect body."

When I work physically hard—becoming aware of my body—I feel most alive, kin to the birds and the bees and whatever else is out there. I may be a slave to technology, wearing pricey shoes or pedaling a 21-gear bicycle, but physically and mentally I am connected to the natural world, to the wild. I am just another animal.

Now that it is warm, the animals are out. It had been seven months since I regularly saw rabbits. Now I see half a dozen every morning. They eat the grass along the path I use. When they see me, they freeze, for a moment anyway, and then rush headlong, and foolishly, into the palmettos. There are eastern diamondback rattlesnakes back in the silent shadows, and they eat rabbits for a living. A friend, walking in the park one afternoon, saw a rattlesnake swallow a rabbit. Some people have all the luck.

Only once have I seen a diamondback during a walk. In the woods north of Tallahassee, I accompanied a wildlife biologist who studied them. Suddenly, near a tall pine, he held his hand up in caution. Then he whispered and pointed. I failed to see the snake. The biologist hunkered and pointed again. It was coiled near the base of a palmetto, maybe six feet away, tongue flicking, trying to pick our scent out of the air. It never rattled. The nearest McDonald's was 25 miles away. It was a moment of startling beauty and clarity.

On a December morning, I accidentally rode my bike over a pygmy rattlesnake at Myakka River State Park. The reptile, sluggish from the cold, was stretched out on a fire road and trying to collect energy from the sunlight. I rolled over it before I could stop. So did my wife. We returned for a better look. The snake slithered slowly into the tall grass. We wished it a speedy recovery, but we knew we had probably damaged it mortally.

Unpleasant things can happen to people who risk the wild, too. An older friend, an extremely active man, was digging fossils in the middle of the woods when chest pains hit him like a lumberjack's ax. He made it back to civilization, to the hospital, to the heart surgeon. But technology can do only so much. The other day his wife, Frances, smiled and said: "Paul's back digging fossils again. And he's been turkey hunting!"

For a couple years, after I was diagnosed with an obscure lung disorder, I worried obsessively about dying. The temptation was to play it safe, to stay on the couch, to watch happy television shows. Exercising hard while seeking the wild became my physical and mental therapy. As Thoreau wrote in his November 18, 1857 journal: "Sympathy with nature is an evidence of perfect health."

So. Picture this: A bobwhite quail leads her family across my path. A gopher tortoise watches from the opening of his burrow. A pileated woodpecker attacks a slash pine like a living jackhammer. I jump a coral snake and laugh/squeal. It's better to run with the snakes than to die on the couch. I'm not dead yet, thank you.

During a bike ride in my neighborhood park, I saw a Sherman's fox squirrel, a thrilling rarity. I saw white-tailed deer during a Panhandle ride along a deserted beach. During a Paynes Prairie State Preserve bike ride I saw a flock of turkeys. Some very sassy blue jays—they must have had a nest close by—dive-bombed my head during a Miami run. At Lake Kissimmee, I saw scrub jays, a threatened species, as I bicycled through dwarf oaks. In the Everglades, I got to see a snail kite, one of North America's rarest birds, as I pedaled through Shark Valley.

As I jogged through St. Petersburg's Boyd Hill Nature Park recently, a friendly zebra longwing butterfly kept me company for a quarter of a mile. It must have been my shorts, redder than any passionflower. I was walking with my wife at the same park last week when we were stopped by a five-foot alligator lying contentedly in the middle of a trail. It grudgingly crept out of our way after one mighty hiss.

Sometimes, as it happens, I lack the time to drive to the park for a run. But it's possible to find the wild among the civilized if you are tuned in. My friend Mary Jane walks along the sidewalk of a St. Petersburg bayou in the morning and sometimes sees manatees, which have survived on this Earth for more than 30-million years. My neighbor, Dave, jogging around our block, shouted to me that he had seen a bald eagle down by the bay. From where I stood on the front porch I could hear wilderness in his voice.

The next morning I jogged through the neighborhood and watched the skies like a bird of prey. I saw no eagle, but I noticed a red-tailed hawk—an exceptionally large raptor—perched on a light pole near the grove of oaks at the nursing home. Nursing home residents feed squirrels there. The red tail, I am positive, was stalking an easy meal of squirrels tamed by domesticity. In the wild is the ever-present possibility of death.

Three times I have fallen off my bike. All were surprises, all were frightening—but exhilarating, too. I always wear a helmet and I seem to bounce. Last time it happened, I flew over the handlebars and landed in a soft fire ant mound. Watching a passing bald eagle, I failed to jump a curb.

In April, while running early one morning on a gravel road, a long way from the nearest human being, I stepped wrong, turned my right ankle and fell hard. For a moment, I was sure I had broken the bone and envisioned a long, painful crawl to civilization. Standing gingerly, I hobbled the mile back to my pickup truck. For a while, even after the ankle was mending, I stuck to flat, sensible asphalt.

But to cultivate the wild, inside and out, you have to risk the wild. I'm back on unpaved trails in the woods. This morning I saw a harmless ringneck snake. Tomorrow, if I'm lucky, I might trip over a rattler. Let me die in my footsteps.

Second coming of a Snake Man

Lakeland
April 1993

Wilfred Trammell Neill, herpetologist, anthropologist, archaeologist, author and man's man, lived for painstaking research and blood-and-guts adventure.

He trapped giant crocodiles. When he caught venomous snakes, he seldom was discouraged when their fangs penetrated his flesh. In the Everglades, he lived among Seminole Indians. In New Guinea, he hung out with headhunters. He wrote college textbooks, scientific reports, newspaper columns and magazine articles. The natural history cartoons he drew for dozens of newspapers educated a generation of Florida children about birds and insects and snakes and mammals.

Then one day he up and disappeared.

A few years later there were rumors he had passed away from the bite of a diamondback rattlesnake. Doc Neill, as people called him, had died with his boots on.

But what happened to him, in a way, was more dramatic, more mysterious.

I first met Doc at his mobile home in New Port Richey in 1978. Drinking bourbon, he sat on a sofa next to his snakeskins, his crocodile and alligator skulls, his tomahawks, his spear, his bust of a Creek Indian named Standing Bear, his magazine centerfolds of naked women, and told stories about his life.

I felt I was in the presence of a legend. I had pored over his articles in *Florida Wildlife* magazine and studied his "Creatures of the Wild" nature cartoons in newspapers when I was a boy. As someone who loathed school, I thought a man who got to roam the woods and draw pictures of what he encountered probably had the best job on the planet.

Neill had worked for Ross Allen, one of Florida's most flamboyant showmen ever, at the Reptile Institute, a Silver Springs tourist attraction near Ocala. Allen, who sometimes doubled for Johnny Weismuller when it came time for Tarzan to wrestle alligators in the movies, collected reptiles all over the tropics. Neill, with his research background, lent scientific credibility to the expeditions. With his flair for writing, he also could spin a yarn to enthrall non-scientific readers.

On the 1978 morning when I visited, Doc's left arm was grotesquely swollen and discolored, a souvenir of his 49th venomous snakebite. The rattlesnake had bitten him twice on the hand as he tried to catch it on a lonely Pasco County highway.

"It was a young, healthy snake," Doc reported, cheerful for a man who had been on his deathbed only a week before. "And I got a full venom load."

It had been his closest call yet. Because he had survived many snakebites, because he was a tough old bird, Doc had decided to ride this one out at home. As he lay on the carpet that day, gazing at the snakeskins pinned to the wall, the enzymes in the venom began breaking down body tissue, the fats and proteins, the red blood cells and capillaries. When he could no longer talk, when he could hardly breathe, when cramps jerked his body, when his gums bled, when he hemorrhaged through every orifice, Doc agreed with friends who wanted to call an ambulance.

When I saw him six days later he was home from the hospital, toasting with bourbon his return from the dead, and talking about the experience with enthusiasm. At 56, he was short and stocky with bushy black eyebrows, a Fu Manchu mustache and flashing eyes. As we exchanged goodbyes, his parting words were: "I may go snake collecting this afternoon."

You didn't have to be a psychiatrist to wonder why Doc did the things he did.

He was drawn to wild animals and wild adventure like a diamondback rattle-snake to a careless rabbit. As a boy, growing up in Georgia, he caught, bought and traded for snakes. As a University of Georgia student, he published his first scientific paper, on mole skinks, in *Copeia*, an important national herpetological journal. While teaching zoology and scientific German at Augusta Junior College, he structured vacations around reptile collection trips.

During World War II, when he was teaching hand-to-hand combat to American soldiers in the South Pacific—he was a karate expert—he always found time to slip into the jungle and harvest interesting snakes, which he kept in a convenient box in the barracks, or to visit with the aboriginal people whose culture sometimes called for shrinking the heads of their enemies. When he went to work at Ross Allen's Reptile Institute in 1949, he'd go on long, difficult hikes armed only with his courage and his mattock, a tool handy for tearing apart logs and locating hidden animals with sharp teeth and nasty dispositions.

"He was a most colorful man," said Dick Franz, a Florida Museum of Natural History herpetologist who was 14 the first time he went snake collecting with Doc Neill. "I was using a potato rake to turn over logs and finding nothing. Wilfred watched me and said, 'That's not the way to do it!' With his mattock he split a log in half and found a coral snake. I always thought of him as 'el tigre.' He was very macho."

He was married once, but it ended in divorce. He could be a volatile or peaceful, depending upon his mood at the moment. He could be charming and outgoing one day, brooding and reclusive the next.

"You never knew which one of him you'd get," Franz said.

Sometimes, for shock value, Neill ended an evening at the local tavern by downing a beer and slowly devouring the glass. His karate skills came in handy if somebody complained loudly about his behavior.

His son Tram, who teaches psychology at New York's Adelphi University, has fond memories of wandering the woods with his father. But Tram also remembers his own fear. "He was a very, very intense man," Tram said recently. "He could be uncomfortable to be around."

Neill often preferred his own company. Oblivious to danger, he'd pick his way through the pines and palmettos where rattlesnakes dwelled. He'd wade swamps in his search for animals that could kill a man. Fifteen times he was bitten by cotton-mouth water moccasins. He became so allergic he broke into a rash whenever he held one. He picked them up anyway.

He was the first scientist to discover and describe the Chipola River kingsnake, the South Florida rainbow snake, Gulf Hammock dwarf siren, an eel-like creature called the one-toed amphiuma and the Everglades rat snake, which he named *E. obsoleta rossalleni*, in honor of his boss at the Reptile Institute. During his career he wrote or co-wrote 228 scientific papers, including some considered definitive a half-century later.

"He knew Florida habitats better than anyone in the state," wrote Dr. David Auth, the collection manager for herpetology at the state's natural history museum, in a short biography of Neill. His expertise extended beyond animals and habitats. In the 1950s, Neill spent two years researching and writing a book, still in print, called *Florida's Seminole Indians*. He learned to make arrow points so authentic that only experts could tell.

Neill had a sense of humor, but sometimes people who cared about him were convinced he had a death wish, too. His son remembers the time his father tried to impress some college students by plunging his arm into a hill of fire ants. He withdrew his limb, covered by thousands of enraged ants, which were sinking their mandibles into his flesh. Neill proceeded to eat the ants off his arm.

"My Dad said they tasted like pepper."

Friends worried about Doc's lifestyle. In 1963, after an argument with Ross Allen—another strong-willed non-conformist—Neill impulsively left the Reptile In-stitute, sold parts of his herpetology collection and moved to New Port Richey to open a gas station.

His friends were stunned that so gifted a scientist had left the fold for what they considered an unpromising future. Eventually, the curator of the state's natural history museum lured Neill to Gainesville to help organize the reptile and amphibian collections.

Soon, at the urging of friends, he entered the University of Florida to pursue a doctorate degree. But Neill, idiosyncratic and proud, got along badly with his profes-sors. They wanted him to take basic courses that Neill maintained were unnecessary for a scientist of his stature.

Rather than endure what he considered the humiliation of taking classes he believed he was qualified to teach, Neill dropped out of grad school. Instead, he re-turned to New Port Richey, broke and bitter. Still, when people put the word "doctor" in front of his name, he failed to correct them.

During the next 13 years he scratched out a living at a number of jobs. He taught science and history classes at Pasco-Hernando Junior College. He wrote a popu-lar column called "Pioneer Past" for the Pasco, Hernando and Citrus editions of the *St. Petersburg Times*, where colleagues sometimes found it impossible to contact him be-cause he had no telephone. In a rage against the phone company, he had smashed it and mailed in the pieces.

Professionally, he continued to be brilliant. Columbia University published four of his textbooks, including *The Geography of Life* and *The Last of the Ruling*

Reptiles: Alligators, Crocodiles and Their Kin. The man who wore a raccoon penis bolo tie to Christmas parties also found the energy to write several historical novels, among them *Wildcat in the West* and *Quanna Parker's Magic Button.*

Still, friends worried about what seemed to be the downward spiral of Doc's life. And things seemed to get worse after the 1978 snakebite that nearly killed him. He lost his house to the bank. He lost his Indian artifacts, skulls and scientific papers to unscrupulous collectors who took advantage of him when he'd been drinking.

A few years later, he entered the hospital again, weak and hemorrhaging and depressed. Surgeons removed a growth from his chest; Neill complained he had not been himself since the bite from the rattler.

He stopped taking care of himself. He was in and out of hospitals and nursing homes. He lost his money.

He lost touch with friends and former colleagues.

He seemed to vanish from the face of the earth.

Whatever happened to Doc Neill? Every once in a while, somebody wondered.

The snakebite took its time, but it eventually killed him, was the most prominent rumor. He died of Alzheimer's disease, went another. His years of hard living finally caught up with him, others swore.

Knowing Doc—knowing how he had pushed the edge of the behavior envelope—made it easy for people to assume the worst.

"There was a general consensus that he was dead," said David Auth, the herpetologist at the state museum.

Auth, 47, could hardly walk through the museum on the University of Florida campus without confronting the inspirational ghost of Wilfred T. Neill. Anyone who did research sooner or later encountered Doc's scientific papers.

"He's definitely a founder of southern herpetology," Auth said. "It was natural to wonder what had happened to him."

Others wondered the same. At New York's Cornell University, Kraig Adler planned a chapter on Neill for the second volume of *Contributions to the History of Herpetology*. It was simple to compile facts about Neill's rich life and his discoveries. It was impossible to find anything about his death. Everyone they spoke to said he was dead, yet nobody could provide details.

Auth started investigating, too.

"I wasn't able to learn when he had died or where he was buried," Auth said. Eventually, he called the New Port Richey police and asked for help. The police could tell him nothing about Neill's demise, but an officer put him in touch with Dewey Mitchell, a former neighbor. In late 1990, Auth dialed Mitchell's number.

"Doc's not dead," Dewey said. "He's very much alive."

At the Health-care Center, a 300-bed convalescent home in Lakeland, nurse Paula Kasparik wondered about the man in Room 301. Wilfred T. Neill, a full-time resident since 1985, was weak and withdrawn. He seldom spoke. He was afraid to leave his room. Estranged from his family, he rarely had visitors.

What was wrong with him? Kasparik, and the other health care specialists, had no idea, really. They knew Mr. Neill had problems remembering recent events but seemed to have a recollection of the distant past—even if he was unwilling to talk about it. They knew from his son that he had been bitten many times by snakes and that possibly the venom had affected his memory. They also knew that alcohol may have contributed to his failed health. But Kasparik, caring for him, always got the impression that Mr. Neill just needed rest, a refuge from the past. She liked to believe that the Lord protects a person by turning off their minds for a while.

JoAnn Carter Summers, the activities director at the center, wondered about Mr. Neill, too. Summers, 48, is a high-energy woman whose enthusiasm for fun is almost contagious. But Neill was unlike the other long-term elderly patients. He wanted no part of bingo, or sing-alongs, or spelling bees. He wanted to read nature magazines in his room, alone.

What had he been like when he was younger? What kind of work did he do? How much education did he have? If Mr. Neill remembered, he wasn't saying.

In 1990, Neill had his first visitor in a long time. It was David Auth, the herpetology collection manager from the Florida Museum of Natural History. From Gainesville, he had tracked down Neill, and there were a couple of hundred questions he wanted to ask about his life.

Doc responded. He was happy to have a visitor who remembered him, who understood the value of his accomplishments, who showed respect. "It made me feel good," he told his nurses. He opened up to them a little, and they were pleased to learn something about his history. Among other things, they learned he had written books.

After work one night, Paula Kasparik visited the Lakeland public library to see whether she could find one. She found *The Geography of Life*. In his room, Doc had no memorabilia—not one of his own books or scientific papers—so he was tickled to get his hands on one. He read it from cover to cover. With the library's permission, Doc autographed the book before Kasparik returned it.

Other visitors—herpetologists who had read his papers for years, or who had met him once as children or young men and been inspired—started making pilgrimages to Lakeland.

"I always kicked myself for not tracking him down," said Paul Moler, a Florida Game and Fresh Water Fish Commission biologist who studies crocodiles, frogs and snapping turtles. "In a lot of my work, what I've done is follow in his footsteps."

Delighted at the opportunity, Moler drove from Gainesville to ask where to look in Gulf Hammock, Doc's old Levy County stomping grounds, for rare amphibians. Doc gave him detailed instructions and advised Moler to go immediately after a big storm.

"A storm will wash things out of the swamp," Neill said.

One day, JoAnn Carter Summers asked Doc if he wanted to go outside. Neill, the rugged individualist who explored wildernesses all over the world, long had been reluctant to leave his room. But this time he said yes.

"We went out and looked at an oak tree," Summers said.

Every day they went on longer walks.

Doc, who had seldom spoken to Summers in the past, now bent her ear. He identified moths for her. He identified plants. One day he picked up a shell that he said Indians used as a scraping tool to make arrow points. Another time he poked a dirt mound with a stick and told her the life history of the ants that spilled out. One day, during a longer walk, they encountered a dead snake.

"*Masticophis flagellum flagellum,*" Neill announced.

"Speak English, Doc," she told him.

"An Eastern coachwhip," he said. "But a very smashed one."

Tommy Allison made his living as a Tampa pianist, singer and comedian. But his hobby, his passion, always had been snakes. He began collecting as a boy, and when he was 14, a friend took him to Silver Springs to meet his idol, Wilfred T. Neill.

The thing Allison remembers about their meeting was how Doc Neill treated him as an adult, talked to him as if he were a real herpetologist and not some dumb kid. At the end of their talk, Neill even gave him a packet of material about snakes. For Allison, now 50, it was as if Mickey Mantle had handed him an autographed baseball. The boy was so inspired he went home and tried to write a scientific report of his own. He wanted to be like Doc.

"For a man like him to spend time with a tall, skinny kid with pimples like me was an inspiration."

Last fall, when Allison learned Doc was alive, he drove to Lakeland after one of his music gigs without taking time to change clothes. Doc had no memory of the handsome tuxedo-clad visitor who appeared in his room, but he was happy to talk to a fellow herpetologist, and even drew him a picture of a rattlesnake to take home as a souvenir. Allison brought a camera, and JoAnn Carter Summers took pictures of him and Doc standing arm in arm.

Then Allison had an idea. He wondered whether Doc might like to attend a meeting of the Tampa Bay Herpetological Association. Doc, whose confidence was slowly returning, said he might.

A few months later, accompanied by Allison and Summers, Doc Neill made a short speech about his life to adoring herpetologists.

"When I brought him into that room," Allison said, "it was like someone had walked into church with Jesus."

Fifteen years had passed since I interviewed him about the rattlesnake bite. I suppose I was hoping to find the energetic, 56-year-old man who planned to go snake collecting that afternoon, but age and illness had changed him. I walked right by.

A nurse pointed him out. Doc Neill was grayer and slower, as was I, but he had more style. Sitting in the deserted dining room, he was dressed in a shiny dark suit, tie and hat. A scarf peeked from a pocket. He wore running shoes. We shook hands and I asked whether he felt like lunch.

"That would be swell," Doc said. "That would be swell."

We drove to the nearest restaurant, a Chili's, where Doc had chicken, corn, and mashed potatoes. Doc ordered coffee—he no longer drinks—but added that he had never had a problem with alcohol. I didn't press him about that. I told him a lot of his old friends thought he had passed away.

"No, no," he said. "I'm swell."

Where had he been all those years?

"In the hospital."

Why?

"A rattlesnake bit me."

I didn't press him about that either.

He spoke fondly about less daunting matters, his boyhood and his experiences with snakes. His daddy had started him as a herpetologist by giving him a black snake. Then his daddy had brought him home a cottonmouth. His daddy built him a cage for the snakes. His daddy didn't mind snakes. They could hurt you, though.

The index finger of Doc's right hand was curved. A copperhead had done it, he said. And the scar on the top of the hand? That happened while he had tried to catch a canebrake rattler under a house.

The strangest bite?

"A New Guinea brown snake during the war. I had one in the barracks and it bit me. I was sure I'd be all right, you see, so that night I went out looking for crocodiles in a boat. Suddenly, my hands didn't want to work. Instead of dipping the paddle in the water, I was putting it in the boat. Then I started going blind. New Guinea brown snakes have a neurological poison, you see.

"I somehow got back to land. Walking, I couldn't feel my feet hitting the ground. I was curious about what would happen to me, but when I got back to the barracks I went to sleep. In the morning I was fine."

We talked anthropology. Doc said he had learned to speak both Seminole languages, Muscogee and Miccousukee, while researching a 1956 book. He told me his first name, Wilfred, in both dialects meant "Red Wolf." The Seminoles trusted him. They let him attend their most sacred ceremony, the Green Corn Dance.

As diners in the modern, fern-decorated chain restaurant turned to listen, the relic of untamed Florida before me sang *The Cat, the Mouse and the Bird* in the Cherokee language he had learned while visiting the North Carolina reservation. Doc grinned at the reaction.

Back at the health care center, where the most ill patients lay in fetal positions or talked to themselves while confined to wheelchairs, Doc hugged a nurse and waved to an orderly. He greeted other patients who said, "All right, Doc." Everybody seemed to know and like Doc. Last year, he was even elected president of the Resident's Council.

He runs their meetings according to Robert's Rules of Order, he pointed out. The council decides on weekly themes and decorations. Doc does a lot of the decorations himself. His drawings of animals grace the activities center. There are alligators and apes and dragons. He also illustrates the monthly newsletter.

"I have the typical scientist's view that productivity is all-important and satisfying."

Since his rediscovery, as he has felt more comfortable around other people, he has entered and won all the spelling bees. The other day, aide Jack Cannon opened the *New Expanded Webster's Dictionary* and tried to trip him with the word "bacchanalia." First Doc spelled it. Then he defined it.

A bacchanalia is a drunken feast.

"Did I show you my room?" I wanted to see it again anyway. He showed me his maps of the Amazon and Central America, his photographs of Indians he cut out of *National Geographic*, his poster of a Pine Barrens treefrog. Doc found a Pine Barrens treefrog once in the Florida Panhandle—a significant discovery. He brought out his collection of *Time-Life* nature books. I asked Doc if he thought he might like to leave this place one day.

"I like it here," he said. "I'm content to be here. I want to stay. It's swell."

He probably will live in the care center for the rest of his life. There are unresolved tensions between Doc and his former wife and their only son. He has a grandson he hasn't seen in 11 years.

Still, as one part of his life has closed, another part has opened. Herpetologists have rediscovered him and his work. They bring gifts and respect. They want to know what he thinks. Resurrected, a man can have a second life.

Doc is among the most marvelously complicated people I have known, and I asked if he had any regrets.

"No, it's been a good life," he said. "The things I did, they seemed reasonable at the time. I guess those could be famous last words. I don't know."

He sat on the bed and looked out the window. A mockingbird lit on the lawn. Then it was gone.

Gatorland

Orlando
April 1994

Tim Williams still owns 10 fingers, though his hands are scarred, and he has what looks suspiciously like a fresh wound on the palm of his right hand. "I kind of like to downplay the bites," says Williams, who teaches young men the fine art of wrestling alligators.

Any job, after all, can be dangerous.

"I tell my boys, a painter is going to get splashed with paint and a carpenter is going to smash his thumb with a hammer," he says, leaning across his desk at Gatorland, a Central Florida tourist attraction. At 44, he has white hair, a neatly trimmed moustache and round eyeglasses. He could almost be an accountant, except for the nasty wound.

"If you wrestle alligators," he goes on, "you have to expect that sooner or later you're going to be bitten."

One of Tim Williams' boys enters the Gatorland pit looking as if he's got the world, if not an alligator, by the tail. He is 21 and his name is Mike Hileman. Only 18 months ago, he had a cushy job at a nearby country club, giving golf lessons. Then he visited Orlando's Gatorland, which bills itself the "Alligator Capital of the World," and answered the call of the wild.

His first assignment, selling fried alligator chunks to tourists at Pearl's Smokehouse, was hardly what he had in mind. Then Tim Williams, who knows a comer when he sees one, invited the boy to a round of golf. On the first tee, Williams popped the question: "When you going to come to work for me?"

For $6 an hour and insurance he jumped feet first—the only way—into the alligator wrestling business. He is tall, lithe and has hair the color of straw. He removes his cowboy hat and climbs into the pit as 800 spectators hold their breaths while wondering if scarlet billows will spread any time soon.

It's always a possibility. Next to the fence at the wrestling pit is the Bite Box, filled with first aid equipment, ropes and a hammer and chisel. If an alligator were to bite, and to hold on, a rescuer might have to hammer the chisel into the alligator's small brain. So far, Gatorland has never used it.

Hileman wades into a moat, picks out a nice gator, grabs it by the tail, jumps back when it turns and hisses, says "He's real glad to see me," grabs the tail again, climbs gingerly backward onto a sand island, hauls the gator out of the water, sits on the gator's shoulders and then holds the jaws closed with both hands.

"I'm gonna let him catch his breath a minute," Hileman pants. The alligator, eight feet long, is not breathing hard. Hileman slides one hand down the neck, just like Williams taught him, and the other hand just over the nose. He pulls back the nose and the alligator's lower jaw falls.

All 82 teeth are exposed.

"People have all kinds of misconceptions about alligators," Hileman tells the crowd. "One is that their tails are more powerful than their jaws. They do have powerful tails, but I've never had an alligator run after me backwards."

Hileman suddenly dips his fingertips into the mouth.

The alligator slams shut its jaws with a terrifying pop.

Spectators scream.

Hileman, grinning, can still count to 10 on his fingers.

There's no business like show business.

Animal lovers in our modern state might not like the idea, but Floridians have wrestled alligators for hundreds of years. The original wrestlers probably were cowmen who got riled when hungry alligators surprised cattle, pulled them into watering holes, and devoured them. Cowmen responded by hauling offensive gators out of ponds, by hand if necessary, and shooting them dead.

Alligators became a tourist attraction in 1893, when the St. Augustine Alligator Farm began charging people a quarter for a peek at a live one. Part of the thrill was watching men work with the gators.

When the nation went car crazy in the 20th century, and tourists migrated into the state by the thousands, alligator attractions sprang up everywhere, from the Everglades to the Georgia border. Gatorland, among Central Florida's oldest tourist businesses, opened in 1949. Even now, in the face of competition from Disney and Epcot and other fantasy worlds, it endures. At a time when urban sophisticates frown upon anything that smacks of animal exploitation, it attracts about a half-million visitors annually by offering tourists a taste of Real Florida and man vs. beast.

Seminole Indians long have delighted tourists by man-handling alligators in the Everglades. But Florida's most famous wrestler was a white man named Ross Allen, who founded the Reptile Institute, at Silver Springs, in 1929. Allen's specialty was grappling with alligators—underwater. When Tarzan wrestled alligators in the movies, it was Ross Allen, actor Johnny Weismuller's double, doing the work.

Allen was elderly when he hired Tim Williams. But he still knew his way around an alligator pit.

"He was the greatest alligator handler I ever saw," says Williams, who stayed with Allen for a dozen years. Allen died in 1981, and Williams became a police officer. Though policing was interesting work, it was not interesting enough—gentle reader, how could it be?

Three years ago, Williams answered the call of the wild and came to Gatorland.

"Everything about them fascinates me," he says. When he was a boy, he looked for alligators along the St. Johns River. He reads about them, consults University of Florida biologists who do research at Gatorland, visits old-time gator wrestlers at nursing homes. On his last vacation, he drove his Jeep Wrangler to the Big Cypress until the road stopped, and photographed alligators. Sometimes he brings them home and stores them in the bathtub. Only once has he forgotten to tell his wife, and she jumped out just in time.

"Alligators," Williams sighs. "They're the last of the dinosaurs."

When Williams speaks, his alligator-wrestling boys listen. Right now he has six working for him. The oldest, a part-timer, is 55. Youngest is 20. No women wrestle at Gatorland, but he says he would hire one if she were willing and able.

"I look for people, man or woman, who are enthusiastic and genuinely interested in alligators. I don't want someone who wants to do this just so he can say 'I wrestled an alligator.' That turns me off.

"The people I hire want to be the best in the business. That goes without saying. They come to me after shows and want to be critiqued. They ask questions about problems they're having with the gators. That makes my job easier. The hardest thing to overcome is bad habits."

Training lasts 90 days. A trainee receives an 11-page instruction manual written by Williams. But reading isn't doing. A budding wrestler learns the natural history of alligators while narrating the tour taken by tourists who ride a train through the 50-acre park. Next the trainee narrates the wrestling show. He practices on a stuffed alligator head. Finally, Williams catches an alligator and lets the trainee put his hands on it.

Then he offers his most important piece of advice:

"When you're around gators, you have to remember one thing. All they have is time. They don't have to go to the grocery store. They don't worry about a job, or washing a car, or going on a date. All they have is time to wait for you to make a mistake."

When Michael Womer started wrestling alligators for Tim Williams, he had trouble pulling them out of the water and onto the island in the middle of the pit. Womer, about five-feet tall, is smaller than Gatorland's other wrestlers.

"Mike makes up for it with his heart and determination," Williams says. "He kept working at it, and the next thing you know he was handling those eight-footers."

He's 20, a native of St. Petersburg, where he grew up. He daydreamed about alligators as a boy. He wrote homework science reports about them. Two years ago, after graduating from Northside Christian School, where he was in the drama club, which had given him the role of the artful dodger in *Oliver*, Womer visited Gatorland for the first time.

"How'd you get a job like this?" he asked a wrestler. The wrestler directed him to Williams.

"It's the best job I've ever had," Womer says. "I get to combine my love of alligators with my interest in drama. My mother would like me to go to college, but I can see doing this my whole life."

Womer shows the signs of being a lifer. He even got married in the alligator-wrestling pit. The wedding party—fellow wrestlers—gathered around the bride and groom while alligators witnessed from the moat. Somebody pulled an alligator out of the moat, and the happy couple, she in her white dress and he in his tuxedo, straddled it for the wedding photos.

•   •   •

As spectators watch the pit in that rarified atmosphere of amusement and fear, Mike Hileman is happy to have his fingers. Just in time he jerked them out of harm's way when the gator slammed its jaws.

He grabs the alligator by the nose and tucks it under his chin, as if he were going to play Beethoven's *Violin Concerto*. While he controls the alligator with his chin, he holds both hands above his head. The skill might be useful should a wrestler need to dial 911.

"Now I'm going to try something a little dangerous," he says, as if he has been sewing doilies until now. He turns the alligator—the alligators hisses—and begins rubbing the stomach. This is called putting a gator to sleep. Actually, the alligator is disoriented. As the alligator lies comatose, Hileman jumps up and pretends to tickle its ribs. The alligator suddenly revives, turns and crawls, defiantly, into the moat.

"I've never been bitten," Williams says a moment later, signing autographs.

He pauses.

"I fully expect to be."

Alligators injure about a dozen people a year, usually swimmers, in Florida. Eight people have been killed since the Florida Game and Fresh Water Fish Commission began keeping records in 1948.

Nobody keeps track of alligator-wrestling injuries. But they happen more than a dozen times a year. At Gatorland, wrestlers just pour bleach on the minor wounds, attach a bandage, and go on. Williams, during his career, has shaken many a bandaged hand.

"We've had only one serious injury here," he says.

It happened to his friend John, a fine man, a fine wrestler, who had a safe record until he let his mind wander one day in the pit. Usually, an alligator will bite once and try to escape. This one hung on to John's hand. In the business, it's called a lockup.

"He needed reconstructive surgery," Williams says. "He came back to work for a while, but when his sister in California got sick, he left to take care of her."

There are enormous alligators at Gatorland, including a 13-footer, and dozens of specimens longer than 10 feet. Williams has jumped on and off the backs of 12-footers for fun, and wrestled a 10-footer once. But he considers a 10-footer too powerful for safe handling. Anyway, a 10-footer will return to the pond and hardly notice the grown man riding on its back. An eight-footer is dangerous enough.

Williams seldom wrestles alligators every day—his boys get paid for that. But sometimes he is needed, or sometimes one of his boys needs a quick lesson. Last winter, one of his boys told him he was having problems turning gators and putting them to sleep.

Williams volunteered to do a show.

"Just watch me," he said.

Williams picked out the largest alligator in the pit, Sassafras, eight feet four inches long. Williams grabbed Sassafras by the tail and lugged him out of the moat. Nothing to it for an old gator man. Then Williams straddled Sassafras and reached for the jaws.

Williams must have been distracted for a second, because Sassafras closed his jaws on Williams' right hand.

"He blew real hard—alligators do that when they're mad," Williams says. "Then he started biting down real hard, with real pressure."

A grown alligator bites down at 3,000 pounds per square inch.

"It hurt so bad! Tears came out of my eyes. But I didn't cry—in a situation like that I always laugh. I said, 'We've got a lockup, folks.'"

Nor did Williams curse. That's one of the first rules he teaches his boys. Performers never, ever should curse in public. Anyway, he was too frightened.

When alligators want to kill something, they shake their heads violently or begin spinning. They can tear their prey into bite-size pieces.

The first thing Williams did was try to control Sassafras. With his right hand trapped, he placed his left hand on the alligator's neck and leaned. Sassafras must have noticed the movement. Sassafras released the right hand and lunged at the left.

He missed.

Williams, with both hands free, grabbed Sassafras and held shut his jaws. Blood dripped down his arm and into the sand.

The teeth had passed nearly through his hand.

Williams finished the show. That's another lesson he teaches. If you're breathing, if you still have your hands and feet—if you still have your wits—you finish.

"The rest of the show was shorter than usual," he says.

Even so the tourists had gotten their money's worth.

Seminole lives,
Seminole art

Big Cypress Reservation
May 1994

At night the pond is dark and the bullfrogs sing. Behind the tan concrete house is the pond, and beyond the pond is the mystery swamp that goes on forever. Bull alligators bellow and gar fish splash and great horned owls fly on silent wings. Bears and panthers prowl nearby, though it has been a while since anyone saw them.

Don Osceola and his wife Mary Gay, who are Seminole Indians, live in the house on the pond. When Don was a boy, nearly half a century ago, the big animals of the Everglades were more abundant, and the Seminoles depended on them for food and spiritual sustenance. Don remembers eating panther, which tasted wild and strong, a match for the best of the people who lived in this hard land south of Lake Okeechobee.

Mary remembers her father and grandfather hunting frogs and fish with spears from dugout canoes. She remembers her mother and her grandmother, sitting in the palm-thatched chickee, cooking and sewing and telling the old stories as the glades whispered all around them.

Mary is a storyteller herself, though in a different way. She paints pictures that tell about Seminoles and the lives they once had in the grassy waters—what they called the Pahayokee—of the Everglades. She sits in a back bedroom Don converted into a studio, gazes out the window at the swamp and paints stunning, colorful pictures that capture a traditional way of life that seems to be vanishing as Seminoles more and more step into the modern world.

"What she does is inspired by her whole life experience," Don explains.

"It is a way of keeping the culture alive," Mary says.

Keeping the culture alive, I'm about to find out, is no easy task.

My meeting with the Osceolas is the result of a chance encounter at a Clewiston festival where Mary is selling her art. I introduce myself, tell her I'd like to visit her Big Cypress home some day and interview her. She says neither yes nor no but smiles shyly and accepts my phone number. I wonder if I came on too strong and fear she will never call.

Two days later my telephone rings in St. Petersburg. Don Osceola invites me down to talk to his wife. But he has an unusual request. He asks if I might interview Mary in front of children at the Seminole school where he is a counselor.

"Maybe you could tell them what reporters do," he says. Motivating children to get an education and learn the skills that will help them compete in today's world is what Don does. "Maybe you could tell them how to become a reporter. We are trying to show the children the things that are possible, the options open to people who have an education. We don't want them to drop out of school."

A week later I climb into my truck and head south on the interstate, all the while thinking about the challenges facing the Seminole people, the challenges of preserving the past while preparing for the future and all of its complexities.

I drive past the shopping malls, trailer parks and suburban sprawl of southwest Florida. At Naples, I turn east on Alligator Alley and speed past the pines and cypress of the Fakahatchee Strand and the Florida Panther National Refuge. Inside the boundaries of the Big Cypress National Preserve, I race past swallow-tailed kites and wood storks and water the color of tea. Finally, after an hour, I turn north on Snake Road, the narrow serpentine highway that slithers 17 miles onto the 52,000-acre reservation.

There is sawgrass and pine, cypress and slough. Great blue herons hunt minnows, and territorial red-wing blackbirds dive-bomb passing crows. Lubber grasshoppers creep over the steamy blacktop; the roadsides are alive with Spanish needle, the white and yellow flowered plant the old medicine people still know how to use.

I drive along wood and pasture, thousands of acres of pasture, where Seminoles on horseback drive cattle. Just before reaching the settlement, I watch a calf walk down a canal embankment for a drink. Suddenly, the calf leaps back and bolts away in terror. The alligator, lying perfectly still in the water, almost had him. A moment later I park at the Ahfachkee School—it means "Happy Place"—and walk inside.

"Welcome," Don Osceola says.

White people came to Florida in 1513. By the 1700s, almost all of Florida's aboriginal Indians were dead, the victims of warfare, smallpox, measles and other European diseases for which they had no immunities.

The few who survived may have left Florida for the Caribbean, though some historians believe a handful of Calusa Indians hid in the remotest Everglades and may have intermarried with the Indians who migrated down the peninsula from the Panhandle, Georgia and Alabama. Those migrants were the Creek, Choctaw, Oconee, Yuchi, Yamassee, Apalachee, Talaisis and Miccosukee who called themselves "people of the distant fires" because they had come a long way. In three wars against the United States to hold on to their territory, they banded together as Seminoles.

By the time the shooting ended in 1858, most Seminoles were deported to Oklahoma or dead. But a few hundred survivors vanished into the Everglades and Big Cypress without surrendering or signing a peace treaty. Today, about 1,500 live for the most part on reservations at Brighton, near Lake Okeechobee, in Hollywood, Tampa and the Big Cypress. The 300 people who prefer to call themselves Miccosukee usually live west of Miami on the Tamiami Trail.

For outsiders, figuring out who is Seminole and who is Miccosukee can be a challenge. Some Miccosukees are registered with the Seminole Tribe and some Seminoles with the Miccosukees. A dwindling number of older Seminoles speak Muscogee, a dialect shared by the Seminoles of Oklahoma. But most of the Florida Seminoles, at least the ones who still can converse in their native tongue, speak Miccosukee. Few young Indians speak it, an alarming situation to tribal elders who believe the end of the world will come when their people no longer are able to tell their stories in their own language.

The Miccosukees are said to be the most traditional—many still practice their nature-centered religion. The Holiywood and Tampa Seminoles are the most cosmopolitan. The Brighton and Big Cypress Indians are the most isolated, though television has brought the urban 20th century out to them. Some still dwell in chickees, the cypress and palmetto-thatched huts, but most live in concrete houses.

Many are Christians and no longer attend Seminole rituals such as the Green Corn Dance, the purification ceremony that binds them to the past and renews their relationship with the earth. Although unemployment is high, many work in the nearest cities as house painters, carpenters and mechanics, or remain on the reservations and raise cattle, make crafts or wrestle alligators for tourists. The Everglades Indians who resisted white ways once were considered among the healthiest native people in the United States; in 1994 obesity, high blood pressure, diabetes, alcoholism and drug addiction are growing problems.

"There are more temptations for the people now than there used to be," Don Osceola says in a Miccosukee accent that sounds to me like soft rain falling on a canvas tent. "Modern times."

The Ahfachkee School is brand new. There are 72 students from kindergarten through eighth grade. They are taught the same subjects as children elsewhere in Florida, but twice a week they receive lessons about their own culture and language.

We visit the classroom of Therese Sullivan, a teacher for 30 years, including two here. "They're wonderful, bright children," she says about her class of 27 fifth-through-eighth graders. After graduation, some of her students will move on to high schools in Clewiston, Hollywood or Oklahoma. But many will drop out.

"My feeling is that in some schools, native American children have never been invited to be themselves, so they haven't been able to show their potential," Sullivan says. "But they can be themselves here."

She claps her hands and the children—they have coal black hair, almond eyes and skin like coffee ice cream—sit at tables or stand in the back of the brightly lit room. The Macintosh computers that the students are learning how to use rest on desks. Their best papers and pictures hang on the walls. Their teacher says, "I keep telling them I want them to graduate from here, go on to college, and to come back and take my job."

I talk to the children about telling stories, which is what writers try to do, and encourage them to write the family stories they hear from grandparents. They listen solemnly, for the most part, though a couple of girls remind me of my own daughters by covering their eyes and giggling when I turn their way. I tell the class about the alligator I saw stalking a calf as I drove in, and about the herons along the road, and how I enjoy writing about animals.

Then I invite Mary to sit next to me, for the interview. She's middle-aged, like me, with glasses and short graying hair. She is dressed in dark slacks and a maroon blouse decorated with the wavy pattern favored by many Seminoles. We're both nervous, talking publicly, but we try. She tells me she was born in the Everglades, near the Tamiami Trail, and has warm memories about living outdoors, surrounded by a loving family.

Men dressed in traditional "big shirts" that reached to the knees and sometimes covered their heads with turbans, she says. Her husband, watching from the back of the room, looks colorful to me, too. He wears jeans and a sky blue shirt covered by a beautiful rainbow-colored vest his mother-in-law made for him.

In the old days, Mary goes on, women were clothed in long colorful dresses and sometimes wore hundreds of beads around their necks. The old people, the heart of the culture, told many stories that always had a moral to them. Some warned children to avoid white people and white ways. For example, Seminole young were forbidden to touch paper and pencil. A reliance on the white man's written word might lead to the eventual disappearance of the Seminole oral culture.

Mary attended a Seminole school in Hollywood, and one day she drew a picture of a river scene she had looked at in a magazine. A Seminole teacher encouraged Mary to draw more. When she was a teen-ager, her parents sent her to the Institute of American Indian Art in New Mexico. She returned to Florida after graduating and sold paintings to tourists. She married, and had a son, and she had to give up painting to take care of him. But as he got older, she had more time, and again picked up the paint brush.

Don and Mary take me to the school's culture center, where last summer Mary painted several large wall murals. Her colors are vivid and her style might be described as Grandma Moses folkart: beautiful and primitive. In one painting, a Seminole man kneels and tells a story to his children. Under a chickee, women cook gar fish stew. Another man walks into camp toting a bundle of firewood. I ask if any of the people in her painting are Mary or her family.

"Oh, they could be," she says. "That's how it was."

In another mural, a dugout canoe sails across the Everglades and carries a heron, toad, otter, snake, wind, panther, deer and bear. They represent the clans of the Seminole people.

"In the old days, you could not marry someone from your clan," Don explains. "When you did marry, you moved in with your wife's clan. Your children belonged to your wife's clan. But it's different now. People can marry anybody they want."

Mary belongs to the bird clan. Don is a panther. In Mary's painting, the heron is in the bow of the canoe. The panther is toward the back. "I wanted her to put the panther in front, instead of back in the economy section." Mary smiles at Don's tease.

We go to their home so Mary can show me where she paints. Her work hangs from the living room wall and decorates her shelves. She calls one painting—it shows a dugout canoe carrying a Seminole family and heading for a village—"Visiting Grandmother." Don's photograph, as a U.S. Marine, also is displayed. When he finished his five-year tour of duty in Vietnam, he used his VA money to continue his education. He's a graduate of Florida Baptist Theological College. A portrait of Jesus hangs near his collection of Bible homilies.

A 19th century portrait of Osceola, the great chief who led the Seminoles in their second war against the United States, gazes across Mary's studio, a jumble of brushes, paint, sketches, blank canvas, Rubbermaid containers, an electric fan, and the radio that plays gospel music as she works.

There are photographs of her grandmother and her son. His name is Christian, he's 22, and he's attending a vocational school in Broward County to learn auto mechanics. But he recently began taking a class to learn his native language.

"I didn't teach him when he was a boy," Mary says. "I didn't think I should."

"Back then," explains Don, who was born in the Everglades, "if you wanted your child to be successful, it meant teaching English. It meant more opportunities."

He still thinks he is right. But now he believes that knowing the native language, and the old stories, are as important. Yet teaching both is increasingly difficult for Seminole parents.

"Now sometimes both are working, or the family is spread out, and there's just not a lot of time to teach both."

Don watches Mary get out a new canvas, her brushes and her paints.

"In the old days," he continues, "everybody lived together, in clans. Now everybody has a vehicle, people can go anywhere, work anywhere, marry anybody. The TV is always on, and some of the young people want to be rock stars.

"Freedom is good; it gives you all kinds of opportunities to better yourself. But in a way, it is also anti-culture. In the old days, it was easier for the Seminoles to keep their culture together."

In her studio, Mary begins a new painting, a Seminole child dressed in rainbow colors, from the era before television, from the era when choices seemed simpler. Mary glances out her window, at her pond and her swamp, and smiles.

"It's loud here at night," she says. "Lots and lots of frogs."

Tom Gaskins,
in the swamp

Palmdale
May 1992

The old man of the swamp walks across a four-lane highway in bare feet. Tom Gaskins does not believe in shoes. He does not believe in modern highways either.

"I remember a Florida where some places you didn't have paved roads," he says as a passing produce truck shakes U.S. 27. "I remember when bridges weren't made of cement." He has lived all of his 83 years in Florida, most of them in the swamps along Fisheating Creek, which drains into Lake Okeechobee. As for footwear, it makes no sense for a swamp man in the Everglades even in the '90s.

"It's an easier life without shoes," Tom Gaskins confides. "Yes, sir it is! I have to go to a funeral, I'll wear 'em, but that's about it. Barefoot is better. The Seminole Indian . . . I don't think he wore moccasins. They would have slowed him down too much if he had to stop and take 'em off when things got wet. Plus, shoes and socks, they're expensive."

Gaskins, the old man of the swamp, has a mind for dollars and cents. He runs the Cypress Knee Museum, a roadside attraction harkening back to the older, more innocent Florida all but gone even here in rural Glades County.

For two dollars a head, Gaskins lets tourists in to admire his collection of knees, the picturesque bumps that grow up from cypress roots and stick out of the water like pointy-headed gnomes. Gaskins calls cypress knees nature's art. They are twisted and tortured, straight and smooth, ugly and beautiful. They play games with the imagination.

Gaskins displays cypress knees resembling elephants and donkeys and grizzly bears. He's got a cypress knee with a nose Charles De Gaulle wouldn't have sneezed at. He's got a knee dressed with eyeglasses and a big cigar *a la* Groucho. He's got a knee which reminds some churchgoers of the Madonna who was famous long before the Material Girl of MTV.

"There ain't many places like this left," roars Gaskins, who is as rare as the dwindling panthers of the Everglades. A woodsman, hunter, inventor, philosopher and shameless huckster, he may be the last of his kind. He's vanishing Florida, and a metaphor for the Everglades that used to be.

Lady, If He Won't Stop, Hit Him On The Head With A Shoe.

Gaskins put that message on a homemade highway sign more than four decades ago. The letters, cut from cypress logs, are falling down now. But passing motorists can still make out enough of the words to figure something extraordinary is ahead. Some even take a chance and stop.

When I was a boy, when U.S. 27 was the state's major interior north-south highway, roadside attractions were as common as gas stations—especially in the Everglades. There were snake farms and places a tourist could stop for a coconut-head doll or maybe a genuine stuffed baby alligator. In good years, as many as 20,000 visitors poured into Gaskins' museum. But I-75 and the Turnpike, and big-time attractions such as Disney World, changed tourism and Florida.

"It's a different place now," Gaskins says. Most modern folks are satisfied to remain ignorant about cypress knees. Or they think cypress trees should be protected from commercial exploitation. To some modern Floridians, the sport of hunting is an act of barbarism. Most think "Florida Cracker" is a racial invective instead of the complimentary description of a native old-timer that it is.

Gaskins is a Florida Cracker and proud of it. He was born March 26, 1909, in Tampa, grew up in Arcadia and sold Gator Roach Killer Spray for a living until 1934. Then he fell in love with Virginia Bible and cypress knees. He married both of them.

In 1937, he and Virginia moved to Palmdale, on the edge of wild Fisheating Creek, because of the cypress. He made everything from lamps to tables to his own home out of cypress. He collected knees by the truckload. In 1947, for variety, he invented a turkey call that hunters by the thousands buy to this very day. It's his moneymaker.

In 1951, he officially opened his museum. He put up a cypress boardwalk through the cypress swamp. He erected cypress signs pointing the way. He didn't clearcut the cypress forests of Glades County, understand. But he used trees here and there because he was in the cypress business. When he started, anyway, everybody thought the natural resources of the state were endless.

In the swamp, on his own, he hunted turkeys and bears. He listened to owls. He ate swamp cabbage. Now even sabal palms, the trees that provide the edible heart of palm cabbage, are dwindling. Some people say it's because of the greenhouse effect. Others say too many people still eat swamp cabbage and kill the trees. What's a swamp man to think?

Tom Gaskins just tries to keep up his strength. He's been known to stand on his head for hours because he believes it improves blood circulation. He still does dozens of pushups a day. He chews coal tar creosote for his health even though doctors have warned him he'll get mouth cancer. They've been wrong so far.

In 1978, he celebrated his 69th birthday by running 11 miles along the creek. His son, Tom Jr., says his father has slowed in old age. Gaskins has shortened his daily run to two miles. Nike has yet to make a dime out of him.

"Bare feet are good enough," he says. Except for a couple of broken toes he's never been bad hurt. "Feet toughen up after a while."

He's walking—make that trotting—along the boardwalk that weaves a half mile through cypress trees and knees and oaks and snakes and deer flies. I have to work to keep up with him. Otherwise, he could not tell me about cypress knees.

"The encyclopedias all say that cypress is hard, hollow and only found in the South," he says. He's short and wizened with blue eyes Joanne Woodward would love.

"The encyclopedias got it wrong. Cypress is soft. It's only hollow if you hollow it out yourself like I did. Hell, I've seen cypress in New York."

He brought cypress knees to the World's Fair in New York in 1939. Twice he talked cypress knees with Johnny Carson on *The Tonight Show*. Then he returned to his swamp. He never cottoned to city life.

"It's wild out here. There are cypress trees. Cypress knees are beautiful to look at. That's what I like about 'em. They're nature's art. They're pretty. People will tell you a cypress knee is hard and hollow and only grows in the South. But they're wrong."

He apologizes for repeating himself.

"My mind's not what it used to be. It's gone to hell. I'm no spring chicken." The boardwalk is as high as eight feet, a foot wide and in places lacks a railing. Looking at the cypress knees below, imagining the damage they might do to my ribs, I inch my way along the boardwalk in fear. Gaskins, meanwhile, walks and hops and spins, protected by the gods of the swamp. With minimal effort he climbs off the boardwalk, his callused feet wrapping around the posts as if he were a monkey.

The old rooster has to wait for a spring chicken four decades his junior to climb down. "No water here now," he says when I join him in the swamp. "You ought to come back later in summer. I seen water deep enough to go right over the boardwalk."

It was true years ago anyway, before all the roads and the buildings and canals altered the landscape. "The steam shovel changed Florida," Gaskins declares. "Draining, draining, draining. We don't get the water we used to get."

Some of Florida's earliest drain-the-Everglades schemes happened nearby. In 1881, a wealthy Pennsylvanian named Hamilton Disston bought four million acres. He dredged the Caloosahatchee River south of here and opened it to steamboat travel into Lake Okeechobee. He drained land for farms and homes. Draining continues to this day.

"The steam shovel, it changed the face of Florida," Gaskins says again. "I don't like it. I wish things was the way they used to be."

Gaskins almost always wears shorts. A big biting fly lands on his bare knee. A swamp man knows you don't slap a deer fly. The fly will feel the wind coming from your hand and escape. He crushes the fly beneath his thumb. "Dear, deer fly," he says, grinning at the bloody splotch.

In the swamp world of Tom Gaskins, there are deer flies aplenty. Mosquitoes swarm in summer. There are moccasins and rattlesnakes fat with poison. He's never been snake bit. "Every snake is different. Some will get out of your way and some you have to get out of their way. Some will coil up on you. I don't know what snakes are thinkin'. They don't talk the English language."

We walk out of the swamp and into his yard. He has two canoes for when the creek is up. He has a snowmobile. Years ago, he discovered that snowmobiles were perfect for getting around the shallow mud of a Florida swamp. For a while, he had the state's only Arctic Cat Snowmobile franchise. Snowmobiles never caught on. His rusts in the front yard near the gift shop where he sells turkey calls.

In Tom Gaskins' hands, it's the Stradivarius of turkey calls. He strikes a two-inch piece of wood against the side of an eight-inch cedar box. The box yelps like a turkey in heat. I listen for a returning yelp, from a real bird, but all I hear is the booming radio of a passing car. And then the rat-a-tat-tat of a pileated woodpecker. The Everglades are like that.

"I've had six friends, I think, shot by other turkey hunters who thought they was turkeys," he says. "Some of these nuts in the woods these days will shoot if they see a bush move. Crazy."

He built the gift shop out of cypress. Fifty-four years ago, he built his home out of cypress. By hand he made 30,000 cypress shingles for the house. "That's how everybody made houses then!" he says with a sigh. He looks tired to me. I don't blame him. Modern Florida must be bewildering when you are the last of the swamp men, when everything you knew and loved is changing around you.

U.S. 27, no longer a clay country road, is four lanes of pavement that nevertheless carries fewer tourists. The bridge across Fisheating Creek is made from concrete instead of wood. Nearby towns have McDonald's and Pizza Huts. The swamp is dry when it should be wet.

People don't care about cypress knees, not like they used to, and they wear shoes when anybody with a lick of sense knows enough to go barefoot. Cars whip by the Cypress Knee Museum as if it were a ghost town.

"You won't see houses like this anymore," Tom Gaskins shouts as we stand in his yard and admire the cypress shingles he made so carefully a half century ago. "I'll bet there ain't a house like this left in the world. My house will be here when the cows come home."

A natural balance

Okeechobee
May 1992

Sonny Williamson says he wants to check for mice in his hunting cabin. They're so hard to catch. They hide in the stove, and he is unaware until the smell of roast rodent wafts through the cabin and everybody runs outside gasping.

So we drive through his pastures in his Jeep, past his oak trees and his cabbage palms, past his deer and his turkeys, and we stop at his cabin, and we go inside, and he opens his oven, and checks his mousetrap.

No mice.

It's one of those humane traps. The mouse is supposed to get stuck on a glue patch and avoid a broken neck. You can release your mouse alive.

"One was here," he says, looking at mouse prints in the glue. "The trap didn't hold him."

I have heard Sonny Williamson is an unusual man. I never figured it meant he had a soft spot in his heart for mice. He's a hunter, after all. He might find it odd, but he confuses people. Just when they think they've got him figured, he escapes the hole into which they've tried to put him and the other pigeons.

It's a warm, cloudy day when I meet Sonny to talk about the Everglades. As an environmentalist, as somebody who grew up playing in the Everglades, I sometimes think about them in black and white terms. They have to be saved, no matter what, no matter who gets hurt. Sonny values the Everglades, too. But he's one of those people who automatically sees the world in shades of gray. A hunter can free a mouse, and a rancher can be an environmentalist.

At 62, he is a rancher and a farmer who believes in property rights and free enterprise. He is also a hunter and a fisher and a camper and an environmentalist who believes in the Everglades. It's a strange combination, especially down here, where people tend to be one or the other.

Free enterprise and property rights—"the American way of life" to many of us—have contributed greatly to the decline of the Everglades, which provides drinking water for 4.5-million people and life to thousands of rare plants and animals.

Is it possible to have both prosperity and a healthy Everglades? A lot of hard-core environmentalists, and a lot of dyed-in-the-wool capitalists express doubts. They see it as one of those nature vs. jobs battles. They see it in black and white.

Saving the Everglades is going to be a bear, Sonny Williamson knows. But he thinks it's possible if we're willing to recognize that the solution lies in the grays.

"Agribusiness and the Everglades are the crown jewels of Florida," Williamson says as we tour his 10,000-acre ranch north of Lake Okeechobee. "We can't afford to lose either of them."

For Williamson, a fifth-generation Floridian, understanding the need to preserve two very different jewels is more than an intellectual exercise. Gov. Lawton Chiles appointed him to the governing board of the South Florida Water Management District.

In the years ahead, the district may have to change the way agriculture does business. Some farmers and ranchers may be required to limit pollution or pay fines. Some might even have to leave. A number of farmers and ranchers, whose families have been working land drained more than a half century ago, retain lawyers just in case. Most are fearful of the pain ahead.

"It's fair to say there's lots of apprehension," Williamson says with a sigh.

Farming and ranching are a way of life in South Florida. In Okeechobee County, where Williamson has lived more than four decades, agriculture is a $150-million business. And it's hurting. A few years ago, the state ordered dairy farms to reduce the water tainted by cow dung pouring into Taylor Creek, which feeds Lake Okeechobee.

Even with government financing to help modernize operations, some dairies ran out of money. They chose to go out of business or sold their property to the state. Nineteen out of 49 dairies eventually closed. Some environmentalists, including me, cheered. Dairies were the lake's major polluter. Sonny Williamson, who counts dairy farmers among his friends, winced.

"It fell like an ax on our economy. People lost jobs. It was a painful thing."

But a necessary thing? You have to break eggs to make an omelet, right?

Williamson sees himself as an agriculture advocate on the water management board. He also sees himself as representing the interests of the Everglades and South Floridians who require clean water.

"I wear two hats," he says quietly.

Some of his agribusiness neighbors are unhappy with him. How can he vote for the Everglades when he knows farmers and ranchers—his own people—might be hurt?

"It's sobering when I hear that," he says. "It's not been easy for me."

He is a quiet, serious, God-fearing Baptist with an old-fashioned rural outlook who has adapted to a fast-changing world. Stuffed deer heads hang from his office walls. He can look out a window and admire a green swamp white with ibis. In a back room, a fax machine hums and spews out the business of the water management district. He's old and new Florida.

He has a long history of public service in Okeechobee County. He's on the board of directors for a drug and alcohol rehabilitation facility. He served on the school board for eight years. He was a member of the Kissimmee River Resource Management Council that recommended restoration. He was chairman of the county planning commission.

The nine water management district governing board members are appointed for four-year terms. They receive no salaries. But the jobs are coveted, especially in the agricultural community, where water is as important as currency. Ranches and farms require serious water.

When Sonny Williamson's name came up as a candidate for a water management job, a strange thing happened. Environmental and agriculture and development interests did not fight about him like pit bulls. They liked his philosophy.

"He's attentive to all sides," said Andy Rackley of the Florida Sugar Cane League. "But he makes it plain that in the end he's going to make a decision based on the facts."

"Sonny's a farmer, and I'm sure he's proud of it," said Florida Audubon president Bernard Yokel. "But he's evenhanded enough to try to understand the whole issue."

"He has what some people call a stubborn streak," said former Okeechobee County Commissioner Elder Sumner. "But all the time, he's listening to the other side."

"Sonny Williamson is a Renaissance man among cave people," said Richard Coleman, an environmental advocate for the Kissimmee River and the Everglades who has bumped heads more than once with agribusiness. "Sometimes I think he doesn't fit in a community that fights to stay ignorant. He looks to the future."

"I don't believe agriculture purposely damaged the Everglades," Sonny Williamson says. "It's only recently that science has been able to tell us we've been hurting our neighboring environment. For the most part, and there will be exceptions, those of us in agriculture are going to say, 'Let's fix things.'"

For the district, Williamson toured a dairy farm that adapted to state regulations and has dramatically reduced the amount of fecal matter pouring into the Everglades system. He's scheduled to address a high school class about the problems of the Everglades. Florida fishing and hunting writers have invited him to their annual convention to talk about the Everglades. He's a busy man.

Meanwhile, he's been hearing turkeys gobble in the oak hammocks in the distant woods. He keeps a 12-gauge in the back of his Jeep station wagon. Shotgun shells rattle on the gear shift console as we drive along. He's hoping for a chance to hunt soon. He'll hide in the palmettos, imitate a female turkey with a caller and wait for an amorous gobbler to come calling. He'll rise, aim, fire.

Wild turkey tastes better than any supermarket bird.

We miss a chance for a free lunch at his wife's history society meeting. As we drive through pastures and hammocks and citrus groves, full of Black Angus-Brahman hybrid beef cattle and wild turkeys and ripe Valencia oranges, we share stale peanut butter crackers.

"We can't lose agriculture," he says. Hard-core environmentalists believe agriculture has to go, especially south of Lake Okeechobee, where it probably doesn't belong. Agriculture moved into the Everglades about seven decades ago after the early "Let's drain Florida" projects. Fertilizers and pesticides now threaten the Everglades, and it sometimes seems right to fit farmers with black hats. On the white hat side, they supply most of the nation's winter vegetables.

"We have to compromise," Sonny Williamson says. "But compromise is often rejected by environmentalists. They see compromise as a perversion of their ethic. I see my role as pointing out the importance of food production to them."

His family settled in Florida before the Civil War. He was born east of Clearwater when the city was mostly woods and a boy could hunt and fish and camp a mile from the nearest paved road. His Christian name is Frank, but a sister dubbed him Sonny. After graduating from the University of Florida, he helped his dad establish their ranch in Okeechobee County.

He married Betty Chandler in 1951. They brought into the world three children. Wes, 36, manages the family ranch. Kim, 37, is a Phoenix attorney who sometimes represents business interests against environmentalists. Karen, 32, is a homemaker and married to an Okeechobee dairy farmer. Sometimes Sonny argues with his children about the importance of the environment.

"In some ways, I'm more liberal than they are," he says.

His roots go deep into the Everglades. More than three decades ago, his dad was among the few people who opposed the destruction of the Kissimmee River. In the name of flood control, the U.S. Army Corps of Engineers replaced the 103-mile river with a 56-mile canal that destroyed wildlife habitat, turned marsh into pasture and helped move polluted water into Lake Okeechobee.

Now the Corps and the water management district want to restore the river. Williamson believes restoration will help the Everglades—"It symbolizes our commitment"—though his son thinks it will waste taxpayer money.

"I think we have to look at the Everglades as one big system," Sonny Williamson says gently. "The Kissimmee, Lake Okeechobee, the Everglades Agriculture Areas, Everglades National Park, Florida Bay . . . they're all pieces in the puzzle."

When he was a boy, Sonny waded in Lake Okeechobee with his father and caught bass they'd bring home in gunny sacks. He hunted south of the lake in the Big Cypress. "You always wanted to kill a young hog early in the hunt," he says. "That way you could eat some fried pork chops and grits and tomato gravy."

He has done well in business. More than 1,600 head of cattle graze on 5,000 acres of his land. He grows three kinds of oranges and two kinds of grapefruit on another 1,000 acres. He left 4,000 acres as a wilderness preserve.

More than 300 deer live on his ranch, according to state wildlife biologists who conducted a census. Flocks of wild turkey patrol the oak hammocks for acorns. Fox squirrels, a species designated as "threatened" by government, scamper up maple trunks. A pair of bald eagles, an endangered species, nest in a slash pine. Williamson stops so I can admire their baby through my binoculars.

Some Florida ranchers get nervous when a protected species shows up on their property. They're afraid government will swoop in and tell them what they can and can't do on their land. It's when the rights of property owners clash with public good.

"What you have to understand is that cattle ranchers are independent in their thinking. They are advocates of free enterprise. The idea of a government entity telling them what to do is a foreign concept to them."

Perhaps Florida should buy their land.

"I think Florida has to buy more land," Sonny says. "But I say that as a landowner who is getting more and more uncomfortable with the idea of public ownership of land."

Why the reluctance? Most people believe buying land is the fairest way to preserve wilderness.

But Williamson sees another gray area.

"I don't know where the money to buy lands is going to come from unless we have a viable private sector to pay for it. Private enterprise is the goose that lays the golden egg. If we banish agriculture, we're truly short-sighted. We have to solve the problems as we encounter them."

It will cost hundreds of millions of dollars to restore the Kissimmee River. It may require hundreds of millions of dollars to acquire land and restore marshes in the agricultural area south of Lake Okeechobee. The federal government, all the while, is negotiating to buy additional land for Everglades National Park. It's expensive to save panthers and crocodiles and manatees.

He softens his tone, switches gears—and directions.

"Farmers are providing food for the rest of the country. But it doesn't mean we should have a license to misuse the land. It's a complicated issue."

A mature bald eagle, its white head and tail flashing in the hazy sun, swoops low over the trees. A crow dive bombs it. Sometimes an eagle will eat a crow. It's revenge time.

"If you're walking or driving, sometimes an eagle won't let you get very close," Williamson says. "But when you fly, they'll get close enough to look you in the eye. It's something to be sharing a thermal with an eagle."

For 35 years he has piloted his own planes. For a while, his hobby was flying in gliders. He once floated 28,000 feet above Pike's Peak in Colorado. In South Carolina, he once crashed and broke both legs. He healed. He also healed after an enraged bull knocked him down and broke ribs and ruptured his liver.

Some people believe saving the Everglades is a life-and-death matter, too. Can a world treasure of bio-diversity co-exist with agribusiness? Can you mix black and white and be happy with the resulting gray?

Williamson doesn't know. But he hopes so. He was encouraged by the way the dairy industry responded to the need to clean up. Dairy farmers were hurt by state rules, but they complied, and most of them were able to stay in business. He hopes the same spirit of cooperation happens south of Lake Okeechobee, where Big Sugar reigns.

"I've got my feet in both worlds," he says.

It takes hours just to see part of his ranch. It's that big. He shows me a cypress forest that might do the Corkscrew Swamp proud. Sometimes he uses its water, but never during summer. In the summer, South Florida stays wet. He tries to use water according to the cycles of nature.

Some ranchers drain year round. "The conventional wisdom used to be to drain as much land as possible." In some areas, he has allowed water to return to lands he once drained. He believes in preserving wetlands.

Unlike some farmers, he's planted his citrus where soil drains naturally and eliminated the need for constant pumping. He monitors his groves for excessive phosphorous, a byproduct of fertilizers that can damage the environment. He buys treated wastewater from the city of Okeechobee to irrigate his fruit. It's part of a cooperative experiment to see whether secondary water will hurt or help crops.

It's his ranch policy to eliminate exotic plants and animals, whether they're water hyacinths or feral hogs. Non-native flora and fauna have damaged the ecology of the Everglades. He says he has tried to balance the need to make a dollar with the responsibility to steward the land with wisdom.

In late afternoon, as raindrops fall, we drive into some of the deepest woods I've seen. He says it's his favorite hammock, a great shady place, good for thinking, good for hunting.

There are oak trees that surely were here when the Seminoles moved down the Peninsula. There are great cabbage palms and hickory trees. Hickories shouldn't grow so well here, but they do. It's hard to believe I'm in the middle of a South Florida cattle ranch. It's a lush rain forest dream.

"The farmers and ranchers of South Florida supply a lot of our nation's food," Sonny Williamson says, interrupting my thoughts. "What will happen if agriculture has to move? Where will it go? Mexico? To a rain forest in South America? The biggest violations of the environment are being done in Third World countries. Do we want to contribute to that?

"We're faced with an interesting set of tradeoffs," he finally says. "We don't want to kill the Everglades. We don't want to kill American agriculture either."

Later, as I drive home, I think about our day together, and what's at stake. For some reason, I keep picturing him in his Piper Super Cub airplane, looking down at the crazy-quilt pattern of agriculture, and the deep blue-green of the Everglades, and loving them both.

Hunting tomatoes

Ruskin
May 1992

"You want to pick some tomatoes? I got tomatoes," drawls the white-haired fellow at the Dodge pickup.

"Now go down that dirt road over yonder and take a left. All right? You'll see a blue Port-O-Let after awhile. Just park somewhere close and walk into the field. You don't have to walk far now. Just ten feet or so. You'll see the prettiest dadgummed tomatoes. . . ."

Joe Robertson tells it straight. On a warm, breezy morning, he is supervising doings at the 125-acre Interchange Farms off U.S. 41 below Ruskin in southern Hillsborough County. Some of the prettiest dadgummed tomatoes of the spring threaten to give hernias to the poor, overburdened vines.

Like many of the farms in Central Florida, Interchange has opened fields to the public. "U-Pick," signs are as common along rural roads in May as wild flowers and honey bees. You park, walk out into a field, fill a bucket or two with plump tomatoes and pay bargain prices by the pound or by the bushel. Then you go home, eat tomato sandwiches and wipe juice from your chin.

Tomatoes bought at supermarkets come from these same fields. But there's a difference.

Supermarket tomatoes are picked green, when they are less likely to perish during transport. They're trucked to warehouses, sorted and gassed to redness. But on the inside they're rock hard and relatively tasteless. Some people say gassed tomatoes eventually ripen and taste as good as vine-ripened fruit. Others who don't worship at the altar of modern technology liken supermarket tomatoes to wax facsimiles.

"I call them plastic tomatoes," Joe Robertson will tell you. "They don't got no taste. There's nothin' like a real tomato."

Of course, he is prejudiced. At 69, he is old enough to remember when only the sun could determine whether a tomato was ripe and ready to eat. Gassed supermarket tomatoes may be further evidence that life has gone to hell in a handbasket.

In West Central Florida, where I live, fields open to U-Pickers for about six weeks in late fall and another six weeks in late spring. Some fields offer sweet corn, green beans and strawberries as well. Many advertise under the "Good Things To Eat" section in the newspaper classifieds.

That's how we find Interchange Farms and Joe Robertson. He waits next to his pickup truck and a shaded stand. Before him is a tomato field stretching nearly to the horizon. About a dozen or so pickers already are at work in this field of tomato dreams.

Customers at U-Pick fields range from retirees who want two or three tomatoes for trailer park pot-luck suppers to ambitious entrepreneurs who arrive shortly after sunrise, pick a dozen bushels and sell them from roadside stands in Tampa and St. Petersburg in the afternoon.

We want tomatoes for at least a couple of sandwiches and enough for a half year's supply of spaghetti sauce. I won't speak for my wife, but I enjoy getting my hands dirty, too. There seem to be few opportunities in the city to commune with the soil.

Joe Robertson, who loans empty five-gallon buckets to arriving customers, and collects their money as they depart, needs not instruct us on the fine art of tomato picking. Grizzled veterans, we're serious enough about our tomatoes to bring our own buckets and other weaponry.

The well-equipped tomato picker should be armed with sunscreen, sunglasses, a wide-brimmed hat and sensible shoes. Joe's fields, irrigated by ditches, tend to be on the damp side. It's no place for spike heels or $200 Florsheim's. We're comfortable in old running shoes too far gone to be ruined by mud.

Though tomato picking hardly qualifies as rigorous exercise, a five-gallon bucket grows heavy quickly. Our strategy is to walk about 100 feet into the field, turn and pick our way back toward the car. It saves wear and tear on the shoulder joints.

Tomatoes, which ripen from the ground up, are often hidden under low leaves. We squat, pick, stand, move down the row to another straining plant and squat again. Concentrating on the image of my tomato sandwich, I bravely ignore creaking knees.

It takes 15 minutes to pick two bushels. Back at the stand, where he has been passing time reading fishing magazines and eating his own tomato-and-mayo sandwiches, Joe Robertson charges us $16. I figure my cost at 13 cents a pound plus gasoline and tolls. In the end, maybe I don't save much money. But I get more than 120 pounds of fresh tomatoes. And Joe throws in conversation for free.

Good talk is among the unexpected pleasures of tomato picking. You get to meet friendly folks. Joe sits in a lawn chair, flicks gnats away from his ears with a Brazilian pepper twig and without urging discusses the fine points of snook fishing, tomato growing and tourism.

I won't tell you where snook are biting—that's Joe's secret. But he says tourist season was longer than usual this year because of a mild spring, and that meant more tomato sales.

"Yesterday I had five Canadians in here in a big old Lincoln Continental. I think they'd been drinkin' cocktails. I mean they had themselves a good old time. They laughed and yelled and even took pictures. I think one of 'em as a joke was tryin' to pick tomatoes wearin' boxing gloves."

Yes, anything can happen in the tomato fields. Joe stands to greet an arriving customer, who to his relief has had sense enough to leave the boxing gloves at home.

"Yes, sir, we got tomatoes," Joe Robertson tells the bare-handed fellow. "Tell you what. Just take a left at that yonder dirt road and follow it to the blue Port-O-Let. Then just walk into the field. You won't have to go far. We got the prettiest dadgummed tomatoes. . . ."

The Real Florida tomato sandwich

Hoagie roll
1 ripe and juicy large or medium tomato, sliced thick
4 thin slices of provolone cheese
4 thin slices of sweet onion
A handful of lettuce
Dab of mayonaise
Salt and pepper
1 bib

Slice hoagie roll lengthwise. Spread mayonnaise and add cheese. Place tomatoes on top of cheese. Salt and pepper to taste. Add lettuce and onions. Close bread. Tie bib around neck. Grasp sandwich with two hands and eat carefully over sink. Wiping chin is optional.

Last of the cowmen

Zolfo Springs
April 1994

The white-haired man they call Judge sits on the other side of a crowded campfire as a bluegrass band plows through *Red River Valley* on a ranch near Zolfo Springs. Judge is not in the band, but he plays along on his harmonica as if he is, and nobody minds.

"Judge is the last of the cowmen," whispers Ray McIntyre, the trail boss, as the smell of horses wafts through the night. "Talk to him."

Judge, who was driving cattle through Florida when Calvin Coolidge lived in the White House, is on the Florida Cracker Trail Association's annual horseback jaunt across the state. Every year, to commemorate Florida's glorious ranching past, Judge and about one hundred others mount their horses at Bradenton, and camp, swap lies, eat vittles, chew tobacco, drink whiskey, cuss a little and maybe get saddle sore before finishing a week later at Fort Pierce. The only thing missing is cattle. Cattle might clog modern roads.

At Zolfo Springs, two days into their ride, I meet the riders for supper. I'm traveling with them tomorrow for 16 miles. As a city boy who cut his buckteeth on *Gunsmoke*, I'm looking forward to it. The chance to talk to an old-time cowman is a bonus.

But by the time I clear my plate of barbecued chicken, beans and swamp cabbage, Judge has vanished. Somebody leads the way to Judge's camp, which turns out to be black as pitch. Real cowmen value society as much as the next man, but they crawl sensibly into their bedrolls when night falls.

It is nine o'clock.

The next day begins dreadfully early. As cowmen stir, barred owls protest from the oaks. Dawn is licking the horizon when the chuckwagon starts serving scrambled eggs, biscuits and all the grits a belly can handle. The coffee, poured from an enormous pot, is perfectly black, greasy and authentically laced with grounds. Well-fortified, Judge is saddling his horse, Charlie. Sure, he can talk a spell.

First off, no reason to call him "Your Honor." "When I was a little baby, I wouldn't smile even when folks tickled my toes," he explains. "My momma said I was solemn as a judge." He smiles now, but the nickname stuck. In the Melbourne phone book he's "Frank (Judge) Platt."

At 79, Judge Platt is a man who has spent his life working hard under the Florida sun. His small body is anvil-hard, and his neck is brown and creased like an old saddle. He wears a cowman's hat, boots, blue jeans and a long-sleeved shirt, the breast pocket bulging with chewing tobacco. He looks at his horse, and at daybreak, through tortoise-shell glasses.

Judge waters Charlie at a shallow pond as an orange sun nibbles the pink fog. "It's gonna be a pretty day," he announces, and Charlie, a fine quarter horse, snorts in agreement.

Judge has been riding Charlie 22 years, and they understand each other. It is only natural that, when Judge offers Charlie a plug of Levi Garrett, Charlie takes him up on it. A long morning lies ahead, and a good chew will make a fine ride even more memorable.

"I don't come on this because it gives me a chance to ride a horse," says Judge, who has never missed any of the seven Florida Cracker Trail excursions no matter what, even if the state is modern now and no cattle go along. "Shoot, I ride at home all the time. I come to talk to people, to hear the old stories."

Seldom can you find the old stories in history books. When the Spaniards left Florida more than two centuries ago, the cattle they abandoned, and subsequent generations of those cattle, became wild. The people who migrated into the peninsula had to catch them before they could use them for meat, milk or turn them into cash. The original cowmen were known as cowhunters.

They hunted the cattle, driving them ahead with cow whips—'bullwhip" was missing from the cowhunter vocabulary—all the way to the coast and waiting ships. Judge's great granddaddy, who drove cattle into Florida from North Carolina in 1821, was a cowhunter. So was his granddaddy and daddy. Judge is of the next generation of cowhunters, called cowmen. Only a Yankee would call a Florida cowman a "cowboy."

No cowman, I have not ridden a horse in 35 years, so I am grateful to join Largo pharmaceutical technician, Mike Lowe, in his wagon. His magnificent Belgiums, 1,800 pounds each and almost 14 hands high, will pull us along.

No wagons for Judge, a member of the Florida Cracker Trail Association Hall of Fame. He and his 10 brothers and sisters were practically born on the saddle. "The only way you could get around," he drawls, spitting. He was born at Wolf Creek—try finding that on a map, or wolves for that matter—when Osceola County was mostly swamp, prairie and woods. Parents worked their children hard. Judge helped drive cattle back and forth across Central Florida.

The days of the long cattle drives on horseback are history. Modern ranches often use trucks and helicopters to maneuver cattle toward the huge trucks that transport livestock to slaughterhouses. Electrified fences keep cattle from wandering. Some cowmen wear trendy caps that advertise their favorite football teams instead of proper cowman hats. They spend leisure hours staring at television in air-conditioned rooms. Most avoid chewing tobacco and even harmonicas.

At 7:30 a.m. horses whinny under their riders who yell "giddy-yap," and a deputy sheriff, vehicle lights flashing, leads the convoy east on State Road 64 out of Zolfo Springs. Mike Lowe's Belgiums jerk our wagon ahead. We ride past a waiting Mercedes, a Nova, an Oldsmobile, a Chevy Blazer and a Hardee County schoolbus.

I think about what Judge told me earlier: "Florida was different when I was comin' up. The big thing was, people wasn't in a hurry then. We're livin' in a high-speed world now."

We ride off 64 onto a county road toward an elementary school. A sign says, "Drug Free, Gun Free, School Zone." Children scream with delight as we approach. Judge touches his hat, the cowman's salute. We turn east on State Road 66, where 15 miles of rural blacktop await. Our destination—the next campsite—is the Kahn ranch near the Highlands County line.

Judge rides ramrod straight, except for when he leans to spit. He is the oldest person on the ride but probably the most at home on the saddle. Other riders, their behinds protesting from two hard days, squirm on their horses. Mike Lowe's wagon is no Cadillac. We sit on hay or folded raincoats and grimace. I take the reins for a while, and Jake and Lucky, the massive Belgiums, have pity by staying on the road.

The Florida of Judge's youth boasted relatively few roads. Who needed pavement if you had a horse? "Only thing is, it could take you half a day to get anywhere," he says. "I recollect ridin' fifty miles to go to a square dance. Different times."

There was no such thing as fast food. His daddy and momma and brothers and sisters hunted it or grew it, and that could take a long time. He ate what momma put on the table. There was no electricity, and the kerosene lanterns were extinguished when after-supper chores were done. Out on the range, whippoorwills called. Lonely cowmen went days without human company. Judge would build a fire and take out his harp—that's what he calls his harmonica—and play *Fox Chase* or *Bark Like A Dog* to cheer himself.

Jake and Lucky, the Belgiums pulling my wagon, take off on a trot. I hold the reins in a death grip. The horses ignore my feeble "whoas," and Mike Lowe takes over. There are no brakes on his wagon, and, even if there were, they wouldn't stop Jake and Lucky. Jake and Lucky would drag the wagon along.

Several hours pass, and the sun is hot enough to make beef jerky, though nobody does. Riders, who include women and a few children but mostly men, adjust bandannas. The shadow of a red-shouldered hawk skates across the road. Judge lets Charlie drink from a ditch and exercises his harmonica after automatically checking first for snakes and alligators.

Judge stepped on a big rattler when he was young. The rattler, tangled around his legs, could not bite Judge because its mouth was filled with a dead rabbit, allowing Judge to squeeze off a precise shot. That's how cowmen treated snakes then, though alligators generally were tolerated unless they ate a cow.

"Gators was different back in the old days," Judge says. "They was wilder, more afraid of people. Now people feed 'em, and they get bold." He is careful around ditches, especially with his livestock. Judge once watched a 1,600-pound steer disappear in a raging boil of alligator-infested St. Johns River. One of Judge's bullets inevitably found its way into the beef-eating gator. The hide stretched 16 feet.

There were panthers in his boyhood woods and bears in the swamps. People hunted bear, for the fur and the meat, and there were no animal rights organizations to raise Cain. Somebody Judge knew shot a bear and was trying to photograph the bear when the bear came to. The bear grabbed the nearest hunting dog and hugged so tight the dog's eyeballs popped. The hunter snapped out of his shock in time to shoot the bear stone dead.

A T.G. Lee food truck rumbles by, then a truck owned by Tony's Frozen Pizzas. A grinning man hangs out the window of his Plymouth Voyager and shoots video, and a blond woman who lives in a rusty trailer next to the road lays wet laundry onto the bowl of a satellite dish to dry. A passing Peterbilt hauling a bulldozer spins off a dust devil. No horses spook, but they could have, so every rider yells, "Slow down!" anyway.

There were thoughtless people in the old days too. Judge used to hear stories from his granddaddy. Cattle and pigs roamed freely, see, and a cowman would catch them and put his brand on them, but maybe the brand would wear off, and another cowman would come along and place his brand, and that could lead to a misunderstanding followed by spilled blood.

"Lots of folks buried back in them pines and the palmetto thickets."

Horse hooves pop empty beer cans and other roadside litter. The water moccasin that startles a horse turns out to be a tire retread. We pass Proctor's (Christ is the Answer) Dairy. Pasture is punctuated by pines and oaks and twisted cypress trees that watch us pass like dark sentinels. About noon, past the creek named for the dead Seminole chief Charley Bowlegs, we pull off the road and into the next campsite, a sprawling ranch.

I look for Judge to say goodbye, but I have to catch a ride back to my truck, and he has vanished again. I want to hear more, about how he still tends his cattle from horseback, and how his 1200-acre ranch never feels big enough anymore, not with the city of Melbourne and all of modern Florida closing in.

"On cattle drives," the last of the cowmen had told me after breakfast, "my uncle, he'd start a story, but then we'd have to split up to work cattle, and all day I'd wonder how the story was gonna come out. Eventually, you know, we'd come back together, and build us a fire, and he'd pick up the story right where he left off."

So long, Judge. Until next time.

The fine art of trespassing

St. Petersburg
May 1994

The other night, as I was creeping through a neighbor's quiet back yard, hoping his dog and his alarm would remain still, and wondering if just now he were aiming a gun with an infrared scope at my forehead, I found myself thinking:

Maybe I am getting too old to enjoy the thrill of urban fishing.

Never did I plan to trespass. When my teen-age son and I waded into Tampa Bay after supper, we only hoped to scare up a few trout with our fly rods. The fish were biting, we advanced against the rising tide, we lost track of time and place—and suddenly the water felt exceptionally cold and deep.

The tide had come in. We hardly relished wading back to our starting point, a neighborhood park, because we might have to swim across the swash channel. "Large animals with teeth come close to land at night," I told my son. We took the path of least resistance—straight to shore, over a sea wall, then tiptoed through a neighbor's back yard.

We managed to avoid triggering alarms, watchdogs or firearms. We trudged, squishing, down the street to my truck. My son leaped into the bed with our rods. Soaking wet and covered with fish slime, I stripped off my clothes under a street lamp, wrapped a dry towel around my waist and drove home.

No cops pulled us over, but it was wonderfully exciting anyway. Maybe too exciting for an angler with graying hair.

The Chamber of Commerce touts a different kind of fishing. In those come-to-Florida brochures, a perfectly tanned couple sip martinis while trolling from their cabin cruiser for Gulf Stream marlin. In another variation, the tanned couple stand in an expensive skiff armed with expensive tackle as the expensive fishing guide points at bonefish.

This kind of angling does happen. I've seen it. But in Real Florida, many of us who wet our lines never hire guides, cast from teak decks or wear the uniforms of L. L. Bean. Who can afford it? We buy cheap tackle, wear moldy tennis shoes and sneak around.

That's because the best fishing spots seldom are accessible to people without boats or the means to hire a guide. Many bridges are guarded by "No Fishing" signs. Fishing holes happen to be the "No Trespassing" water hazard on a golf course. Or else they are a canal or a river that meanders, not through the cypress or saw grass of wilderness, but the asphalt jungle of a city. To fish those spots, you develop the skills of a cat burglar.

In Miami, where I grew up, trespassing was an art.

The canal on the other side of the railroad tracks weaved through an exclusive neighborhood and a country club that harbored a wonderful game fish known as a snook. Snook anglers were about as welcome on the golf course as chinch bugs.

We snook commandos climbed fences in the dead of night with our tackle; during a daylight raid a friend once toted a golf bag as a cover, stopped at the canal and dangled a No. 3 Reflecto Spoon from a two-iron. At the footbridge near the 12th tee a big snook swallowed the lure. When the line popped, it sounded like a gunshot.

The ranger often chased us, either on foot or in his golf cart. Once, as I made my escape over a fence, he grabbed my leg. I pulled loose, but he got a sneaker. A sneaker was a small price for a snook.

Sometimes there were larger penalties to pay. In the Keys, a high school classmate sneaked onto a "No Trespassing" bridge near Marathon and dropped a live crab bait in front of a giant pompano known as a permit. He lost the permit when it severed his line on the pilings. He lost his freedom when the cops put him in jail and made him call his dad.

After I bought a canoe, I often paddled in Everglades National Park. But the best fishing was often outside the park, in the many canals dredged by the Army Corps of Engineers to drain the 'glades. Those canals cut through the city. Drifting among back yards, I'd cast popping bug lures at the banks as housewives in curlers hung laundry and scolded me.

As I reeled in bass, neighborhood kids sometimes lobbed mangos and grapefruit at the canoe. A friend of mine, surviving one such bombing, paddled his canoe directly at the sharpshooters and asked them to stop. In peace they offered him a marijuana cigarette.

We caught big bass next to abandoned shopping carts rusting near bridge pilings. Under the bridges, homeless men—we called them hobos back then—slept off whiskey hangovers.

In West Palm Beach, we visited relatives during a recent holiday. A brother-in-law, fishing commando extraordinaire, developed a battle plan. Only one fishing spot involved a visit to public land. His best places were owned by private individuals. I expressed reluctance to trespass.

"I know this golf course where there are tarpon," he said, throwing out the bait, and I was hooked.

Tarpon are among Florida's most fabled fish. Well-heeled tourists pay guides lots of money for a chance at casting to them. The idea of sneaking onto a country club golf course in the dark and pulling a tarpon out of a water hazard was impossible to resist.

These would be small tarpon, not the 100-pounders you read about in magazines. But size mattered little. A 100-pounder, leaping out of the water, its gill plates rattling like castanets, would attract too much attention. A two- or three-footer on fly rod would do us just fine.

"You don't mind getting arrested?" my brother-in-law teased. I looked at my son. His eyes were as wide as mine.

The tarpon were in a series of small ponds, connected by a creek to a small lake that fed a canal that led to the Atlantic Ocean. As the sun disappeared, and the golfers vanished, we began casting streamers and looking over our shoulders for the ranger.

My brother-in-law snagged a green with a backcast, and my son got tangled on a fairway marker. I spanked a couple of palm trees with my fly line. The fear of arrest does nothing for your casting.

Two hours passed without the hint of a tarpon. My son sneaked across a fairway toward a distant pond. My brother-in-law and I flailed at the same water in hopes of waking up a fish.

We heard the world's quietest yell. Trespassers never like to advertise.

We ran toward my son, whose flyrod was bent double. Line buzzed off his reel. Something the size of a coffee table, but as flashy as a mirror, launched into the air, then crashed into the water, too loud for comfort. My brother-in-law and I were generous with advice, which my son wisely ignored.

Soon the tarpon—about 30 inches long—lay gasping on the fairway. My son unhooked it, and held it steady in the pond, until it regained equilibrium. Then it swam away.

We left too, before the light in the distant trees materialized into a police officer. I don't run as fast as I once did, though I work at staying in shape.

Gandy dancers

White Springs
June 1993

The gandy dancers who sweated and laughed and bled and sang while working on the railroads of America are a thing of the past. They worked with their hands, legs and strong backs maintaining rail, replacing ties, shoring up the railroad bed. Replaced by machines about a quarter century ago, they deserve to be in museums.

"We're almost extinct," Cornelius Wright Jr. is saying. Dressed in overalls and chain-smoking Viceroys, he stands next to a railroad track with a nine-pound hammer in hand. He and four other African Americans who devoted their lives to maintaining the rails are showing how they did it at the Florida Folk Festival.

They are old men from Birmingham. Wright, the baby in the group, is 65. He spent 35 years and three months working on railroad tracks in the South. Elder Brown, 66, spent four decades. Allen Jones, 68, gandy danced for 37 years. Charlie Vinson, 69, was a gandy dancer for two decades. John Mealing, 85, spent close to half a century. For the last eight years they have toured the country showing people how things used to be.

Gandy dancers took their name from the company that built their tools and their own rhythmic dancing, chanting and singing as they used those tools. The calls and songs took their minds off tedious work and kept up spirits.

There were rowdy songs about honky tonk women and religious songs about Jesus at Galilee. Sometimes a caller made up a song about the white, often racist, foremen who led the crews. In the calls or songs were instructions that choreographed every move a gandy dancer made. A man whose mind wandered might end up with a two-ton rail on his foot.

"To move rails you had to be agile, mobile and hostile," says Cornelius Wright, who worked all over the South, including Florida. "You had to have agility to move about, and the mobility to move instantly, and being hostile was the only way you could stay in this work. The men took no pity on somebody who couldn't keep up."

Summer-like heat has arrived in time for their Florida visit. They don't complain. They've seen worse. They pick up their tools and toil on a 37-foot section of track installed right before the performance. They hammer and pull spikes. They wedge long bars under the rail and click them against the metal in a one-two, one-two-three rhythm. On the third count they move the rail six inches. Only then do they stop and wipe their brows with red bandanas.

"You had to work hard in this line of work," says John Mealing, who was 13 when he started working on track more than 50 years ago, "but hard work won't kill a man. I worked for ten cent an hour, ten hours a day, six days a week. It never snowed or rained on the railroad.

"We was proud of what we done. It was men's work."

Sometimes white bosses made the work even more trying. But gandy dancers had ways of coping.

"We had a foreman, a bad foreman, who drank," Mealing says. "A fella and his whiskey, they's hard to get along with. I said, 'Fellas, we got to do something about him. We ain't no monkeys, and we ain't no dogs.' What we did is fix the track so no train could come by. The foreman got blamed. That got his attention."

A song told the story:

Captain can't read
Captain can't write
Captain can't tell
if a track is right

Gandy dancer callers and singers were part psychologist, part sociologist. "In the mornin'," says Cornelius Wright, whose father worked on the railroad for a half century, "the caller would go around and talk to the men. He wanted to know who'd been to a honky tonk the night before. He wanted to know who was having trouble at home. 'Hey, man, how you doin?' he'd ask, and a man would say, 'Well, my baby been sick three days.' That was important to know. See, now he knows where to position that man so he won't get hurt."

Gandy dancers got hurt. They got heatstroke. Their bones snapped. They were bitten by rattlesnakes. They had heart attacks. In Oklahoma, a gandy dancer's jack stuck under a track. He was trying to withdraw it when the weight of a passing train fired the jack through his body. "He stood there with the jack bar completely through him," says Cornelis Wright. "He just stood, normal like, and talked to us, but when we pulled the jack bar out he made this gasping sound. Then he was dead."

A good caller never let the men dwell long on unpleasant matters. Outside of town, where there were no women or children around, the caller would sing earthy songs about what sometimes happens between males and females. "He could bring the men's minds right inside a honky tonk," says Wright, lighting up another cigarette.

Mary wore a red dress
Sally wore blue
Yon comes Suzy in a yellow dress
Just think what you can do

"Now I cleaned that one up for you," he says. "We had songs that would really cause a man's mind to go ramblin'. Gandy dancers, they could be rowdy."

Now many of them are old, ill or dead. Their time is past. When Wright began putting together a crew to perform at festivals and museums in 1985—they have appeared at the Smithsonian Institution and at Carnegie Hall—he had trouble finding even a small group of men who had done the work or felt fit enough to even demonstrate it. Eight years later, it is even harder.

"Gandy dancing is dying," he says.

The work today is done mostly by million-dollar machines, including lasers, operated by highly trained technicians. Four men with machines can do the work that 40 gandy dancers once did, but the songs that used to echo down the tracks have all but disappeared. A part of Americana, and Floridiana, has vanished.

"Gandy dancing was a thing I lived through," Wright says, "and it's a thing that never leaves you." He takes a deep drag of his cigarette and blows. The smoke floats into the pine trees and is gone.

His daddy taught him how

White Springs
June 1992

The old man of the woods is telling me about his daddy, long dead but not forgotten. Dowlin Morgan says, "My daddy was the best dowser in these parts, and he was generous with his time."

When neighbors needed help finding a well, Dowlin's daddy, Lonnie Morgan, picked up a forked stick and went dowsing. In his hands, the stick led to the best place to dig for water.

"He found lots of wells," Dowlin Morgan says. "No, he didn't take no money for it. He did it because it was the neighborly thing to do, like playing the fiddle for people if you knew how to play the fiddle."

I meet him at the Stephen Foster State Folk Culture Center on the Suwannee River. Dowlin Morgan, who lives along the river, is showing me all he knows about dowsing, or water witching, the art of using a stick to locate underground water. His daddy taught him how.

"I learned pretty much everything I ever needed from him," he says. At 64, he wears long pants, a dress shirt and a baseball cap declaring his status as a "Couch Potato."

"Some of these young-uns I see here, they have a chance to learn things I never did in school," says Dowlin, who dropped out in 10th grade to chop trees, fix roofs, and drive heavy equipment. "But they miss the kind of education you just can't get anymore. You can learn a lot in the woods. I was the luckiest feller in the world."

People knew how to dowse in Real Florida. Old Lonnie Morgan would take his stick, bend it back in his hands and start walking in a likely spot. When he reached a place holding good underground water, the stick plunged dramatically toward the earth. "And when it happened, there was nothin' anybody could do to stop it. The stick just went down."

In the city, where I'm from, most of us know nothing about dowsing. When we want a well, we hire somebody with specialized equipment to just dig deep enough. And we don't drink the water, which may be polluted. We use it on our lawns. In the Florida of Dowlin Morgan's youth, the water had to be drinking quality.

"How does dowsing work? I don't rightly know," Dowlin tells me. "If enough people tell you it's raining, you begin to think it's raining. I just know it works."

When he was growing up, sons learned living skills from their fathers and daughters from their mothers. The industrial age—progress to most of us—took many parents off to the workplace and away from their offspring. But not Lonnie Morgan, a sharecropping farmer who worked with his hands and his children.

"One time, when we needed to buy a sack of flour, and we didn't have no money, he said, 'Boy, we got to kill us a gator.' It was legal then and he could always sell a hide. We went walking through the woods to this swamp. It was August, but dry, and the gator had dug himself a hole that contained the only water for miles. The gator had dug himself a cave in the side of the hole. He was hiding."

Lonnie Morgan and his son waited for the alligator to emerge. Hours passed.

"I was so thirsty. Daddy took pity on me and gave me directions to this well he knew about. I listened good and went to find it. Had to walk two miles. I dippered up water until I didn't want any more."

Then he thought of his father's thirst.

"There was this bucket used to prime the pump. I filled it and toted it back the two miles through the woods. Daddy drank his fill. And then he said, 'Boy, now put this bucket back exactly where you found it. It ain't ours.' I don't know if kids today get that lesson or not. I don't know if modern folks would send their kids back two miles with that bucket."

Dowlin Morgan's sister died of kidney disease when she was a child. A brother died of spinal meningitis. Dowlin was seven before he ever saw a doctor. He never received proper dental care.

"I got happy memories. We never went hungry. We always had a garden. Lima beans. String beans. Collards. Turnips. Cabbage. There were wild huckleberries in the woods. My mother was the most resourceful person I ever saw. She put everything up. I remember the first Christmas I ever smelled an orange. Got one in my stocking.

"What's most valuable to you when you get older are some of the most insignificant things, like the smell of an orange on Christmas morning."

As we talk, Dowlin Morgan puts up the dowsing stick and brings out a catfish basket his father made. A catfish basket is shaped like one of those big conga drums Ricky Ricardo used to play on *I Love Lucy*. On the wide end of the basket is a trap door. A catfish swims into the trap door looking for the stinky cottonseed-meal bait. Once a catfish swims in, it lacks the intelligence to figure out how to swim out.

"My daddy used to catch catfish for all the restaurants in Lake City," Dowlin Morgan brags. "He had seven boats in different places on the river. He had baskets like these in the water everywhere.

"Today, you couldn't leave boats or baskets lyin' around along the river. Somebody would steal 'em, sure as anything. Sometimes I'm glad my daddy's not around to see what's happened to society. He'd shoot somebody for sure. Florida ain't what it used to be. People don't have the same character."

Two decades ago, Lonnie Morgan went down to the river to gather his traps. He was in his 60s, and he had a bad heart, and the doctor had warned him about lifting heavy equipment. He didn't want to give up his catfish for anything.

Late in the day, when it was time to go home, Lonnie Morgan started hauling his heavy baskets up the river bank to his car. It was hard work; he probably needed several trips. He went back, a final time, for the outboard motor and his rifle. He carried the motor and the rifle about halfway up the bank and stopped to catch his breath.

"He didn't come back home," Dowlin Morgan tells me. "I was out of town, so my wife, Betty, went lookin' for him. She knew where he liked to fish. She found him, lying next to the river, in the woods.

"My daddy died the way he wanted to die."

Gator thoughts on a spring day

Myakka River State Park
May 1995

Up ahead, near the bridge, in the middle of the river, floats a true leviathan, a very large alligator watching and waiting, probably for something edible.

With luck, my son and I won't be on the menu.

Facing the cane-pole anglers who stand so confidently on the shore of the Myakka River, the 10-foot alligator initially takes no notice of our canoe. I'm seldom anxious while paddling near wild alligators, but I'm alert around large tame ones, and this one seems unnaturally friendly. I'm wondering if this gator, having been thrown hot dogs, fish heads and marshmallows, has lost its natural human fear and awaits larger prey.

I'm on guard for another reason. During winter the cold-blooded alligators hardly move and hardly eat. In the spring, their metabolism and their hormones heat to a boil. Hungry and horny, they can be a tad aggressive.

As my son and I drift closer, we stow our fly rods and quietly pick up our paddles. We try to take the widest path possible around the river's dominant animal. But it notices, turns and swims in our direction. I leave the seat and kneel, the most stable paddling position, just in case.

The alligator slowly sinks beneath the surface.

What a strange place is Florida. Our state has 13-million residents, large cities, professional sports franchises, major universities, cable television, state-of-the-art hospitals and interstates connecting everything. But launch your canoe into any lake, river or canal and there is a possibility, extremely remote, that a very large animal, related to the dinosaurs, might try to eat you.

My son and I pass the Myakka River alligator without incident, as I knew we would.

I'm relieved. Disappointed, too.

But spring hasn't ended yet. As my son and I continue paddling down the river, I can't possibly know that before spring is over I will have a close encounter of a far different kind with a very different alligator.

Alligators nearly disappeared from the United States in the 1950s, the peak of the poaching era. When I was a boy, the sight of an alligator was a thrilling event to my father and me as we fished, from shore, in the Everglades. My dad would grab my hand, pull me away from the canal, and almost run for our parked DeSoto, where he kept a Brownie box camera on the back seat. The alligator always was gone by the time he returned to the water to take a picture.

Conservation laws and law enforcement saved the species from extinction and, by the late 1960s, alligators no longer were scarce. My parents' South Florida neighborhood, built on what once was an Everglades pine forest and swamp wetland, was crisscrossed by canals patrolled by the growing alligator population. Sometimes they even showed up blocks from the water in storm drains. Seminole Indians were hired to remove them.

When the federal government built a new road across the Everglades in 1967, the local name, inevitably, became "Alligator Alley." The canals and marsh that paralleled the highway were a paradise for alligators and husky largemouth bass. My younger brother and I would drive out in my rusty Studebaker, pull off the road, grab our fishing rods and race each other to the canal.

Sometimes, as we made our way slowly through the saw grass that grew along the canal, we'd startle the huge, unseen alligators lying on the banks ahead of us. They crashed into the water like Buicks. Wild animals, they were afraid of even teen-age boys.

Only once were we scared.

Arriving at a dead-end canal, my brother decided to fish along one bank while I worked the other. Our plan was to meet back at the car in an hour. I showed up on time. Where was my brother?

Finally, from the other side, I heard his quiet call. Blocking his path was perhaps the largest alligator we had ever seen, about 12 feet, maybe even larger, lying on the bank like a cypress log. Big Boy was unimpressed by our presence, and we wondered if maybe he'd been lurking in the grass nearby when my brother passed earlier.

We shouted and waved our arms. The alligator didn't blink. We tossed pebbles. He ignored us. Finally we heaved big rocks. Grudgingly he rose on stubby legs and crept into the water. The moment he submerged, my brother ran by—and we had a story we still enjoy telling.

How dangerous are alligators? Probably not very. Since 1949, when the state began keeping statistics, gators have killed eight people. Dogs and lightning—blah, blah, blah—have taken many more human lives.

Still, knowing the facts, people fear alligators far out of proportion to the actual dangers. We're horrified beyond rational thinking at the mere possibility of being attacked and devoured by a wild animal. At the same time, we who sometimes find life in the civilized world a bit tame, are oddly thrilled by the idea of a creature— already ancient when dinosaurs first appeared on Earth—stalking human beings in the computer age.

In the spring of 1987, a Florida State student swam away from a roped-off area at Wakulla Springs State Park near Tallahassee and was taken by a very large alligator. Tourists in a glass-bottom boat saw the body, mistakenly identified by the guide as a deer. I had been snorkeling in the river only a week earlier and also had been tempted to sneak out of the roped-off section. But it was spring, alligator season, and I didn't.

A year later, a child walking her dog along a pond in Southwest Florida was pulled in and killed by an alligator tamed by humans who had enjoyed feeding it. Once, while visiting my parents in South Florida, my brother carried my youngest child to the canal to feed ducks. A large alligator he hadn't seen, hadn't remotely expected, exploded from the water, almost at his feet, and grabbed a duck.

In 1993, a boy accompanied his parents on a canoe outing to the Loxahatchee River, a primeval wilderness that nevertheless is 20 minutes from Palm Beach County's poshest mall.

It was a Saturday, busy on the river, a hot day, the kind of day that tempts you into slipping overboard and cooling off. Lots of kids were doing it. The boy went in. An 11-foot alligator killed him. On my previous canoe trip to the Loxahatchee, I had done the same, with my son, on the very same patch of river. We jumped overboard to cool off. We were in the right place at the right time; the dead child was in the wrong place at the wrong time, a hot day in the spring.

On Easter weekend, we visit our West Palm Beach relatives. My son and I, of course, pack fly rods. We find time to meet my brother-in-law and drive out into the Everglades.

We find a fishy-looking canal, walk along the banks, and begin casting. To our delight and surprise, the bass are ravenous. We've lucked into the classic great-spring-fishing-in-the-Everglades scenario. Rainy season is a month off. Water in the marshes grows shallower and shallower by day, forcing bass to concentrate in canals where there is not enough food to go around.

I've never been more than a mediocre fly fisher. Yet I catch bass on four consecutive casts. My son loses a big one. My brother-in-law catches a four-pounder, a fine bass. I catch a big one too. My son, the best angler among us, hooks one so heavy even he can't control it on his light tackle. The line breaks.

I cast my little lure along the shoreline where bass, hiding under lily pads that face deep water, hope to ambush passing food. I retrieve my lure slowly and erratically. It resembles a small frog. My concentration on the lure, and the possibility of bass at any second, is body-and-mind total.

Suddenly, an alligator I failed to notice leaps off a lily pad into my field of vision, attacking my lure. Instantly I try jerking the lure away. You should know that it's actually hard to hook a fish, much less a leathery creature such as an alligator. My lure misses the alligator's open jaws but somehow snags its tail.

It's a small alligator. Two feet at the most. It is terrified. It begins a series of heart-rending yelps. "Goonk, goonk!" it cries. I know a call for help when I hear it. Standing in the grass, I look behind me for the alligator's mother.

I haul the little alligator to the bank. It thrashes pathetically, then opens its jaws, careens around and tries to bite me. Now I yell for help. An alligator bite, even from a small one, is dangerous. A state trapper I know who was bitten by an alligator suffered more from the infection than the wound. He was a month in the hospital.

My son and my brother-in-law come to the rescue. With sticks they pin the alligator's jaws, gently, to the ground. Kneeling on the bank, I'm able to work the hook out of the tail. The gator leaps into the water, doesn't look back, swims to the canal's far bank, disappearing into the tall grass.

I experience an adrenaline rush followed by a huge portion of guilt. Alligators have more reason to fear us than we them.

In twilight we return to the car and head back into a different world, passing the new VA hospital, a golf course and a series of strip-shopping centers that all seem to feature windowless adult bookstores. We get home just as dinner arrives, pizza from Dominoes.

The gospel according to Willie

Lakeland
May 1995

The Rev. Willie Eason is a gospel musician who sings like an angel. When he plays his steel guitar, the guitar talks. Yet tonight he is strangely anxious about performing. He is fidgeting. He is fussing with his food—says he lost his appetite—and his wife Jeanette has to coax him into eating. He takes a few bites of chicken, a forkful of potatoes, and pushes himself away from the table.

"When you eat too much," he tells her, "you begin to feel that heaviness in your chest. You can't get the right notes out."

Willie Eason is the headliner at the Tenth Street Church of God's Pentecostal gospel show at a Lakeland Holiday Inn. The old church needs money for renovation, and Willie's name on the marquee can draw a crowd. On a hot Saturday night the room swells with a couple hundred diners who wear their Sunday best. While they finish their suppers, they steal glances at Willie's table, where he sits fretting about how he will entertain them.

"I'm not exactly sure what I'm going to play," he says. He discusses song ideas with Jeanette. She nods at some choices, shakes her head at others, gives him an everything-will-be-fine smile. She knows God will lead him. Willie agrees.

"I'm led to my songs more by the spirit of the moment than anything," Willie finally says. "How that happens, I don't rightly know. It's just unexplainable." He leans forward and taps the knee of the person he's talking to.

"You can't explain it! It comes from God! God uses me as his instrument!"

He is 74. Born in south Georgia, he moved with his mother to Philadelphia when he was a baby, hurt his back in an elevator accident that left him unable to move, and was cured by God through the intercession of his aunt, who anointed him with olive oil and prayed over his body. He learned to play Hawaiian steel guitar—the kind used by country and western musicians in the 1930s—and brought it into certain black Pentecostal churches across America.

He recorded original music, sang on street corners, and watched segregation end in the deep South, praise the Lord. He got married, had children and saw his first wife die young. God had mercy, and he married another fine woman and raised a second family. He suffered what could have been a career-ending injury when a car fell off a jack onto his face, but God healed him again and his voice returned strong as ever. He prospered in business. He saw his children grow into fine adults. He had everything, he thought.

A son was murdered, a tragedy he can barely contemplate.

The gospel, and the music that went along with it, gave him the strength to carry on, as it always has, from the time he was called "Little Willie and his Talking Guitar," to now that's he's old, bent, crippled by a circulatory disease and worried about his voice, more delicate than it used to be.

Retired, a St. Petersburg resident, he makes few public appearances. But when he has to, when the cause is good, when a church needs him, when his God has called upon him, he finds the strength. To believers, his bent guitar notes do sound like the great words in the good book.

"I don't know about you," he roars into the microphone at the people who've come to hear him, "but I'm feelin' somethin' tonight."

They roar back.

"Amen. AMEN!"

A few years ago, a south Florida music store owner was surprised by how many African-American men came in to buy Hawaiian steel guitars or to have them repaired. If you believe stereotypes, the steel guitar is a country-western instrument played only by lily-white musicians. One day the owner asked a black customer about his steel guitar. He learned that the weepy-sounding instruments were a staple in certain black churches.

The guitar technician wisely passed on the information to a state folklorist named Bob Stone. Stone began tracking down the old musicians. It can be difficult, tedious work—these men belong to no musician unions—but he got lucky. He found a guitar player, who told him about others, who told him about even more. The trail led to a House of God church in Ocala, where Henry Nelson had been the gospel-steel guitar player for decades. When Henry retired, his son Aubrey Ghent took over. Aubrey was teaching younger men to play too. It turned out that Willie Eason was the inspiration for all of them, and for other steel guitar players at other churches, in other towns, in other states.

"Willie is the pioneer," Stone says.

In certain House of God churches, the Hawaiian steel guitar is the lead instrument instead of the organ. The guitarist plays driving jubilee music and accompanies vocalists. Sliding a steel bar up and down the strings with one hand, the guitarist uses the fingers of his other to pick out a melody or to play a chord. The music has a bluesy feel to it, though some numbers jump like Dixieland jazz.

Services last hours. Touched by God, audience members sometimes speak in tongues, or leap up and dance with joy. Preachers lay their hands on sickly church-goers and try to heal them. Sometimes, during a lull in the music, somebody in a pew stands and breaks into song. The guitarist's job is to pick up immediately on the melody, in the same key, with the same feeling. A good guitarist, reaching down to twiddle volume and tone knobs while working the slide up and down the strings, can bend a note until it almost sounds like a human voice. At least that is how somebody filled with Pentecostal spirit hears it.

"I make the guitar talk," is what Willie Eason says.

By the time he was 10, he already had taught himself how to play the organ. His brother Truman came home one day with a Hawaiian guitar, of all things, and a music teacher. Why the steel guitar? Willie can't remember why Truman was attracted, except that some famous country-western artists, Jimmie Rodgers, Tex Ritter and Gene Autry, were very popular at the time. For Willie it is not important how or why. All he knows is he absorbed his brother's guitar lessons, practiced a lot, and soon was good enough to play in church.

At 15, he visited Florida for the first time as the steel guitar player on the tent-revival circuit. It was the middle of the Depression, but in Washington, Roosevelt was holding the nation together, giving hope to the poor. In Florida, the Deep South was alive and unwell. Willie remembers his rude introduction to the state: Bending to drink from a fountain, he was jerked roughly away by the preacher who was his chaperone. The sign above the fountain said "White." Folks with black skin were permitted to drink only from fountains labeled "Colored."

"I was scared," he says now. "It was instilled in me back home that in the South, if they didn't like you, they could hang you by the neck."

Willie headed north where times, and money, were better. He played big and small cities, often on street corners, passing his empty guitar case until it was filled with coins and even dollar bills. At night, he usually found somebody in black neighborhoods to give him a meal and a bed. Then he was off to another city, another street corner, and, come Sunday, another church. Atlanta was good to him. Chicago and New York were even better. He recorded there, and sometimes other gospel groups recorded his music, including The Soul Stirrers, later made famous by a young singer named Sam Cooke.

Some of Willie's original songs were *Remember Me, Lord*; *No More, No More*; *Standing on the Highway*; *Does Jesus Care?*; *I Thank You, Lord*; and *If I Could Hear My Mother Pray Again*. Perhaps his best known song, one that many Depression-era black people still request, was about his favorite president.

> *During Hoover's administration Congress assembled*
> *All the poor folk began to tremble*
> *The rich rode in their automobiles*
> *The Depression made poor people rob and steal*
> *I would look next door to our beloved neighbor*
> *He wasn't getting anything for his hard labor*
> *Great God Almighty! they were moonshinin' and stillin'*
> *Brought about a crime wave of robbin' and killin'*
> *After Hoover made the poor man moan*
> *Roosevelt stepped in and gave us a comfortable home*

"There was this street corner in Chicago," Willie says, "I think it was 47th and Prairie, where this undertaker used to come and listen to me. He liked *Tell Me Why You Like Roosevelt*, that one verse especially. Whenever I sang it he threw five dollars into my guitar case! When I saw him, I'd drop the other verses and just do the one he liked!"

His first marriage lasted 11 years and produced seven children. When Alice died he thought the grief was going to kill him too. In Ocala, where he made an appearance at a House of God service, a little slip of a girl, a young teen-ager, shoved a note into his back pocket. On the way back north Willie found the note and laughed. It was a marriage proposal. He was old enough, after all, to be the girl's father. Four years later they married. He and Jeanette have been together 40 years. They had eight children of their own and adopted six others. More than a wife, Jeanette is Willie's best friend, adviser, nurse, cheerleader, and, when he needs it, drill sergeant. In 1987 they retired to St. Petersburg.

"We've had a wonderful life," she'll tell you. "We've had fine children. No drinking, no smoking, no drugs. Hard workers. God has blessed us." Photographs of their children, grandchildren and great grandchildren form a choir on their living room piano. They're a musical family, and she can list who sings and who plays instruments.

In her heart, their son Michael has a special place. When he was 11, a neighbor child, playing with matches and gasoline, accidentally ignited him. Michael never surrendered to the excruciating pain. He recovered and grew into a fine man. He played the drums so well. He could play those complicated jazz riffs, she says. Why, Michael could play just about any percussive instrument. He also knew his way around a computer. He was making a living fixing them. He had a wonderful future.

"He was a sweet, young man, he was our great joy," she says. "After he was burned so bad, God let us have him for another ten years before taking him."

Jeanette will tell you the heart-breaking story, in her strongest voice, about the terrible day in 1990. Michael was crossing a street in Philadelphia when a gunfight broke out between rival gangs. Four bullets pierced his chest. At age 21, he become another sad statistic in America's urban war. . . .

"Sometimes I can console myself when I play my music," Willie says quietly. "If I'm down, I can cheer myself up, you know, relieve the pain, with my music. God is good. Without Him I'd be drifting like a ship without a sail."

In Lakeland, at the gospel show, as the crowd watches with apprehension, Willie is in trouble. His amplifier is buzzing like an nest of angry hornets. When he quiets the amp, the microphone acts up. The performance he was so anxious about to begin with is in jeopardy. But here comes Preacher Arthur McCloud—he's a musician too—and he calmly fiddles with the wires and gets everything working again. Willie smiles and blames the faulty wires on the devil. And he tells his life story, from the time he was a boy to now, about how God gave him talent and strength to carry on.

"Amen!" somebody yells. "Praise God!"

Willie plays an old spiritual, *The Old Rugged Cross*. There's more shouting. He says "Maybe me and this guitar can understand each other." Next he sings *Take Your Burdens to the Lord and Leave Them There* and he throws back his head and his voice sounds raspy and warm like cane syrup and everyone who hears him knows he's telling the truth.

He sings one about having never heard a man speak like God before, and plays guitar notes that seem to echo the lyrics. Listening, folks can't be sure, at least for a moment, whether the words they're hearing in their heads are from Willie's voice or Willie's guitar.

Willie sings that God spoke to him one morning and told him never to be afraid, that He would make his burden lighter and his pathway brighter, too. Willie sings that he has never heard a man speak like God before.

Some folks stand and sway. Others dance in place. Some hold their hands high and sing along. Some clap. Cooks slip out of the kitchen to listen.

"I see all these people!" Willie shouts, and his voice is almost buried under the avalanche of returning "Amens." "It makes me want to play!" he roars. "Yes! Praise God! Something's happening to my fingers!"

They begin their magic, picking out another sacred melody.

God is walkin' with me, Willie is singing, and he is talkin' with me.

Nobody doubts it. Not even for a second.

The lion at dusk

Gainesville
May 1991

Inside the VA hospital, inside a small cheerless room, Jim Fair lies in bed with his pain and his memories.

A nurse tries to find a vein with a needle. "My veins are shot," Fair tells her. "You're an optimist."

She gives up on the arm and stabs the other. It proves to be just as difficult. "You need to warm my arm with a towel before you do that," Fair advises. "I've been through this before. Sometimes a warm towel will bring out a vein."

Tampa Bay's most infamous blueblood, friend of the poor, gadfly, eccentric, political activist, wronged mental patient and pain-in-the-backside rabble-rouser needs a transfusion. At 73, Jim Fair suffers from acute promylocytic leukemia. Tired, weak and depressed, he is feeling his mortality.

"I'm whipped. I'm dragging. I wake tired."

At the same time, he is, as usual, fighting mad about everything—his past, present and future. The possibility of death has failed to mellow him, but it has given him a sense of urgency. Before he goes, he wants his story told one more time.

Even at dusk a lion can roar.

"The greatest thing I should be admired for is my inner strength. I never kissed anybody's ass."

Jim Fair, born into a powerful Tampa family as J. Searcy Farrior, Annapolis graduate, World War II hero and engineer, metamorphosed in the 1950s into The Man Who Never Tired of Fighting The Establishment.

For two decades he took on all comers. He fought city hall. He fought electric companies, phone companies and just about any other company, or individual, who had money, power and the will to use it. If city movers and shakers wanted a new bridge, or a new building, or a new tax increase, or a new rate increase, Fair opposed it in the name of the poor and downtrodden who always ended up paying the bill. He was not a thorn in the side of Hillsborough County wheeler dealers. He was a javelin.

"I was a patriot."

If a big shot told him to sit, he stood. If a judge told him to hush, he shouted. He was no stranger to jail, where he passed contempt-of-court sentences by writing poetry and plotting future mischief.

Jim Fair was no lawyer—he loathes them—but he hand-wrote hundreds of court briefs and filed hundreds of suits for "the little people." He won for them, among other things, the right to vote in bond issues even if they owned no property.

Jim Fair's fight, boiled down, was this: Make it easy for people to exercise their right to vote, for pity's sake, because the right is fundamental to democracy. If someone wants to run for office, don't charge an arm or leg in filing fees. Otherwise, only the rich and powerful, only the stinking and corrupt lawyers, will be candidates. And you know they'll only represent themselves and their rich friends and the unjust status quo!

"I don't think any lawyer should run unopposed," Fair rumbles from bed. "There's no such thing as an honest lawyer. There's no money in democracy."

Money. Talk to anybody about Fair and money comes up. He was a Farrior, a member of a family of wealth and means that long has been a sturdy beam in Tampa's power structure. How could a Farrior choose to become a Jim Fair, ranting and raving and going to jail and writing strange poetry and choosing poverty instead of wealth and power?

At Tampa Plant High School, he was voted most popular. He belonged to the right country clubs. He won a scholarship to the University of Tampa. Then he won an appointment to the Naval Academy, where he graduated with an electrical engineering degree. During World War II, he distinguished himself on battleships, cruisers and aircraft carriers. He won seven combat stars. His hearing was damaged in battle, he developed a spastic colon, and he admits he was burned out. He got a medical discharge.

"I came back to Tampa," he says. In his hospital room, the nurse is prodding his arm. "I remember walking by the police station—and they had a car parked there, and there was a pool of blood next to it. There'd been a gangland slaying. That should have tipped me off about Tampa."

Engineering held no appeal for him. Instead, he opened one of several strange department stores that catered to the poor. The best known was a four-story Franklin Street business called the A-1 Catalog Discount House Department Store Get It For You Wholesale Co. Swap Shop and Rent All—Salvation Navy for short. His customers included punks and poets, tourists and natives, winos and teetotalers, straight-arrows and weirdos.

He dealt with people who looked for bargains because they could afford only bargains. Fair wanted to help. He was sure politicians were in league with utility companies that wanted to raise rates and make life difficult for the poor. He was equally confident that judges and lawyers were conspiring with organized crime when the city decided to build a bridge from Tampa to Davis Islands. Fair was not quiet about his concerns. He went from being a fly in the ointment to being a B-52.

"I was raised to be fair. Fairness was a big thing with me." James Searcy Farrior chose to become Jim Fair. He wanted a name that matched his ideals. "I wanted to make a new name for myself. Things people work for all their lives—wealth and material goods—I worked to get away from. Because of my values."

He was a media celebrity of sorts, a man whose picture was before the public without relief. He wore funny hats. He wore baggy suits. He wore a beard and long hair. A single dreadlock snaked its way to his shoulders. He said colorful things. Once, after he lost a lawsuit, a judge asked if he wanted to poll the jury. "How big a pole do I get to use?" Fair wondered.

He entertained Tampa Bay while appalling the establishment, old friends and family. He didn't march to a different drummer as much as he rhumbaed, limboed and slam-danced. He has three ex-wives.

Some people were sure he was wonderfully mad. Fair painted his own portrait: Don Quixote, tilting at windmills, forcing a corrupt America to face its own promise.

"I thought he was bright, even brilliant," says Bob Turner, a *Tampa Times and Tribune* reporter who covered Tampa and Jim Fair for almost three decades. "But he was erratic. He didn't think the way other people thought."

He seemed to run for a political office every time he saw or heard a reporter's notebook opening. He ran for Tampa mayor. For secretary of state. He ran against Lawton Chiles as a write-in candidate for U.S. Senate. He never accepted campaign contributions—just in case anyone offered.

"I remember hearing him make a mesmerizing speech," retired Tampa newsman Turner says. "He had the crowd. Just as he got to the climax, he bolted off the stage and said—'Let's go get a beer!' That was Jim Fair."

He was off center. He seemed to be the St. Bernard of publicity hounds. Yet people—his beloved "just folks"—trusted him. After all, he had once raised such a fuss that the phone company returned to consumers $2-million in old fee hikes. Twice his court actions and hijinks delayed power company rate increases. In 1968, his believers elected him Hillsborough County's elections supervisor.

"It was a shock," says Turner. "I'm not sure how it happened. I always thought that voters thought Fair had paid his dues. They knew he was eccentric, but they said, 'Let's give him a chance to see what he can do.' They also held their breath."

For politics watchers, it was a strange sight: Jim Fair, the perennial outsider, on the inside. Even Fair was surprised. "We're talking about 1968. Nixon, Agnew and Mitchell were in office. Well-groomed men in blue suits."

Among his first accomplishments was discovering 3,000 names on the voting rolls who turned out to be quite dead. Yes, dead people had been voting in Hillsborough. The scandal made the national news, embarrassed the county and delighted Fair.

"I stepped on toes," he says.

He also ran a looser ship than the political establishment was used to seeing. He rode a battered bike to his office. He let homeless people sleep there. He encouraged Vietnam vets and war protesters—he opposed the war—to use his office as a gathering place and cafeteria. He put American flags in flower pots. On a tape recorder he played the *Star-Spangled Banner*. Endlessly.

He drove the Establishment crazy.

What happened next was probably inevitable. At the urging of the state elections supervisor, Gov. Claude Kirk, citing "misfeasance and malfeasance," ordered him out of office. The Florida Senate impeached him as being unfit for the job.

"Here's a poem," Jim Fair says in the hospital room. He recites from memory, slowly, so his visitor can write it all down:

> *John Doe vs. Joe Blow*
> *It's justice gung ho*
> *It's just folks vs. big bucks*
> *It's people (that) power plucks*

"Notice how I cleaned that up for your readers?"

Did Jim Fair quit fighting after being kicked out, after being shamed, after being laughed at? Did he get a shave and a haircut and go straight?

Of course not. He was angrier and more colorful than ever. He took his case all the way to the U.S. Supreme Court, where it failed. He continued running for other political offices. He got into fistfights. He made a spectacle of himself.

Eventually, he was arrested for trespassing in front of Tampa's Curtis Hixon Hall, where he was gathering signatures necessary to get his name placed on the ballot. He planned to run for Congress.

"In the USA they arrested me for that!"

He was hauled into court. In 1973, after consulting with a psychiatrist, a judge declared Fair paranoid and schizophrenic and sent him to Chattahoochee, the state mental hospital, in leg irons.

"They sent me to the nuthouse," Jim Fair announces to the hospital room. The nurse has a warm towel around his right arm. She takes it off and tweaks his pasty skin. Where is that vein?

"I was in the nuthouse from January fifthteenth to August tenth," Fair says. The nurse blinks. Nuthouse talk has her attention. "It was an injustice. When you challenge power, step on toes, they have to crush you."

At Chattahoochee, psychiatrists wondered why he had been committed. He was eccentric, true, but not clinically insane. They returned him to Tampa. The judge sent him back.

Fair was hardly your everyday mental patient. He spent his time writing strange but somehow persuasive law briefs designed to free himself. Finally, his case came before a state hearing officer.

"Evidently, this man was sent to the hospital for some other reason (than insanity)," said hearing officer Jon Caminez in his report. "Political systems opposed to democracy use these tactics."

Fair had won.

Fair had been vindicated.

Fair had shamed Hillsborough County. Again.

He was discharged from the hospital. Friends urged him to return to Tampa, so the judge could restore his civil rights by declaring him mentally competent." No sir! Fair refused to return to Tampa on the grounds that he should never have been declared incompetent in the first place.

Instead, he moved to Tallahassee, to the seat of state government, to a university community, to a whole new audience of reporters and their readers, to a place where he might win new friends, influence people, and, most certainly, irritate the big shots.

His first priority: Regain voting rights and run for office. The problem continued to be his legal mental status. As far as some people were concerned he was "mentally incompetent" until a judge in Tampa said otherwise. But he wouldn't go back. For 15 years the man who had always considered the right to vote as the keystone of democracy was disenfranchised.

"When you're adjudged mentally ill you're stigmatized forever. You lose your right to vote. Your right to drive. I had been a gunnery officer on a Naval ship, but I couldn't own a gun. If you have syphilis, if you have a gonorrhea, people will accept that. But not mental illness. Your word loses value."

He kept filing petitions claiming sanity. He kept nagging Leon County voting officials to let him vote. In 1987, Leon's new elections supervisor did what predecessors refused: Register Fair. On the big day Fair tied his hair back in a navy-blue ribbon and signed his name in purple into the book.

He wants it known: He never crawled back to corrupt Tampa to beg for his voting right! Got it?

"Write these words," he commands from his hospital room. "Get interested! Get indignant! Get involved! Get entangled! Get infringed on! Get injustice! Get incarcerated! Get incompetent! Get institutionalized! Get insolvent! Get disenfranchised! Get in limbo! Get in exile!"

Peace eludes him.

The nurse has coaxed a vein into accepting a needle. Now another nurse arrives with blood for the transfusion. "Can you warm the blood?" Fair asks. The nurse says the blood is supposed to be served cold. Fair says, "Sometimes, they'll run the tube along my leg and let body heat warm it up some." The nurse says the tube is too short for that.

"I can feel it," Fair says. He drags his gold and blue blankets—Navy colors—over his legs. "It's cold."

Fair came to the hospital from Tallahassee in March. He knew he was sick, but didn't know how much. He had a high fever. When he stood, he feared he might faint. He bummed a ride with a friend to Gainesville. Doctors discovered leukemia.

"My fever is down, but my doctor says I'm a sick, sick man." Light hurts his eyes so he wears a rain hat—he has a penchant for weird hats—low on his forehead. "My veins are hard now. Feel them. The inside of my mouth hurts. It hurts when I talk to you."

For the first time in 18 years, he has seen members of his family. Against his wishes they visited him at the hospital. "In case anybody asked about me, they wanted to say they'd seen me," he says cynically. "They've hurt me so much."

Fair has five siblings. Fair says none of them understands him. He has never thrown away the letter he received in 1989 from his older brother, J. Brown Farrior, among the nation's most prominent ear doctors. Even in the hospital, Fair rereads it and smarts:

> *Dear Searcy:*
> *In the past, you have suffered many injustices but all of the world's power and money could not reverse these injustices. You have isolated yourself. Quiet down, get a shave and a haircut and come home. You will find a welcome from your hundreds of friends and your family.*

"My family has no grasp of the political," Fair says. "They're part of the power structure. They never supported me. I have no closeness to them."

As the blood drips into his arm, as he talks about the old hurts, his energy returns. It's amazing to watch. First he sits in bed. Then his bare feet find the floor. He stands, totters, keeps his balance. Soon he's walking around dragging his IV. He's about five feet nine and extremely thin. But his eyes, as blue as the Gulf Stream, are alive with rage.

"I cried wolf," he says. "But only because a wolf was there. People get tired of you when you cry wolf."

He's searching for his records. He brought them to the hospital, in a bulging briefcase and grocery bags. They contain newspaper clippings, the public record of his life. Piled on chairs are a week's worth of newspapers. His dresser holds a copy of *How to Legally Defeat Probate Fraud.*

Fair contends he was cheated when his Tampa department store was seized in an eminent domain case so the Crosstown Expressway could be built. He got $75,000— it's still in a bank, untouched, he says.

He has a $1,000 monthly military pension and has lived frugally. In Tallahassee, in some ways, he has feasted. At times he was the toast of the press corps with his lawsuits on behalf of the poor. In a town where most people measure their words as carefully as a nuclear engineer talks about a new formula, he delivered A-bomb quotes on request.

On his 70th birthday, friends gave him a plaque.

To Jim Fair—In appreciation for a lifetime of courage and patriotism and for his tireless dedication to the ideals of liberty and justice and the principles of the United States Constitution.

He opposed construction that would destroy a favorite oak tree.

He sued the city for not letting him pay his utility bill because he walked up to a drive-in window.

Last year, though, he slipped on a figurative banana peel. In his campaign for a City Commission seat, he ran a newspaper ad urging white residents to vote as a block to offset votes of African-Americans who he says always vote as a block. He says it was a joke based on his concern that people vote on the basis of race and not issues.

Nobody laughed. Editorials blasted him. Old friends were disappointed.

Another city seemed to be tiring of Jim Fair.

He has filed suit against the Tallahassee police. He says police beat him after a 1986 arrest for trespassing in a restaurant when he tried to pass out party favors.

"I know what hate is. I hate. I hate."

It is late afternoon. Outside, storm clouds are gathering. Soon it will rain. Jim Fair is restless.

"I want peace of mind," he says. "Somebody—a learned man—asked what I was up to. I said, 'Pursuing justice.' He said, 'But justice is not reality.' I'm pursuing justice anyway."

He can't find justice. He can't find it anywhere, even as he waits on his leukemia and what could follow. He says someone came to his hospital room one night and removed his potted plants and his basket of fruit.

"They said the plants were putting pollen in the air and the fruit was attracting flies. It's the same old story: always a Little Hitler, hurting little people."

He shows his visitor more clippings, including one describing him as Don Quixote. He offers another drink. He wishes he had a peanut-butter sandwich to share for supper. He says there could be a Pulitzer in his life story. It would be about Tampa, and corruption, and how he was mistreated for trying to uncover it.

"The one thing I'd like before I die is the correction that I'm a kook. Nobody was more serious about the government than me. I was a patriot. My whole life has been one of misunderstandings. I just tried to help people, and everything I did was twisted around by the cynical."

The lion shakes hands. Dusk is coming.

"I don't want to be buried in this state," he says before the door closes. "Not in a state that insults men who fought for their country."

The nature of kindness

Floral City
May 1995

We are riding bicycles on the Withlacoochee State Trail, where pasture fence posts along the way play host to birds the color of the sky. Cheer, cheerful charmer, comes the high-pitched chirp. If my brother-in-law and I were wearing hats instead of helmets, we'd tip them.

It is mid-morning, already hot. But we have seen bluebirds and we are cheerful enough to ignore the wilting heat. Also, we are moving fast enough to generate our own breeze. The trail—eventually it will stretch 47 miles through Citrus, Hernando and Pasco counties in North Central Florida—lies ahead of us like a magic carpet. We're on a nine-mile leg, Floral City to Nobleton, and it is as country as an apple pie cooling on a windowsill.

Pay attention, I tell myself, take advantage of your day of bike-riding in the country: You might learn something important.

Cows moo. Horses trot across a pasture. Sand pines line the edge of a scrub. A gopher tortoise, watching us pass, retreats into its burrow. We stop and come back to look. The tortoise is gone, and then we are too.

The bike trail used to be part of a railroad line. Now it is paved and smooth. It begins near Dunnellon and is scheduled to end south of the Withlacoochee State Forest near the little town of Trilby on U.S. 301. The trail connects a number of small towns, but mostly it passes through rural Florida.

Tom, my brother-in-law, squeezes his brakes hard. I squeal to a stop, too. "Fox squirrel," he whispers. Fox squirrels, much bigger than the grays we see in city parks, are a threatened species. This squirrel lumbers across the pasture and hunts something to eat.

Doesn't the squirrel know how vulnerable it is out in the open? In their Darwinian world, careless squirrels become food for bald eagles, red-tailed hawks, bobcats and coyotes. "Fox squirrels are soooo slow," says Tom, a zoologist. "Even we could run one down out in that field."

The fox squirrel stands on hind legs, sniffing the air and looking our way. We don't move a muscle, and the squirrel returns to scavenging. When I brush a love bug away from my face, the fox squirrel notices and looks in our direction. Anxiously it hops across the pasture and disappears into the dark woods.

We get on our bikes again.

A giant swallowtail butterfly darts above the path-side carpet of blushing-pink phlox. A dragonfly crashes into my chest. We stop and admire an abandoned old house, half hidden among Virginia creeper, green briar and laurel oaks. It has a tin roof, a front porch and a cook shack, separated from the main house by a walkway. Did someone raise a family here, make a living, lose a fortune when the orange groves froze?

Did someone die here?

Every once in a while, the trail crosses a lonely country road. Motor vehicles at crossings have right of way. At one crossing, I'm so confident of our solitude that I nearly run the stop sign, just as a Cadillac barrels around a curve.

Ten years ago, when the trail was still a railroad line, a speeding train hit a Ford Thunderbird at a crossing here. The driver survived, but the children died. Tom and I, fathers both, talk about it, shuddering.

Slowly I regain my good cheer. The open country is the land I love the most, and one I too often drive through with my truck windows closed and my air-conditioner blasting. On my bicycle, smelling the lemony magnolia blossoms, I feel like a country boy.

At noon, we reach Nobleton and stop at the River Oaks Grocery for something cold to drink. A man sitting on a bench outside the store sells tomatoes, new potatoes and yellow squash. Inside, as we fish drinks from the cooler, we're watched by a stuffed largemouth bass that hangs from the wall. I almost expect Sheriff Andy to walk in with Opie.

Intending to pay for the drinks, I reach back, grab my fanny pack, and swing it to the front. The pack yawns open like the jaws of a dead animal.

My wallet is gone.

My wallet contained about $120, credit cards, licenses, important papers and treasured photographs. Now it's out there on nine miles of trail. Somewhere.

We hop on our bikes and head back, pedaling hard, working up a sweat. I look on the left side of the trail, Tom on the right. I hear the bluebirds chirping cheerfully, but I don't look up. Tom, trying to distract me, asks if I just heard that rufous-sided towhee. Drink your tea! Drink your tea! it sang.

I heard but I did not listen. I'll need to cancel those credit cards. I imagine some punk finding my wallet and rejoicing, running to the nearest convenience store to buy lottery tickets and potato chips, then heading for the electronic emporium in Tampa to charge a stereo system to my Visa.

"People are no good," I tell myself. "Why was I so careless? The wallet is gone for good."

Tom skids his bike to a stop and points right. On the edge of a clearing, near a small grove of live oaks, I see, not my wallet, but three wild turkeys pecking at acorns. Wild turkeys are wary birds, and I'm lucky to see one or two a year, but I feel disappointment now. For all my love of nature, I must be a materialist at heart: For a moment I only could be excited at the thought Tom had found my wallet.

Who would return it in this day and age? I watch the news on crime-blotter local television. I read my newspaper about mad bombers, paranoid gunmen, child abusers, carjackers. At home, I lock my doors with deadbolts. I've installed high-intensity lights over the garage. We live in a wicked world Darwin never could have imagined.

When we reach Floral City, I comb Tom's two acres for a wallet I know in my heart is gone. I stomp through his house, looking under chairs and beds, muttering. Irrationally I check my fanny pack for the 10th time.

I call the sheriff's department. My wife calls Visa and reports our card missing. Next call will be to report my missing gasoline credit cards.

But sitting at Tom's dining room table, I impulsively dial my St. Petersburg home number first. Somebody has left a message on my voice mail, an operator at the newspaper where I work. Heart pounding, I call her. Her message is simple but heavenly:

"Murray Bennett of Inverness found your wallet."

A half-hour later, I meet Murray in a parking lot of the Inverness McDonald's. He hands me my wallet, which he and his wife Jackie found along the path during their 25-mile morning bike ride. He apologizes that he looked through it, but he needed to see who it belonged to.

He asks me to check to see if anything is missing. I hadn't checked when he handed back my wallet, afraid the act might be taken as an insult, but I do now. Everything is accounted for. Murray tells me about the time he lost his wallet and how awful he felt. He didn't want another person to have to go through that.

Murray is tall and fit and has graying hair. He says he was born and raised in Inverness, went away to pharmacy school in Georgia, but came back. Inverness is bigger and more sophisticated now, but it's still a nice place to live, he says, it's still a nice little town, with mostly good people.

"Oh, no," he says, when I offer a reward. "It's not necessary. I'm just glad to give you your wallet back."

Driving home, Tom and I agree it's nice to encounter honest people in 1995. Too bad there are so few of them. Later, lying in bed, I realize how cynical I've become. There are lots of honest people, more honest people than dishonest ones. We just don't hear about them. If I were a careless squirrel, Mr. Darwin, I'd be dead. But human nature makes room for kindness in a way the rest of nature does not.

Lesson learned after a day of bicycling in the country: Believe in bluebirds, by all means. Believe in human nature, too.

"Murray Bennett of Inverness found your wallet," the operator said.

Cheer, cheerful, charmer, sang birds the color of the sky.

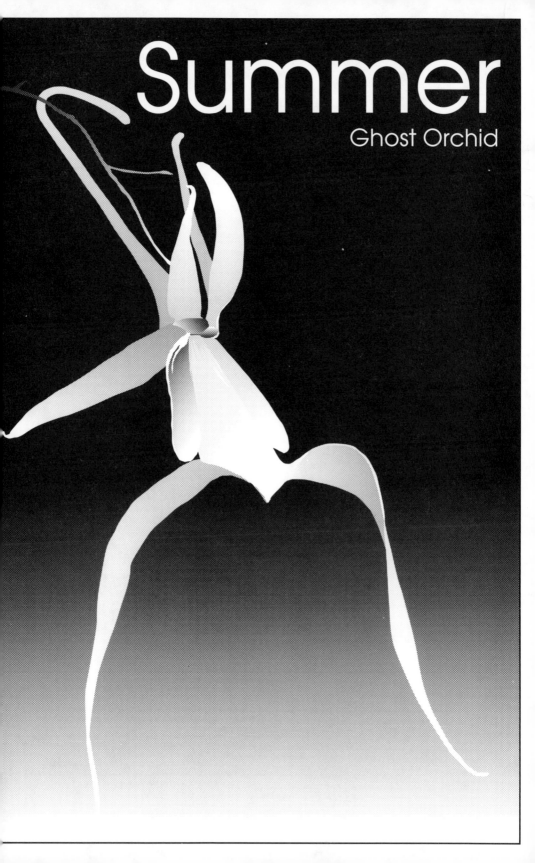

Summer

Ghost Orchid

The Lightning Stalker

Orlando
September 1995

The earth shakes when lightning strikes really close. Sometimes there is sizzling, and sometimes there is an explosive snap in the air, above his head, right before the thunder. "Yes!" is what David O. Stillings shouts when lightning excites him. As he backs away from his metal camera, as he retreats from his metal tripod, he shouts "YES!"

BLAM!

"DID YOU SEE THAT?" David shrieks at Judy, his wife. "WHAT A TREAT! AND I MISSED IT!"

He opened his lens a microsecond too soon. He will try again if the storm will give him another chance. Again comes the Tempest.

CRACK!

It could be any summer night, any summer night in Central Florida, where Stillings stalks lightning, photographs lightning, and lives for lightning, which, so far, has spared his life, but just barely. When will his luck run out?

"DAVID! DAVID! DAVID!"

Now it is Judy who does the shouting, but not with glee. Terrified, she hides in their vehicle. "IT'S CLOSE!"

"Yeah, yeah, yeah," her husband says. "Just one more, just one more. JUST ONE MORE!" He points the camera at the heart of the storm.

KABLOOOOM!

The lightning streaks just over the trees, but on his side of the lake, down there by the municipal airport runway in Zellwood. He hunkers, then thinks better of it. He grabs his camera and sprints through sandspurs and cactus toward his vehicle.

"Crazy is one thing," he says as he runs. "Stupid is another story."

He likes to think he has the best job in Florida. Self-employed, he is The Lightning Stalker. During the last 20 years he has chased lightning about 140,000 miles and taken 80,000 photographs. Most he has thrown away. But the handful of photographs he deems acceptable are spectacular enough to qualify as art.

As storms rage, he'll climb to the top of Orlando's tallest buildings to get a better view. Or he'll stand in an open field while shouting with joy and clicking his camera as the sky erupts hellishly. He has done all the things experts say will get you killed by a bolt from the heavens.

A couple of times he was sure it was going to happen. The air was so charged with electricity his long hair began to twitch. Lightning was stalking him. He crouched low and ran, crab-like, to his vehicle. Another time, when he ignored Judy's prayers that he return to their vehicle, a streak crashed into the ground so close he was knocked off his feet.

"David has always been a little strange," says Judy, who met him in 1968 at the Tiki Dance Club during the song, *In-a-Gadda-Da-Vida.* They danced, he recited a poem about God, and she fell in love. Twice during the last 26 years she has married him, this time, she knows, until death do they part. "He still is strange, but I love him more than ever."

Her husband agrees with Judy's assessment of his psychological makeup. His mind is different and always has been. As a boy, he was an impossible student who could barely sit still. After he quit high school, he joined the Navy, which discharged him after 14 months for having an "immature personality." He believes he is incapable of working a nine-to-five job.

His key ring is engraved with the words, "Certified Crazy Person."

"I'm not another Ansel Adams! I'm not another Clyde Butcher! I don't copy anyone!" he roars, thinking about those prominent landscape photographers.

"I am an original! I am The Lightning Stalker!"

It is David O. Stillings' only job. At 48, he has not become wealthy. He sells his photographs at only one art gallery, Casselberry's Black Oak Art Studio, for anywhere from $19.95 to $695. In his best year, he made about $3,000.

He considers himself a success. His work has been featured in galleries. Even Epcot invited him to do a show. He talks to lots of schoolchildren and civic groups. The Learning Channel did a segment about him.

"Isn't life great?" he asks. "Only in America can a man stand out in the middle of a lightning storm and be paid for it."

Judy supports them with a full-time job in the hearing-aid business. She is happy to do so. Years ago, when he seemed to lose confidence in his dream, she got angry at him, divorced him and married someone else. After that marriage ended, she began seeing David again. At a party, he proposed to her with another poem.

She has no regrets. The other day, she cooked him one of his favorite meals, beef and gravy over rice. Then it began thundering. He apologized, jumped into his rusty old station wagon, and disappeared into the night. He had to go to work.

Before he fell in love with lightning, he tried other things. He did landscaping. He pumped gas. He became an apprentice iron worker. One of life's great innocents, he wanted to be a poet.

He always had hated the poetry classics that schoolteachers made him study. But he loved poetry that rhymed, about everyday subjects, poetry that average people and not just snobby English professors could understand. So he wrote hundreds of poems, poems that he liked, and Judy loved, poems that touched the heart of his mother, and drew applause from friends. Sometimes he laminated his best poems to pretty pieces of wood and tried to sell them as wall hangings. Few sold.

One day, when he was feeling sad, he realized it was within his power to feel happy. He picked up a pen and wrote this poem:

Life is beautiful, if you let it be;
I try not to let people get down on me,
When you're down, you're alone—
it's a long way to run,
When you're up, it's nice,
you're with everyone.
You see the colors of nature, as I see each day—
But sometimes I'm blind,
'cause I made me that way.
I let myself down so the colors all fade—
Then I'm depressed . . . then I'm afraid.
You know, when you're down, you're so much alone;
You've got to reap the seeds that you've sown;
You've got to get out of the rut you got in;
You've got to start over, and know where to begin.
And then you see the colors, as I;
You'll see the green of the grass,
and the blue of the sky;
You'll wonder, "Where were the colors yesterday?
But, then I was blind,
'cause I made me that way."

The *New Yorker* and *Paris Review* avoid publishing such poetry. So do most book companies. Still he kept writing. He had a saying, "Wouldn't it be neat if . . ." and then would add whatever he wished for.

"Wouldn't it be neat if I could make a living writing poetry?" he asked Judy. Then it happened. A kindly shopkeeper at Orlando's Colonial Plaza Mall let him write poetry for anyone who happened to need a poem, perhaps an anniversary poem, or a birthday poem, or a Mother's Day poem.

"Give me a minute," David would tell a customer, and write them a quick poem. The job lasted about a month, he sold some poetry, and then the mall closed. He needed a new dream.

"Wouldn't it be neat if I had a camera?" he said to Judy. He got one and began photographing butterflies, birds and sunsets. One dusk, in his rear-view mirror, he saw a storm brewing. For some reason he did a U-turn, parked and got out his camera. His fourth exposure captured an awesome bolt. It was July 1, 1976.

"That was the day I became The Lightning Stalker."

He is tall, has a beard, and wears glasses. His t-shirt has a picture of lightning on the back, and the words "The Lightning Stalker" on the front. He tucks his ponytail inside a denim tam-o'-shanter. He drinks caffeine-laced Mountain Dew constantly, which may or may not account for his scatter-gun approach to conversation. Sentences tend to branch off like lightning streaks.

"If I were wealthy, people would call me eccentric. I'm not wealthy so they say I'm obsessed . . . Jimi Hendrix DIED when he was twenty-seven, man. My life BEGAN when I was twenty-seven, when I discovered lightning. I made this one picture, in honor of Hendrix, I called *Purple Haze*—'Scuse me while I kiss the sky.

"Lightning is so neat. It's a living dinosaur. IT'S FLORIDA!" He quiets down. "Florida is the lightning capital of the United States. It's a natural resource. The chamber of commerce should PROMOTE lightning. Wouldn't it be neat if Disney had a ride called 'Florida Lightning Storm.' I know how they could do it. It'd be a scary ride."

Stalking lightning is easy. Getting a good photograph is hard. Sometimes David O. Stillings believes that everything is against him. Rain obscures the lightning. So do clouds. Sometimes he is premature with his shutter, or too late.

Recently, he and Judy bought a bucket of chicken, jumped into their vehicle, and chased a storm through Orlando into the countryside. He stayed on the interstate and then took a two-lane road. The road ended. He sped back to the interstate. The storm continued to play hide and seek.

Finally, near Lakeland, he gave up. As he headed home, the sun rose. He had taken no photographs.

Most nights end that way. If he gets a dozen usable shots in a year he is happy. Some years he gets only one or two. This summer, he has made several hundred exposures but printed only two photographs.

"I am not interested in just any picture of lightning," he says. He wants to capture lightning just after sunset, when there is a hint of yellow in the clouds. The hardest thing in the world to do, he thinks, is capturing lightning, sunset and the crescent moon in the same photograph. He has done it only four times.

He usually prefers stalking lightning from about five miles away, at an open horizon. But he will take advantage of any opportunity. On Sept. 20, 1991, huge storms erupted over downtown Orlando. He pulled off I-4, parked and ran into a 14-story hotel.

"Can I get on your roof?" he asked breathlessly.

"No," said the manager, noting the desperation in David's eyes. "We don't want anyone jumping off our roof."

A young clerk came to his rescue.

"Aren't you The Lightning Stalker?" she asked.

He got his picture.

"A lot of people who have seen my work want to try taking their own photographs," he says. They ask what kind of camera he uses. A Minolta SRT. What kind of film? Kodak ASA 100. How long an exposure? Usually one second.

Sometimes they send their photos. To David, they're just streaks in the sky, nothing special. He writes a thank you note, and maybe thinks of a few kind things to say about the photograph. But he considers the well-meaning photographers as "Lightning Stalker Wannabes."

"People think getting a good picture is a matter of having the right equipment," he says. "It's not. It's a matter of getting out there IN THE MIDDLE OF A BIG STORM. You can get KILLED!"

The barometer has been high all day, boding fair weather. There's not a cloud in the sky. David O. Stillings is not happy. Late in the afternoon, he sits in front of his television, tuned to his favorite station, the Weather Channel. What he waits for is the local radar. There's one skimpy cloud. But wait a minute. Barometric pressure has dropped a little since morning. Maybe he'll luck out and get a couple of storms.

Sometimes, just about sunset, just to be safe, he takes a short drive. He checks the horizons, in case local radar has missed something. "We'll go out, but I'm not optimistic," he says to Judy.

They climb into their 1978 Jeep Wagoneer. David traded a photograph for it last year. The engine didn't work, but a mechanic who owns a couple of David's photographs got it running. The odometer says 89,000 miles, but David believes it is at least 100,000 miles wrong.

"Look! Look at this!" David says, craning his neck out the window. Just above the horizon is an anvil-shaped cloud. He says to Judy, "Can you imagine if I had a job at Seven-Eleven right now? I'd tell the customers, 'We're on the honor system! GOTTA GO!'"

"He WOULD," Judy agrees, smiling.

David says to notice the sharp edge on the south side of the cloud. Also, the top of the cloud has some nice humps. It is growing.

He drives past shopping centers and apartment buildings. Pretty soon, there are fences and pastures. Sticking his neck out the window again, he chases the storm past Apopka.

"Ah, it's DYING!" he shouts at the cloud. "It's defused, you know, falling. It is falling apart. SHOOT!"

He does a U-turn, heads back toward supper.

On August 17, 1985, he and Judy were stalking lightning in Casselberry. At first, the lightning was on the other side of Lake Kathryn. Then the storm moved toward them. David continued shooting.

The lightning struck the lake. Then it struck the shore near where David was standing. He told Judy to get in the van. She shouted for him to come with her.

"Just one more!" he said.

It was the answer she had learned to dread. He pointed the camera and tripod into the storm. A bolt crashed to the earth a quarter-mile away. The air was sizzling.

"Come on, come on, COME ON!" Judy cried. "DAVID!"

David felt his hair rising.

A tremendous bolt crashed to earth. Judy screamed. David was gone.

He wasn't where he should have been. He was 15 feet from his camera, stunned and lying on his back. Groggy, he staggered to his equipment. A small hole in the ground near his camera was smoking. He was burned on the right side of his face and on his right arm.

That night he told Judy that his days as The Lightning Stalker were at an end.

But the next night, when the thunder began, he told Judy he had to go. She went with him. And the next time a storm drew dangerously near, got close enough to be frightening, Judy held her ground. She stood with him.

"If David's gonna get fried," she says now, "I'm gonna get fried with him."

Bad memories of a deadly blow

Okeechobee
July 1992

On the day hell came to Lake Okeechobee, Vernie Boots built himself a windmill. He found a boat propeller, impaled it on a fat nail and pointed the toy at the rising wind. He was 14.

"A kid," he says, "don't have a lick of sense." The propeller whirled fast enough to burn a groove in the nail. The big blow was coming. One of the biggest blows of all time was on its way.

On Sept. 16, 1928, the only thing between the wood-frame Boots home and the massive lake was 300 feet and a four-foot dike constructed of mud. When dawn broke, and the hurricane had passed, his father and mother and brother were gone, dead by drowning. So were more than 1,800 other people. He and two brothers survived the storm by clinging to debris and floating two miles into the Everglades.

"I can remember everything," the 78-year-old Belle Glade resident says now. "Just ask me."

In 1992, the lake is hidden behind the massive Hoover Dike, which means you never glimpse Okeechobee while you drive along U.S. 441 on a day so hot the air shimmers and shakes like a ghost dancing on a barbecue.

Love bugs pepper the windshield like shotgun pellets. Turkey vultures, the sentinels of the Everglades, patrol the blue and gray skies. Possums and armadillos lie pancake flat on the road, vulture fast food. The Everglades—and Lake Okeechobee—is one hard land.

Down the highway from Blue-Gill RV Park and Bob's Big Bass Camp, I see the turnoff at Port Mayaca. I follow the pavement up the 40-foot Hoover Dike and stop at the top. Then I gasp. Whenever I get a look at the lake I gasp. It's like seeing the ocean after a long time spent living inland.

Within the borders of the United States, only Lake Michigan is larger than Okeechobee, the Seminole word for "Big Water." It covers almost 700 square miles of South Central Florida. You could float two counties the size of my own, Pinellas, on the lake and still have room to fish.

Laughing gulls fly headlong into a 20-knot wind that slaps tops off waves high enough to invite surfing. Gazing at this big, turbulent lake—the other side, 45 miles distant, is beyond sight—I can easily imagine being seasick. I'm glad I'm standing on the dike instead of plugging for bass or hanging onto the roof of a house knocked down by a hurricane. Vernie Boots, God bless him, had to hang on all night in 1928.

Lake Okeechobee can be a killer.

Everyone knows its potential now. In the three decades after the storm, the U.S. Army Corps of Engineers constructed a 150-mile dike around the lake. In places, the dike is 45 feet high and 150 feet wide. Built out of mud, sand, grass, rock and concrete, and named after President Herbert Hoover, the dike has withstood a handful of hurricanes, though none as powerful as the 1928 storm that blew across the lake with estimated 140 mph winds.

Thousands of people have built homes and farms and ranches within the shadow of the dike. The dike has allowed agriculture, especially, to prosper. Years ago, land south of the lake was swamp. Water flowed from the Kissimmee River into Lake Okeechobee and into the swamp that became the river of grass that was the Everglades.

Thanks to the dike, and other flood control structures, more than 700,000 acres of Everglades have been converted from swamp to sugar cane and tomatoes and beans and melons. The Everglades Agricultural Area, as it is formally known, is sometimes called the nation's winter vegetable basket.

But there's a price for the prosperity. The South Everglades is virtually cut off from the Kissimmee River and the lake. Without a natural water flow, the Everglades no longer functions the way it should.

The 1928 hurricane, and what resulted from that hellish day, changed the way America's greatest wetland wilderness, the Everglades, was managed. It changed the ecology of a beautiful natural system.

It changed lives.

Ask Vernie Boots, people here say when they hear you're interested in knowing about the 1928 hurricane and Lake Okeechobee and the Everglades: Go ahead and ask him.

So I do.

"The Everglades ain't what they used to be," says Boots, when I track him down at the Belle Glade hydraulics firm where he builds machinery though he is long past retirement age.

His parents, William Henry and Mattie Mae Boots, moved to Lake Okeechobee in 1916, tried Arizona for a while, and returned to the lake for good in 1925. The Boots family grew beans, potatoes and cabbages outside of Belle Glade in a community known as Sebring Farms. Roads, few and crude, were built from mud and sand. Some folks found it easier to get around by boat.

For many free-spirited people, though, life on the lake represented a kind of heaven. Only incompetent fools went hungry. Practically anything grew in the rich black muck surrounding the lake. Adjacent woods and swamps were blessed with deer and turkey. In the winter, ducks by the millions landed in lake marshes. A good man with a shotgun could fill a sack in an hour. A good man with a net or cane pole could cover the bottom of a skiff with largemouth bass, bream and channel catfish before high noon.

Today, the lake is polluted by storm runoff from farms and cities dotting the lake. A good angler can still catch bass, but it's work. The marshes no longer produce such impressive numbers of ducks. Fertilizers, rushing into the lake, have encouraged an abnormal growth of cattails, which crowd out duck-friendly vegetation.

Away from the lake, some woods have been logged to make way for development. Swamp has been drained for farmland. No wonder Vernie Boots tells people the Everglades has changed.

Many things, of course, have changed for the better around Lake Okeechobee. There are hospitals, schools and libraries in the growing cities of Belle Glade (17,700 people), Pahokee (10,200), Clewiston (6,100), Okeechobee (5,000), South Bay (3,600) and Moore Haven (1,400). Modern paved roads crisscross the land. In 1992, evacuation at least would be possible in the event of a hurricane. In 1928, evacuation was difficult if not impossible.

Like many September storms, the '28 hurricane was born in the Atlantic Ocean. Winds were howling more than 100 mph when it slammed Puerto Rico, killed hundreds of people, and took aim at South Florida.

Mass communications were unsophisticated, and many Lake Okeechobee residents were unaware of the coming danger. There were no space satellites to pinpoint storm locations, and no hurricane hunter airplanes to actually fly into the black clouds and collect data. Most information was gathered by ships at sea. Information frequently was wrong or obsolete within hours.

On Friday, Sept. 14, word reached Okeechobee about a possible hurricane. Some people made preparations. Some even moved to higher ground. The Boots clan did. They traveled to South Bay, where a big seaworthy barge was moored in a canal. The barge was thought to be the best place to ride out a hurricane even if the dike burst.

When the hurricane failed to arrive as the experts predicted, people headed home. They went home and looked at the lake and whistled. Heavy rains in August had swelled the lake.

What if a big storm hit?

"There was a little dike, maybe about four feet tall, by our house," Vernie Boots says, sitting in his office. "You could stand on it and look down into the lake. The water was only a few feet from the top."

On Sunday afternoon the hurricane savaged Palm Beach with 140 mph winds. Fifty miles inland, at Lake Okeechobee, breezes grew into gales and gales grew into hurricane winds. At nightfall, gauges at Belle Glade broke apart at 96 knots. Nobody knows for sure the actual strength of the winds, but barometers dropped to 27.43 millibars, making the hurricane the fifth most intense Atlantic storm ever.

The Boots family—mother and father and four sons—decided to spend the storm in a neighbor's sturdier house next door. Some 60 people in the community had the same idea. They fought through the wind, entered the two-bedroom home and prayed.

"There was a lot of weight in that house," Vernie Boots says now. "We figured all that weight might keep the house from floating off the foundations."

The storm advanced.

Its counterclockwise winds drove the lake at, and over, the four-foot dike. As historian Lawrence E. Will later wrote:

The wind was howling with that hollow roar only a hurricane can make. The windows of the heavens were wide open like a lot gate, and rain almost horizontal, stinging like sleet, drove down in endless torrents in the pitch-black night. Then came the water. . . .

The dike had given away.

Water 11-feet deep swept over the land.

"As it came into the house, everybody moved to the attic," Vernie Boots says now. He pauses and takes a deep breath. Sixty-four years have passed, and he still fights his grief when he tells the story. He continues only when he has regained his composure.

"I was one of the last into the attic. . . . .The house kept shifting, and a window broke, and the glass cut a piece out of my hand. . . . .The house became buoyant. . . . Floated off the foundations."

In the attic, terrified people wailed and prayed and wailed more. Outside, hell worked to enter the humble wood house.

"We floated over to where the government had been building a road. The wind smashed the house against the road bed. We rocked badly and smashed into the road bed again. The third time we hit the road the house fell apart.

"The last thing my mother said was, 'Whatever happens, stay together.'"

Vernie Boots grabbed a piece of ceiling as the house crumbled. It became his life raft. The hurricane, like the whale that swallowed Jonah, wanted to devour him.

"The wind liked to have turned me over. The big thing I tried to do is keep my head pointing at the wind. That and keeping my balance. I kept rotating on that thing, keeping my balance, all night.

"It was dark, real dark, except for lightning. I mean, you couldn't see nothing. The wind was a constant screech."

For hours it continued.

"Finally, about daylight, the wind started to die. I yelled for help. Two of my brothers answered. We'd been real close during the night but we hadn't seen or heard each other. They'd been hanging to other pieces of wood, too."

The Boots boys were about two miles out in the Everglades.

They waded toward civilization.

Devastation was complete. Belle Glade, Pahokee and South Bay were virtually destroyed. Bodies, livestock and lumber floated everywhere. Some survivors used bloated cows as rafts and splintered lumber as paddles.

"Nothing was left of the community where I lived except for four palm trees. Whatever you was wearing is what you had. . . . They found the bodies of my father and brother—they're buried in a cemetery near the Caloosahatchee River—but my mother was never found.

"I never saw my mother again."

Again he has to pause for breath.

Bodies were stacked in makeshift coffins and wagons and carted to cemeteries. As days passed, and other decomposing bodies were discovered, a new strategy was developed to counter the possibility of disease. Bodies were quickly buried in mass, unmarked graves or burned on the spot. Vultures floated above the stench.

The official number of dead was set at 1,838. But many dead probably were never counted. Many storm victims were vegetable pickers from foreign lands who had no loved ones to ask about them or search for them. Most people who have studied the storm believe the official death toll is low.

Even so, in the annals of natural disasters, only the 1900 Galveston hurricane and the 1889 Johnstown Flood took more American lives.

Vernie Boots and his surviving brothers were raised by an older stepbrother in South Bay. When Vernie was old enough to support himself, he did. He farmed and built roads and helped construct the Hoover Dike, among the mightiest public works projects of its kind in America.

"I feel pretty good about that dike," he says. "I'm proud of it. I think it'll hold up. But I wouldn't blame anybody for leaving because a hurricane is coming.

"The big thing is the water. If you have wind and water you have trouble. Lot of people in Florida now, they don't understand what a hurricane can do."

I find the cemetery at Port Mayaca after lunch. It's five miles east of the Hoover Dike and Lake Okeechobee, on State Road 76, among slash pines and sabal palms and ranches and groves of mangoes. It's Father's Day and many of the hundreds of marked graves are graced with fresh flowers. Elderly ladies in church clothes wander among the tombstones to pay respects.

I park and stroll through the graveyard and search. It takes awhile to find what I'm looking for, but I find it near a storage building and an American flag and a pair of cedar trees.

The tombstone on the earthen mound reads:

In Memoriam
To the 1,600 pioneers in this mass burial who gave their lives in the
1928 hurricane so that the glades might be as we know it today.

I pray a silent prayer and return to my car and drive toward the lake. The clouds, black and gray and puffy, are building high in the west, over the Big Water, over the Everglades.

It looks like rain.

How to beat summer

Fort White
July 1987

North Florida's woods are steamy even in the morning. We're driving a two-lane country road and have flicked on the air conditioning. The weather forecast calls for temperatures in the high 90s. A scorcher.

Then we start seeing the tube shops. They're all over the place. Hole-in-the-wall restaurants rent inner tubes. Gas stations rent inner tubes. Junkyards on the road-sides rent inner tubes. We stop at CB's Inner Tubes and the proprietor emerges from a wood shack to wait on us himself.

"You all want some tubes?" CB asks, a cigarette defying gravity on his lower lip.

You bet we want tubes. We want five. We want to carry them down the road, take a right into Ichetucknee Springs State Park and float down the river. We intend to beat summer, and tubing on an ice-cold river is the way.

We poke through CB's inventory of 100 or so tubes. He has big ones and small ones, fat ones and skinny ones. Some look like they originated on Model Ts and have been patched a couple thousand times. Others look as if they were jerked off some shiny Peterbilt last week.

"Now this here is a nice enough one for a little girl," CB says, grabbing a small tube that does look right for youngest. CB rubs a three-day stubble of whisker and nods to his pit bulldog, which walks at his side. As we pick tubes CB grunts his approval. I hand over a few dollar bills.

He takes a gander at our vehicle, packed to the roof with camping equipment, and frowns. "You too crowded. I'll take your tubes to the park in my truck."

We jump into our own vehicle, and CB steps gingerly into his, an ancient pickup that probably looked good a decade ago. Staring vacantly out the side window, CB valiantly tries to coax the engine to life. It sputters and dies, backfires a couple dozen times, then rumbles into being with a great belch of smoke. Thank heavens.

At Ichetucknee, a park ranger waves CB through the gate. We stop and pay a modest admission, park, and unload our tubes from CB's truck. He tells us to leave the tubes in the picnic grounds when we're finished. "I'll send a boy around to pick 'em up."

We board a tram that rolls down the road toward the launch site. The driver tells us we're the first of the day and drops us off at a dirt path that leads into the woods. Minutes later, sweating in the shade, we spot the river among the pines. Just seeing it we feel cooler.

Although narrow enough to be described as a stream, the Ichetucknee is one of Florida's most popular rivers. It begins in a spring that spills 230-million gallons of crystal-clear water a day, then meanders through a beautiful swamp and a forest that ends almost six miles later at the Santa Fe River. The first part of the Ichetucknee streams through the state park.

Folks have been swimming, paddling and tubing this little river for hundreds of years. There are Indian mounds in the woods, and the ruins of a Spanish mission. Farmers once piped water to their tobacco fields from the river, and ranchers once watered their cattle here. But for many years the river has been used for recreation.

For a long time, recreation was a problem. No Florida river was more crowded. Until the state took over in 1970, the river was filled every weekend by tubers who tossed beer cans into the water, uprooted vegetation and painted graffiti on trees. Poachers shot alligators. Feral dogs massacred deer. Tubing the river was hardly a peaceful experience.

Now park use is controlled. Each day, only 1,500 tubers are allowed on the shallow, sensitive upper part of the river. The lower part of the river is deeper, so more tubers are permitted.

"There still are some problems," says ranger Leonard Bundy, who has lived on the river for five decades. "We still catch people grabbing vegetation to slow themselves, and we see people up on the banks. People get a little excited and don't think too clearly. Overall though, things are a lot better than they used to be."

The water bubbling up from the earth is 72 degrees. Because our bodies log in at 98.6F., the water feels like it has been waiting for tubers since the ice age. My wife, the brave one, slips deliberately off the dock, disappears into the water and pops up, eyes wide. One-by-one we take our cold medicine. Then we crawl into tubes and are off.

The current is strong. We can't paddle against it, so we drift, steering with our hands to keep away from overhanging bushes that might harbor, say, a nice mess of water moccasins.

That's how your mind works when you first enter a wild place such as the Ichetucknee. You are sure snakes are waiting to drop on you from trees, and that around the bend alligators are prepared to slide down the banks as they do in the Tarzan movies. The Ichetucknee has gators, and snakes, but I have never heard of anyone being menaced. After a while, even city slickers relax.

Because we are first on the river, and quiet, we hear nothing but forest sounds. Birds we can't see serenade each other. Squirrels leap from branch to branch. A red-shouldered hawk flaps out of an oak tree, flies ahead and lights in a cypress. We float beneath his new perch. We look at him, and he gives us the eagle-eye so hard I am glad I am not a rabbit.

Our senses, dulled by living in the city, are bombarded. Gnome-like cypress knees seem to peek at us as we float by. Mammoth trees that have never felt a chain saw's bite tower above us. We catch glimpses of little springs that boil out of the river bottom. Caves hug the higher banks. And I haven't told you about the water.

Thirty minutes into our run, I work up my nerve, pull on a mask and fall off my tube. The cold takes my breath away, but the water's clarity makes me forget the chill. I can see a long way. Largemouth bass hang suspended under algae-covered logs. Bluegill bream the size of a frying pan watch from openings in the grass. Sucker-fish, fat lips working on invisible cigars, patrol white patches of sand. And then you come up for a breath and are told that a hawk has landed on the bank, and if you look over there, between the cypress knees, you'll see it, too.

Back underwater, this time with my teen-aged daughter. I point out bass. She's taken by sucker-fish. I swim below her little brother and pinch his behind. He yells but remains in his tube. I think about pinching my youngest daughter, and my wife, but I want to live long enough to enjoy my next birthday and so I resist.

When I come up for air my teen-ager is shrieking. "I just saw a giant crayfish. It's nappy." I miss it—I always wanted to see a nappy crayfish—but I do see a turtle sunning on a log, and I see an old man in a straw hat who has hiked through the woods to fish with a cane pole. "I been comin' for thirty-seven years," he says. As we wave, he holds up his stringer of bream.

Time moves too fast on a river. Way too soon we see a dock ahead. We paddle over, and glance with longing at the river.

We drop off CB's tubes where he told us and take another tram ride back to the parking lot. Other tubers are arriving in trucks, buses and cars whose trunks are stuffed with inner tubes. We envy them. But at least we're cool. At least for now we have beaten summer.

The fish in the clouds

Tampa
July 1991

When you finish reading this story about Mario Sanchez you should walk into your back yard and study the clouds. You can see fish in the clouds, you know. You can see a grouper or a yellowtail snapper, or, if you are lucky, a washtub full of grunts.

Mario Sanchez, 82, sees fish clouds, and they usually remind him of his boyhood in Key West, where he was born, or Ybor City, where he lives for part of the year. A folk artist, he sometimes puts fish clouds into his work. They represent innocence and pride: The old-timers were a tough, resourceful people.

"We ate a lot of grunts during the Depression," he says. "They're a nice little fish. You ever have them? You fry them until they are very crispy. You eat them with hominy. Grits. I would like to have some grunts right now."

One day, Mario is going to create some grunt art so modern Floridians can appreciate old-fashioned cracker cuisine. He may do a nice tub of grunts, which is how vendors displayed them in Key West, or he may hide a few grunts in the puffy clouds that float above an Ybor City street scene from 1930. Mario Sanchez can make magic happen. He can put anything he wants in the clouds.

He is an imaginative man, a humorous man. What he does is lie in bed, shut his eyes, recall a scene from his youth, and then convert memory into art. With a chisel and hammer he carves the memory onto a plank of red cedar. Then he paints it and then he sells it. His art is simple and complex, childlike and sophisticated, happy and sad, realistic and surrealistic. The bas-relief paintings are a colorful history of Florida's Cuban-American community.

"I know that my modest work isn't good," he tells people who disagree completely. "But it pleases."

You want to know what Key West and Ybor City were like? His paintings are better than any photograph. They capture emotion.

"This is a very nice thing," he says, pointing to an award he won from Florida's Department of State. He and Rosa—they married in 1929—have hung it next to a portrait of Jesus. "What is nice about it is I am still alive. Many get no recognition until they are dead and buried. I am watching all of this happening and it is wonderful."

He was born in 1908 when the three-by-five-mile Key West island was among Florida's most vital cities. There were fishermen and spongers. There were pirates who scavenged ships that ran aground. But mostly there were cigar makers. Key West, for a while, was the nation's cigar city.

"It was a fine place to grow up," Mario Sanchez says with a trace of Spanish accent. He and Rosa speak Spanish rather than English unless they have Anglo guests. He wears baggy, ragged clothing with spots of paint near the knee. His hair is still dark, and a caterpillar with poor eyesight might try to mate with his bushy eyebrows. "I used to be tall," he says. "Now I am shrinking."

His grandparents migrated to Key West from Cuba in 1868. Mario was surrounded by a loving family. He had four brothers and sisters and many aunts and uncles and cousins and friends.

He played marbles and tops, dived into the harbor, shined shoes behind his father's cafe, filled his belly with lobster and grunt and conch, danced the samba, plucked the bass in a sextet, acted in amateur vaudeville, drank water from cisterns, flew kites, made cigars, marched in street funerals, watched cockfights, rode the train to Miami and pitched in semi-pro baseball games.

All of this is in his art.

"This is my father," he says, looking at a bas-relief painting of the inside of a cigar factory. A stocky man stands on a scaffold and reads to cigar makers. "He would read the newspaper in the morning and then a novel in the afternoon." At the end of the week, each man would contribute 25 cents to the reader.

The cigar business was in decline by 1920, which is when Mario visited Ybor City for the first time. Many Key West cigar makers were working at least part of the year in the sister Latin community in Tampa. Some of the old ones, like Mario, continue to maintain twin residences out of tradition.

"Ybor City–in the old days it was wonderful, too," he says. Rosa has turned down a soap opera to listen. "It was . . . it was America. You had all kinds of people living together. Spanish. Italians. Cubans. You could smell the different foods. In the summer, you'd sleep on the front porch to get away from the heat. You never locked the door. You heard music on the streets. There were all these vendors . . . ."

All of this is in his art.

"This is Ybor City in the nineteen-thirties," he says, looking at another carved painting in progress. "It's not like this now. Most of these buildings are gone. This fellow here—he sold newspapers and a dog always followed him. Here's a truck the Poinsettia Ice Cream Co. had. Their slogan was The Smile Follows the Spoon. Back there, between the buildings, you can see a train. It was famous. The Orange Blossom Special. You have, of course, heard of it."

Mario Sanchez began painting in 1929. His first medium was canvas. "But there were so many people better than me." Then he tried carving fish on the white pine boxes tobacco came in. His mother-in-law liked them, but she encouraged him to duplicate Key West street scenes instead of fish. Mario, a good son-in-law, listened. Tapping his memory he recreated the life on the streets in his carvings.

Mario's mother gave him her old Singer sewing machine table for an easel. He set it up in the back yard, under the fruit trees, and worked in the mornings. He also talked about baseball in Spanish to friends, gossiped, smoked cigars and laughed when the cats attacked the mangos that were always falling. Every once in a while, he looked across Whitehead Street and saw his famous Anglo neighbor, the one who liked to box.

"Hemingway," he says.

"He liked to fish," says Rosa, a tiny woman with dark eyes.

"Yes," says Mario. "That is true. One day Hemingway knocked on our door with sailfish fillets. Cubans did not eat sailfish. We were used to the cream of the crop. We ate yellowtail and grouper and muttonfish and the grunt."

Rosa turned Hemingway down.

"We just didn't eat sailfish," Mario says with a laugh. Rosa laughs too. They hope they did not hurt Hemingway's feelings. They meant no harm.

Mario was happy in his work. People smiled when they saw it. They laughed. They knew those places. Mario had caught them, and caught all the humor.

His work still pleases. Mario is not rich, but he and Rosa live comfortably if they are careful with their money. Some of his paintings are worth thousands. Famous people own them. Cary Grant, the actor, bought one.

But art speculators who buy and sell old art have made more than Mario. Paintings he sold for $75 and $150 a half century ago bring five-figure prices today. Mario says he is not bitter.

"Money means nothing," he says. "Health is everything."

Mario Sanchez believes himself to be healthy. He doesn't know for sure, since he refuses to see a doctor. He worries that Rosa might worry about him. "It's important to think positively," he says. "I don't like to think negative."

He believes the old Key West and old Ybor City were better than the new tourist cities of the young. But he does not criticize them. What would be the point? What would it accomplish? "Times change," he says with a shrug. Yet he misses the old friends, the old family, mostly gone. Every week, he and Rosa visit their favorite restaurant in downtown Ybor. She orders the garbanzo beans. He likes the boliche. At least the food is unchanged.

At his Tampa home, he works in the utility room next to Rosa's washing machine. His sculptures of Martin Luther King, and the old Cuban war hero, Jose Marti, hang from the wall next to another picture of Jesus. There are bars on the window. Crime has come to his neighborhood as it has come to so many others. He is finishing an Ybor painting and getting ready to start a Key West one.

He begins every painting the same way. He gets a brown grocery bag and carefully cuts it apart until it is a two-foot long rectangle. He draws his art in pen and ink on the grocery bag. Next he puts tracing paper over the bag and copies the drawing. Finally, he traces the scene onto the red cedar. Then he is ready. He picks up the hammer and chisel. He mixes his paints.

Folk art follows.

His next painting is already set in his mind. It will be fish. Grunts. Of course grunts. Vendors sold them from washtubs or from wheelbarrows for 25 cents. They advertised their fish as "Almost Alive." A bunch of grunts would taste good to him.

But right now, they are only in his head and in the clouds as he waves goodbye from the porch and walks back into the house. Yes, the clouds have scales this morning.

A storm arrives shortly after noon and the rain comes down with a vengeance. For a few minutes, it is raining grits and grunts. Later, the weatherman on TV will claim it was hail.

Honest John

South Melbourne Beach
August 1995

Barbara Arthur was wearing shoes the day I visited the ancient fish camp she and her husband Roger own near the Indian River, Honest John's.

Barbara is a modern woman and dresses accordingly. Her daddy, Honest John Smith, wore shoes only under tremendous social pressure. He wore them to the weddings of his children and to the funeral of his ex-wife.

One time he showed up hungry at a nice new steak restaurant in nearby Melbourne Beach but was refused entry when the manager noticed his dramatic lack of footwear. The next day, when the manager opened the restaurant, there was a mysterious burlap sack next to the door. Approaching the sack, the manager heard an ominous buzzing. Coiled inside was a rattlesnake.

"Now I don't know for sure daddy left the rattlesnake in that sack," Barbara Arthur will tell you, mischief in her startling blue eyes. Yet seldom was she surprised by her father and his antics. When he died last year, at the age of 89, the newspaper in Cocoa called him "the cracker of crackers."

Honest John's is among Florida's oldest fish camps, founded a half-century ago on South Melbourne Beach when Honest John hung a fruit jar on a pole next to a sign that said, "Boat Launch. $1. Put Money in Bottle."

Honest John's daddy, Civil War veteran Robert Smith, started farming collards on the property way back in 1888. In the state history museum in Tallahassee, there is a photograph of Robert Smith, and his brother Charley, standing in front of a chickee home holding hoes and pitchforks.

When Honest John got old enough to take over the homestead, he grew pole beans and citrus. He also made moonshine whiskey, and smuggled rum into Florida from the Bahamas until he got into trouble with gangsters. He shot black bears, listened to panthers yowl, gill-netted mullet, hook-and-lined sharks, harvested oysters, ate turtle eggs, supped on the occasional rattlesnake, got married, had a family, got divorced, and became known as Honest John, for reasons nobody can explain today, except to say that Honest John knew how to tell a story, and that some of them turned out to be true.

I never knew him. But whenever I visit South Melbourne Beach, I like to stop at the fish camp, a relic of Real Florida. Driving along A1A, I pass mansions, new condos and golf courses. At Mullet Creek Road, I turn west and drive through a subdivision.

When the paved road ends, I keep going, through an orange grove where shacks have tin roofs, and through a gate. Inside are giant oaks and cedar trees, and a pond, and lots of herons. Then, looming ahead, is the two-story cracker house where Honest John was born, where he slept with a Colt .45 under his pillow, where he sometimes sat on the porch and drank National Bohemian beer, smoked a corncob pipe and held court, where somebody once asked him what church he attended, and he stretched out his bare feet and said: "My religion is knowing right from wrong. It's watching a fish hawk learn its babies how to catch something to eat. Ain't no way it can do it. But it does. That's God. He's all around here, if people will leave Him alone."

Beyond Honest John's house/church are sheds where outboard motors are still repaired, a trailer where Honest John's daughter and her husband live, and then, on Mullet Creek, the little fish camp itself. The odoriferous bait tanks hold dozens of live shrimp and little pigfish, which grunt in fear when they are impaled on a hook and cast in front of a big tarpon, snook or spotted sea trout. There are fish-cleaning tables and rental boats tied up to a dilapidated dock, and stacked rental canoes, and Honest John's grandsons walking around in bare feet.

Inside the crowded little store there is a cold-drink refrigerator, racks of hooks, lines and sinkers, jars of hard-boiled eggs, and a cantankerous black cat known to bite folks who try to get friendly. Hanging from the wall, looking down on everything, are a couple of black bear skulls and a mounted spotted sea trout that weighed 12-pounds, two-ounces when Barbara caught it, a world record. You can ask her where she caught it, and she might even tell you. Then again, she might look you in the eye, show you a smile as nice as pie, and whisper "in the mouth."

Barbara was born about a half-century ago. Back then, there were no causeways connecting the island to the mainland. There was no electricity, but her daddy, Honest John, did provide an indoor toilet, though he was against them himself. There was little money, but Honest John's family never knew hunger. Mullet were fat and grits plentiful. Honest John knew where to find the largest, most succulent oysters in Florida. Barbara still has some shells. The oysters were a foot long.

Barbara worked at the fish camp, even after her parents divorced. "My mother was a Yankee," she says, as if that explains it all. "Mother always was trying to get daddy to wear shoes. He didn't take to her trying to change him." As a little girl, Barbara bailed boats and sold bait. As a teen-ager, she tried to help her father endure the modern world.

In 1960, a letter arrived at the fish camp from the state. The state wanted to know why it never received tax revenue from Honest John. Honest John, of course, didn't cotton to bureaucracy. Grudgingly, with Barbara's help, he started adding the state sales tax to fees paid by folks who launched their boats or rented them.

"It wasn't exactly like business was booming," Barbara says. "There was one month when we only sent in 51 cents, and another month when we only sent in 75 cents." About a year later, Honest John received another letter from the state, which wanted to surrender. The state admitted it wasn't collecting enough revenue from Honest John to justify maintaining his file.

For a time afterward, Honest John was excused from collecting sales taxes.

That Honest John had tried to comply with government was a kind of progress, Barbara thought. As a young man, her father usually ignored laws with which he disagreed.

During Prohibition, he would cruise to the Bahamas, buy rum for $18 a case and sell it in Florida for $125. Eventually Al Capone's boys found out, Honest John liked to tell Barbara, and threatened to kill Honest John and his brother, Bill.

Bill fled to the Keys, where he became a fishing guide famous for catching the first bonefish in history on a fly rod, while John retreated into the mangroves of Mullet Creek, where he took to moonshining and whatever else he could do to make ends meet.

After high school, Barbara attended Florida State, and she graduated with English and business degrees. She married Roger Arthur, a University of Florida engineering graduate. Barbara said good-bye to her father. For the next 10 years she and her husband worked for oil companies all over the world.

In 1979, tired of traveling, they came back for good. Honest John, elderly, was happy to see them. Barbara helped him with his records, which he kept in beer cases, and tried to memorize his stories about moonshine and giant sharks, and bears digging up turtle eggs on the beach, and hurricanes, and mosquitoes so thick you could cut them with a knife, and how Florida was the Garden of Eden before the developers came, with their condos and causeways and infernal appetite for civilization.

Civilization has taken dead aim on South Melbourne Beach. In 1991, the federal government created the Archie Carr National Wildlife Refuge to protect the premier sea turtle nesting beach in North America. But Congress has been slow to appropriate funds, and the land speculators have been racing the government to choice parcels of undeveloped beach. The people are coming, and resorts are going up. There are golf courses and even a polo field.

What would Honest John think?

A good talker, Honest John would have something to say about "progress." He might even take action to protest. Even in old age, he liked to stir up trouble. He enjoyed dropping by beach taverns, bellying-up to the bars, and roaring: "When Honest John drinks, everybody drinks!", an announcement greeted with enthusiasm by thirsty patrons. Honest John would drain his glass and declare: "When Honest John pays, everybody pays!" an announcement greeted with shock followed by naked threats.

The old man grew frail with diabetes. Barbara drove him to the office of a podiatrist who wanted to examine Honest John's extremities for signs of circulatory disease. Honest John, of course, went barefoot.

The podiatrist was astonished to see Honest John's feet, covered with corns and carbuncles and calluses that erupted out of his flesh like so many volcanoes. They were strangely healthy feet. Eyes popping, the podiatrist called in his partner for a consult, and they took notes and made photographs of the feet for a possible story in a medical journal. When the nurse was helping the old man get ready to leave, she asked him a ridiculous question.

"Mr. Smith, where are your shoes?"

"I'm Honest John," he said. ""I don't wear shoes."

He went to his grave without them. On the day of his funeral, his grandchildren acted as pallbearers, and when they went to the hearse to remove the casket, they first took off their shoes.

"I had told them they couldn't do it," their mother says. "But I was glad they did."

The Highwaymen

On a sultry summer day, with clouds puffed up above the Indian River like surreal cotton candy, Al Black should be painting. He should have his easel out, and his canvas, and his good paint. Not the cheap house paints he once had to use, but expensive paints, fitting for a real artist.

He should paint the oak trees on the shore near his home in Fort Pierce, over by Jack Island, on the other side of the causeway. He should paint the moss-draped oaks and add a few cabbage palms for good measure. He ought to paint some herring gulls, three to be exact. Al always liked his gulls to come in his trademark threes.

When he finishes the painting, Al Black should head inland, to the pond he knows about, the one where two slash pines stand tall, blocking out the sky at sunset. The sunset will be an otherworldly combination of red and orange, and the clouds will be gray and moody. The egrets will be large and white, and they will be patroling the shallows, hunting for frogs to eat before dark.

Al could sell the blazes out of either painting.

"Mister," he could tell a potential customer, "my name is Al Black and I'm an artist. I do paintings of Florida. I was noticing you don't have any paintings on your wall. I thought you might be interested in one of mine."

Anybody who ever saw Al work customers door-to-door knows he has a silver tongue. And Al needs money. If he had some right now, Al could buy himself lunch, some clean clothes and maybe rent himself a nice place to live. He still could realize the American Dream and all of that.

But word is out that Al Black has stopped painting. Al's American Dream has gone up in smoke. He is the Highwayman who took the wrong turn and got lost.

There is a white historian who is always asking Al questions. His name is Jim Fitch, he lives in Sebring, and once he even drove over to Fort Pierce to interview Al in jail. Al fascinates Fitch, who has spent years investigating one of Florida's least known artistic traditions, a tradition Fitch calls "The Highwaymen."

For more than four decades, the Highwaymen—African-American landscape artists—have painted Florida nature scenes, loaded their work into their cars and taken it on the road, stopping in small towns and big cities to sell door-to-door at businesses and sometimes busy corners.

Highwaymen, by tradition, work fast and sometimes talk even faster. Some paint three or four pictures a day and have a smooth sales pitch. They seldom waste an ounce of paint or an extra brush stroke on a picture. They usually paint generic Florida landscapes—rivers, beaches and forest—and price them to sell quickly.

For most, painting was, and continues to be, a way to escape minimum-wage jobs or welfare. Even so, few have struck it rich or won any fame.

The handful of Highwaymen still painting for the most part avoid the public eye and do nothing that might draw the attention of tax collectors, bureaucrats who might ask to see occupational licenses, or policemen looking to enforce "no soliciting" ordinances.

Most of the painters go to their graves without recognition. The one painter who has made it big is Jim Fitch's friend Robert Butler. When he started so many decades ago, he cranked out hundreds of paintings and sold his art at the standard Highwayman price, $35.

Now only the rich can afford a Robert Butler. Robert still spends much of his time on the highway, but only when he wants to and only on his own terms.

For the other Highwaymen, the road has been a long and sometimes difficult one.

Al Black has been in and out of trouble for decades. While his art is appreciating in value—collectors are paying hundreds of dollars for his paintings—he lives in poverty and struggles to keep out of jail.

Sometimes his highway seems destined to lead to oblivion.

Sometimes Jim Fitch thinks he spends enough time on the road to qualify as a Highwayman himself. At 60, Jim is still curator of the Museum of Florida's Art and Culture in Sebring. He intends for the art and history of the Highwaymen to have a prominent place. He has been collecting their art for years. He has 10 Al Black paintings.

Jim—and you should know this about Jim—is a man of many talents. Jim studies art, theology, archaeology, nature, history and anthropology.

"I don't want someone to write on my tombstone, 'He was a good merchant,'" Jim explains, in a staccato twang that sounds like Ross Perot.

For now, Jim is collecting Highwaymen paintings. Maybe today, if he is lucky, he will get another Al Black.

The Highwayman tradition began in Fort Pierce in the 1950s. It began with a white artist named A.E. Backus and a black art teacher named Zanobia Jefferson.

Backus—everybody called him "Bean"—probably was Florida's best-known landscape artist at the time. He was a kindly alcoholic who loved Florida and had a knack for capturing it on canvas.

Among his black friends was Mrs. Jefferson, just beginning what was a productive teaching career that continues to this day.

Mrs. Jefferson sent her most promising art student from Lincoln Park Academy High School to Bean Backus for special lessons. His name was Alfred Hair.

A fast learner, Alfred would go home after his lessons and teach about 20 of his friends what Bean Backus had taught him. Soon, in Alfred's back yard, all were painting landscapes.

Florida was not known as a state that supported the arts. There were more poor people struggling to make ends meet than rich people who could afford the luxury of buying art from a prominent painter like Bean Backus. In fact, there was little true Florida-inspired art even available for sale.

Alfred Hair, and the other African-American painters he had taught in his back yard, began trying to sell their work. Merchants, they found, were enthusiastic buyers of cheap Florida landscape paintings they could throw up on the walls of their banks, businesses or motel rooms. For the young artists, painting was a ticket out of the orange groves and the tomato fields.

It was hardly the kind of work that causes professors of fine art to break into applause. But common folks who wanted a painting that captured something of real Florida liked it.

"The Highwaymen," Jim Fitch says, "filled an important niche in Florida art. They produced inexpensive art that appealed to people who ordinarily didn't buy art. They developed a market nobody else was working."

The Highwaymen cranked out paintings using materials at hand. Lacking canvas, they sometimes painted on the back of cheap boarding used in house overhangs. They built picture frames out of carpenter's door trim. They used house paints instead of the expensive art store colors.

Alfred Hair held back-yard barbecues and beer fests for his fellow artists; sometimes they produced 35 paintings in a day. Often they used an assembly-line approach. One artist might paint the water while another did the sky. Some Highwaymen were river specialists, beach specialists or forest specialists. Al Black always thought of himself as a bird specialist.

Eventually the Highwaymen began selling the $35 paintings beyond the city limits of Fort Pierce. They moved up and down along the east coast on U.S. 1, and then traveled two-lane country roads leading into the Florida interior.

You would think it'd be easy for Jim Fitch to find the Highwaymen, to find Al Black. You'd think he'd roll into Fort Pierce, put out the word, and the painters would flock to him, a man who wants to highlight their work and their lives. But that has not happened.

He has had to work hard for scraps of information about the artists. Finding the paintings has been less tricky. Jim goes to garage sales and thrift shops and east coast galleries. He has bought 22 paintings for as little as $1. The most he has paid is $450.

The paintings are signed by the artists, though some paintings only have a last name, or only a first name, or only a nickname on them.

Jim thinks there have been at least 21 Highwaymen. Some have passed away. Some got discouraged and quit as more cities required expensive occupational licenses or started enforcing "No Soliciting" laws.

Most of the working Highwaymen have eluded him, a white man who looks something like a bespectacled Andy Griffith, carries a legal pad and asks blunt questions that may scare shy folks into thinking he has come to make their hard lives even harder.

Initially, he found it difficult making any inroads into the close-knit black community of Fort Pierce. Nobody seemed willing to believe he wanted to help the artists. But he persisted. Zanobia Jefferson, the woman who knew Bean Backus and taught many of the Highwaymen in high school, has provided a few names to go with the paintings.

The Highwaymen, Jim has learned, were more interested in production than they were art, and more interested in being paid than artistic acclaim. The signature sometimes signified who did the art, but not always. When a painting was a team effort, the signature might simply indicate who completed it or did the most work.

Some Highwaymen—and there is one woman, Mary Alice Carrol, who still is active—were content to paint almost by formula. The archetypal Highwayman painting, a generic Florida river scene, always was a big seller. Only the most ambitious artists risked losing sales by developing their own styles.

The original Highwayman, Alfred Hair, was among the most gifted. He loved woodland scenes, and painted marsh grass that looked almost angry. Jim Fitch owns some Hair paintings. Two clearly are Hair's work because they show his characteristic vivid paint strokes. The third painting, which looks nothing like the other two, is signed A. Hir.

Who actually did the painting?

Jim doesn't know.

Jim considers driving a car a grueling affair, a disadvantage when you're hunting Al Black or Highwaymen paintings. On a steamy afternoon, he has drafted a volunteer who likes to get behind the wheel.

Heading for Fort Pierce, we drive the back roads through citrus groves and pastures where red-shouldered hawks glower from the tops of cabbage palms. Jim points out the location of lost Indian mounds and old graveyards. He talks non-stop about art, about life.

Jim says he reads mostly non-fiction, history, archaeology, and the most important book of all, the Bible. At 4:30 a.m., after some inspired reading, he sometimes writes essays about God and man for like-minded friends at his church, Grace Brethren. He hates exercise, but he hops around to a Richard Simmons video every morning.

Here are other things you can learn about Jim during a long road trip: He grew up in Fort Lauderdale, then a paradise for hunters like him. Eventually he and his wife moved to Okeechobee, where he raised quail and had a paint contracting business.

One day, 25 years ago, he saw a striking painting—it was a flock of turkeys in a swamp—hanging in a hardware store. The painting spoke to Jim's deepest feelings about the natural Florida he loved. The price: $35.

"I couldn't afford that painting," Jim says, "but I had to have it. I paid for it in three installments."

Jim met the artist, Robert Butler, and they became friends, unusual for Okeechobee—and the deep South—at a time when black and white folks seldom mixed. But they had a lot in common, from their love of Florida to their love of the Bible. Jim began building picture frames for Robert and giving him advice about his career.

Jim's interest in Robert contributed to his decision to open an art gallery. Then he became fascinated with the Highwaymen tradition to which Robert belonged.

Today, on this hot afternoon, curiosity puts him on U.S. 98, and U.S. 98 puts him on State Road 68, and State Road 68 carries him into Fort Pierce.

"There it is!" Jim says sharply. He has just spotted the "Sometimes Beautiful" antique shop.

He has gotten a tip about this place. The musty little store has a $75 Highwayman painting of a royal poinciana tree, in breathtaking orange bloom. The painting is signed by R.A. McClendon.

"Roy's a will-of-a-wisp who wanders around Fort Pierce," Jim explains to the red-haired owner. "I haven't caught hold of his coattails yet."

Jim admires the painting but declines to buy; the owner tells him she thinks her pastor has some Highwaymen paintings he might be willing to sell.

"You have to follow a lot of rabbit trails," Jim says. "Some of them don't lead anywhere."

This one does.

Jim meets the white-haired pastor at the First Assembly Church of God. The pastor has two paintings hanging in the church hall, a river scene by Alfred Hair, and a boathouse scene by Sam Newton, whose brother, the late Harold Newton, was among the best of the Highwaymen artists, known for his spectacularly stormy beaches.

"The gentleman used to come around every Christmas and I'd buy a painting from him," the pastor says. "He always brought two—said he wanted to give me a choice—but I know that rascal was hoping I'd buy both."

Jim follows the pastor home.

The pastor's favorite painting hangs in his living room in a dark corner. It is among the largest Highwayman paintings Jim has seen, about 48 inches long and 24 inches deep. Like so many other Highwayman paintings, it is a somewhat formulaic river scene, with moss-draped oak trees and stately cabbage palms and three gulls floating in a perfect sky.

Jim can't read the signature.

The pastor fetches Fitch a flashlight.

"Al Black!"

In his prime, Al Black would knock off a painting and hit the highway.

"He paints for money," Jim wrote in an anthropology report last April. "Not willing to invest any more of his time, talent or material in a painting than is absolutely necessary, he has developed a style that is free of laborious toil. He puts it down and lets it be."

Jim Fitch interviewed Al Black for the first time in 1994, when Al was staying in the St. Lucie County jail on a cocaine charge. That day, Al enjoyed talking about his art, and Fitch gave him a snapshot-sized print of an old painting. Al was thrilled. With the snapshot he could prove to fellow inmates that he was not lying about being an artist.

A year later, Jim has new questions, but Al no longer is in jail and is harder to track down. With his lifestyle, he might even be dead.

From a convenience store pay phone, Jim calls a woman who has helped him and Al in the past. She gives him a lead.

Al is living in the most depressed building in what is probably Fort Pierce's most depressed neighborhood. It's a two-story shack. Some windows of the sky-blue boarding house are boarded; empty bottles lie in a gravel parking lot. Jim Fitch leaps out of the truck and strolls toward the back of the boarding house. Five young men, drinking beer hidden in paper bags, walk sullenly toward him.

"Hey, Al," Jim addresses someone in the crowd.

"Hi, Mr. Fitch."

Jim Fitch climbs into the back of the small pickup truck and invites Al Black to sit in the cab. It seems simple enough, but Al looks guilty as his eyes dart toward his friends, who watch him intently, as if he were a police informer or something.

"I'd rather ride in the back of the truck," he whispers to Jim. Jim shrugs; he doesn't understand what makes Al tick; Jim yields the back of the truck to the artist.

Through an open truck window, Al directs Jim and the driver down one side street and up another all the way to U.S. 1, to McDonald's. Al gets a Quarter-Pounder and a vanilla shake. Al, who is six-foot-two and weighs 180 pounds when healthy, looks emaciated and ill. His eyes are watery. He doesn't mind talking, but his words are lethargic.

He says he was born in Mississippi 49 years ago. He was a boy when he came to Florida. He says he went to work as a salesman for Alfred Hair's original Highway-man team as a teen-ager in the early 1960s. "I knew how to talk to people," he says. "I could sell them anything." Then he started painting.

Al Black says he sometimes was part of a team of artists who would work on a single painting. Alfred Hair would tell him, "Jump on this painting for me" and Al might add a couple of flourishes, maybe three sea birds. Three sea birds were his specialty, he says: one bird for the Father, one for the Son, and one for the Holy Ghost. But most of the time, Al painted his own pictures. Then he didn't have to share his profits.

Jim shows Al a snapshot of an old painting.

"Al, it's a beautiful job you did. I can tell you wanted to work that day."

"Yeah, I did. That was the south fork of the river. I saw the gloom on the water, you know, the fog, and I wanted to get home and paint it right away. When I was painting good, I could do ten paintings a day! I could make five thousand dollars a week! I sold paintings everywhere, in Florida, east coast and west coast; Tampa and St. Pete; New York City; Montgomery, Alabama; Jackson, Mississippi."

Al says he has a lot of painting left in him. He's interested in trying a new technique, layering paints, to create a moody feeling. He saw such a painting in Key Largo once, and he never has forgotten it.

"I could do it just as good," he says.

Al says he no longer is painting.

He says somebody walked off with his paints and his easels and his canvases. Big shots claim they'll loan him the money for new equipment, Al says, but they want too much of his profits in return. He says one fellow offered to pay him a $300 a week salary if Al would assign him rights to all his paintings.

"No way, man."

"But at least that would be steady income," Jim Fitch says.

Al shrugs.

Jim asks Al to show him where Alfred Hair lived and worked and organized the other painters. Al nods and walks out of the restaurant to the truck. Al calls out the directions all the way to Dunbar Street. Alfred Hair's modest house is in a quiet work-ing-class suburb. From the street you can see how he turned his carport into a studio.

In 1969, Alfred Hair visited a jook joint on Avenue D called Eddie's Drive-In, which is now the Reno Motel. Hair usually stayed out of night clubs—by most ac-counts, he was a God-fearing family man—but on that night he made an exception. A brawl broke out between strangers, who pulled pistols and began firing. Alfred Hair, the original Highwayman, was slow to duck. He was just 32.

Al Black says to let him out on the corner; he doesn't want to return to the boarding house just yet. Too many bad men there who will beg him for money—or plain steal it.

"Mr. Fitch," he says, "I have to ask you for three hundred dollars, just so I can get started again. With three hundred dollars I can get me some paints and brushes and be an artist again."

Jim is moved by Al's plight. But he also is cautious. Even if Jim were rich and had an extra $300, he'd be reluctant to invest in a man who has been in jail on drug charges and looks troubled even now. Jim tells Al he would rather mail him painting supplies. How would that be?

Al Black looks disappointed.

"How about a check?, Mr. Fitch. Can you give me a check for a hundred dollars? Mr. Fitch, that would help me so much."

Jim reaches into his wallet and hands Al $10.

Al says thanks and disappears around the corner.

The Highwaymen Roster

Curtis Arnett
Hezekiah Baker
Al Baker
George Buckner
Ellis Buckner
Robert Butler
Mary Alice Carrol
J. "Hook" Daniels
Fox (first name unknown)
James Gibson
Alfred Hair, aka "A. Hare" and "A. Hir"
Israel Knight
Lewis McDaniel
R.A. McClendon
Harold Newton
L. Newton
Sam Newton
Livingston Roberts, aka "Castro"
Charles Walker

A Highwayman goes to Africa

Lakeland
August 1995

An endless highway. A doctor's office. A struggling artist.

The highway could be any Florida highway, but this one is U.S. 27, along the spine of the peninsula. It could be any doctor's office, but this one is in Sebring, in the middle of the state. The struggling artist could be a number of other African-American artists, but this one is Robert Butler.

The year is 1965.

Robert walks into the doctor's office and talks to the nurse.

No, he tells her, I don't have an appointment.

Ma'am, I'm not sick either. Ma'am, I just want a moment of the doctor's time, if he can spare it. I want to show him something.

Robert got a tip to come here. Somebody told him the doctor likes to hunt turkeys on his days off. Robert paints nature scenes, and he happens to have a fine turkey painting in the back of his 1960 Oldsmobile Catalina.

He introduces himself to the doctor—tells him a little about himself, his background and how he works—and then shows the painting. The doctor is delighted, not only about the painting, but about the price: $35.

The doctor buys.

Robert returns to the highway, an endless highway that many years from now, will take him to incredible heights and incredible places. Africa.

A former Highwayman, Robert, now 52, struggled in his early years. But no longer. Through talent, ferocious work habits, a winning personality and good luck, he has become one of the state's best-known natural landscape painters.

No longer does he drive 50,000 miles a year in worn-out cars on sales trips. He doesn't have to sell his paintings for $35 either.

Some Butler originals now go for $7,500.

At heart he may still be a Highwayman, but today he drives a Saab.

Robert moved to Okeechobee with his mother when he was four. They were dirt poor. Annie Tolifer Butler picked tomatoes and waited tables in restaurants. She even found a third job, cleaning motel rooms.

"I know now my mother was a unique, unique woman," Robert says in a crisp baritone that always sounds formal. "She was one of those people who believed you could accomplish anything if you worked hard enough."

In 1955, a white businessman lent her $5,000. She invested in a boarding house. With her profit, she bought a restaurant. She liked visiting demolition sites to buy the best of the used lumber at cut-rate prices. With the lumber she'd put up other boarding houses, saving money by laying building foundations herself.

She lived long enough to see her work ethic take root in her son.

As a boy, Robert sat in the school playground and drew pictures. He loved hunting—mostly rabbits, but some hogs and deer—and he is convinced his hunting background helps him as an artist. He says a hunter, like a landscape painter, has to be attuned to the environment in a special way. He has to be able to "read" the land.

He graduated from an all-black high school, but the only job he landed was mowing lawns or doing maintenance work at dairies. Still, he kept painting.

One lawn customer was so impressed by Robert's art that he bought him a set of oil paints. Then the man got Robert work as a hospital orderly. Robert sold paintings to hospital doctors, who referred him to other potential customers.

Okeechobee's librarian gave him $25 to take a correspondence art course. Another doctor commissioned Robert to paint a picture of a favorite Appaloosa horse. Robert painted the picture 40 times before the doctor bought it. "What that man taught me was the importance of detail," Robert says.

Good ol' boys gobbled up his inexpensive hunting scenes. Jim Fitch helped too. They became friends after Jim bought one of Robert's paintings. Later, Jim built frames for Robert's paintings and advised him about his career. Jim opened the Kissimmee Valley Gallery in Sebring and hopes to establish Florida's Museum of Art and Culture. He researches the Highwaymen and remains one of Robert's biggest fans.

Okeechobee, some folks will tell you, might be the heart of Florida's redneck belt. But many who helped Robert along the way were white.

"We all know there was racial prejudice in Florida in the 1950s and 1960s," Robert says. But he cannot remember—says he has chosen not to remember—ever being the victim of racism.

"Okeechobee was the deep South, you understand, and the Civil Rights era was going on, and there was so much anxiety about race. But that town just about adopted me."

Robert says he sometimes asks himself why.

"I'd like to think it was the art that bridged all those potential conflicts."

Robert quit his hospital orderly job so could paint full-time. He was married and the first of nine children had been born.

"I had to take the chance," he says. "I was swimming in this fantastic psychological soup at the time: I came from this poor background and yet this door was opening wide for me, to this universe that could be explored forever.

"I wanted to paint as much as I could, as often as I could. I stepped through the door and never looked back."

As Robert began painting full-time in Okeechobee, other African-American painters were busy in Fort Pierce, which is where the Highwayman tradition was born.

Like Robert, the other men worked quickly, priced their art cheaply, traveled state highways widely and sold their work aggressively.

Robert was in it for the money too. But unlike the others, city men who often worked together as a team, Robert felt most comfortable in the wilderness and painted alone.

He would paint furiously for weeks, load his art into one of his chewing-gum-and-baling-wire station wagons and stay on the road until every painting was sold. Robert is tall and handsome, with prominent cheekbones and a moustache that makes him look like Otis Redding. He's a sharp dresser and always took pride in his appearance on sales trips. He'd stop at doctor's offices and lawyer's offices and motel offices and banks.

If someone bought a painting, Robert always asked for a referral. Then he'd go there. Ranchers, he found, especially loved his landscapes. They'd invite him to their spreads, he'd make a quick sketch, maybe make some field notes and come back a few days later with a painting.

Sometimes he made random stops. One time his old Oldsmobile began whining like a monstrous swarm of yellow jackets, and he pulled into a filling station in Haines City. A new rear wheel bearing was going to cost more money than he had. He traded a turkey painting and $20 for the mechanical work.

Turkey paintings were his bread and butter. Turkey hunters loved them. He jokes that when a landscape was giving him trouble, he'd simply paint a turkey into the scene and it would sell.

He advertised in outdoor magazines, and began selling prints of his work by the hundreds. His work improved and his career caught fire. Eventually he moved to Lakeland and opened his own gallery.

Robert and Dorothy Butler have been married 32 years. They live in a pretty Lakeland suburb. There is a nice pastel rendering of a waterfall in the living room and a painting of a rose in the bedroom. Robert didn't paint them. "We can't afford a Butler painting," Robert says.

A cheerful, soft-spoken woman, Dorothy has had to be mother and father to their children when Robert has been on the road. "I know how Robert works," she says. Dorothy likes to think she has given Robert the freedom to become the best artist he could be.

Some Butler paintings manage to celebrate natural Florida while at the same time mourning its passing. The places he paints are still there, but they are disappearing under what some people in Florida call "progress." Robert says he wants to paint these wonderful places before they're gone.

Robert is an unusual artist, Jim Fitch likes to say, one who is left-brained and right-brained. In other words, Robert is artistic and coldly analytical. His paintings have an otherworldly light to them; the light almost gives them a churchlike quality. At the same time, his work is finely detailed. He is famous for interviewing biologists, botanists, zoologists and even soil specialists for details he can use. If he knows the soil, he knows what plants grow there. If he knows the plants, he knows the animals.

He remembers the time he was commissioned to paint a bear hunt for the cover of *Florida Wildlife* magazine. He researched for days, finding out that many hunters used dogs, and that sometimes those dogs were branded with the initials of the hunters.

Robert painted an angry bear, surrounded by hunting dogs, all of them wearing brands. He drove to Miami and delivered the painting to the printing company. On the way home, he began to worry that maybe painting the dogs with brands on them was a mistake. Maybe animal rights people would see the painting and protest. He might be blamed for the controversy.

He drove back to the printing company and painted out the brands.

He felt better until the next day. Then he realized he had made the wrong decision. He had changed the facts. He drove back to Miami and painted the brands back onto the dogs.

For Robert, life has an improvised quality. Sometimes he jams canvases and paints into his prized 1972 four-wheel drive Chevy Suburban and backs out the driveway with no destination in mind.

"I just point the car and go."

Sometimes he goes for days.

"When I see an interesting landscape I'll stop and start painting. I want to document Florida. I think of myself as a historian with a paintbrush."

Robert did a series of paintings on the Myakka River and a series on cattle ranching and cowboys. He painted the Okefenokee Swamp, where his easel fell off a dock into the dark water, never to be recovered. His latest project involves organizing the state's finest landscape artists to do the definitive series of paintings on the Everglades.

Sometimes Jim Fitch can't find Robert, who doesn't answer Jim's phone calls. Dorothy can't help Jim. Often she doesn't know where Robert is, either. It can be irritating, but they both understand. When Robert's brain is boiling with ideas, he up and disappears. He hides in a motel, unplugs the phone and sets up his canvases.

"Creativity, by its very nature, is about exploration," Robert says. "You have to have at least the illusion of being free to explore your ideas. For me, that means going to a place where I can shut out all distractions. Nobody can call me. I don't watch TV and I don't listen to the radio. I paint."

One evening he ends up at a Howard Johnson's in Tampa. It might seem odd to people who'd expect Robert to do the nitty-gritty of his work in the middle of the deep woods, or a great swamp, but he considers a motel the perfect place to pull an all-night paint marathon. Referring to field notes or quick sketches done in the field, he will work without distraction, unaware of either the clock or the outside world.

"I can do as many as five paintings in a good night," he says, eating a hot dog at Mel's while rush hour traffic streams by on Busch Boulevard. "I work on them at the same time, a little at a time. I'll start one and then move on to the next and then on to the next. If a particular painting inspires me, I may finish it before moving along. I've worked as long as eighteen straight hours—I want to take advantage of the inspiration when it's there. I once did twenty paintings in four days. I worked so intensely I hurt my shoulder. It still bothers me."

Jim Fitch worries that Robert's normal urge to paint frequently—a habit from his early Highwayman years when he had to—may be bad for his art.

"Do you truly want to be a painter?" Jim asks him.

"What Jim means is, are you painting because you want to make money or are you painting from the heart?" Robert says.

"When I first started painting, making money was everything. It was the driving force. Dorothy and I had nine children. Listen, there is nothing in the world like nine children to get you up on your feet and out the door painting and selling."

Those days are mostly over, he says. Now customers come to him. He has an agent to market his work and to schedule appearances at galleries and art classes. He tries to go on the road only when he wants to. He paints less, he likes to think, but he paints better.

He thinks his masterpiece lies ahead of him.

He has felt that way since he made the ultimate Highwayman journey, to Africa.

He brought his paints and brushes. He felt he was on some kind of beautiful mission. Six or seven generations ago, people in his family were taken from Africa and shipped to America as slaves. Now, in the summer of 1993, Robert was going back.

"I was going to re-experience Africa for my ancestors through my paintings."

In Tanzania, in Southeast Africa, he hired someone to take him into the country. Miles outside of a big city called Arusha, he stopped on the Masai Steppe. The high plains are about 3,000 feet above sea level. He could see a long way, but not the 85 miles to 19,000-foot Mount Kilimanjaro, invisible, for the moment, in the African haze. He painted the high plains that stretched toward the mountain, and the ostriches on the plains and the dust raised by Masai warriors driving their cattle.

Then Robert moved on.

At his next stop, a small village, he began painting again.

A mighty crowd gathered around him, a black stranger dressed like a foreigner. Nobody spoke English, and he couldn't speak their Swahili dialect. Tuning out their murmurs, he painted background first, the plains and the scrub trees rising on foothills giving way to distant mountain ranges. Then, into the foreground, he painted the stone huts of the village. The murmuring grew louder. As he painted, a woman carrying a baby on her back walked between huts. Robert quickly painted the woman and her baby into the scene.

The crowd erupted with joy. They recognized themselves. A small child, a boy, pushed in front of him and stood inches from the painting. He looked back at Robert and then looked at Robert's painting again. The boy reached up and touched it, as if to see whether the painting were real or an illusion.

"I don't see light the same since Africa," Robert tells people now. "I see colors I didn't see before. I'm capturing more emotional flux in my work. I'm so fired up I'd like to repaint every painting I've ever done."

Through an interpreter, an African man asked where Robert had come from. Robert hunkered down and used his finger to draw a picture on the ultimate canvas, the Earth. He drew the North American and African continents and the ocean separating them. Robert pointed to Florida.

The African looked confused.

He wanted to know: How many days' walk?

Robert, the Highwayman who had come so far, in so many ways, looked the man in the eye.

Robert didn't know how he could possibly explain.

Where the sea turtles crawl

South Melbourne Beach
July 1994

Keep moving and you thwart the blood-thirsty sand flies. Stop for even an instant and the microscopic insects burrow into flesh. Focus a dim light on the skin and you'll see nothing, all the while feeling an intense burning sensation. When you can no longer stand it, hike briskly away from the sea oats, swatting bare legs and arms and neck until reaching the beginnings of the surf and the saving breeze.

Trey Porter has the right idea. Standing next to a sand dune, he wears insect netting from head to foot. His partner, Manuel Moto, has no protection except for his ability to hop and scratch while still managing to record data on a clipboard.

"Sometimes I just walk into the surf up to my neck to get away from them," he says, somewhere in the dark.

He and his partner, students from the University of Central Florida, are working within the Archie Carr National Wildlife Refuge, studying nesting sea turtles. A huge loggerhead, perhaps 250 pounds, lies before them, burying eggs with painstaking care. That she is surrounded by scientists and spectators has no apparent effect. She goes about her business without concern, throwing sand this way and that, hitting, as often as not, the legs of the those who have hunkered down to watch in awe.

When she finishes, she turns and crawls seaward, stopping to rest, then lumbering a few yards, then stopping again. When she catches the scent, or the sight, of the Atlantic Ocean, she moves steadily down the slope, gravity in her favor. The backwash of the surf takes hold of her, and she paddles aggressively. In a moment she is gone.

"She's practicing a behavior pattern that goes back millions of years," says Trey Porter, the science student hidden behind the insect netting.

Modern Florida beaches, with their waterfront homes, souvenir shops, restaurants and parking lots, seldom offer the solitude and the darkness that sea turtles have required since the time when dinosaurs roamed the earth.

But this beach still does.

It may not last.

Most summers, sea turtles crawl ashore and build about 13,000 nests on barrier islands in south Brevard and north Indian River counties, almost all within the boundaries of the 20.5-mile federal refuge, named after the late biologist and natural history writer, Archie Carr. The refuge features the most significant nesting beach in the western hemisphere, possibly the entire world, for loggerheads, a threatened species. It has the most productive nesting beach in the United States for green turtles, an even rarer species, considered endangered.

The reason for the wealth of turtles isn't entirely known. But without doubt the refuge lies along one of the most natural remaining beaches in Florida, despite some development and a population of about 12,000 people. Somewhat remote, parts of the island until recently offered little in the way of services for residents or tourists. Anti-erosion seawalls, sandbags, boulders and other barriers—the kinds of structures that have destroyed natural beaches and eliminated turtle nesting habitat in most of coastal Florida—are almost entirely missing in the refuge. Counties here have the most aggressive lighting ordinances in the state. At night, the beach is dark and attractive to turtles.

Despite all the good, the Archie Carr National Wildlife Refuge, and the turtles that need the beach to reproduce their species, may be headed for trouble.

When the refuge was designated in 1990, Congress announced it would spend $90-million to acquire more than nine miles of undeveloped beach and more than 800 acres within the boundaries. Since then, working within a shrinking federal budget, Congress has spent less than $10-million. The race for the best remaining parcels is being lost to developers and land speculators. At risk is a sea turtle nesting beach of global importance.

Long, uninhabited contiguous stretches of beach, and the stunning forests across the highway from the beach—the very areas government has made a priority—more and more are becoming homesites and subdivisions. In the last few years, more than 100 new developments have broken ground, including a sprawling shopping plaza that will open this fall in the heart of the refuge. Population on the thin barrier island is expected to increase 40 percent by century's end.

In the ocean, beyond the dunes, in the heart of summer, sea turtles gather by the thousands, waiting for dark, waiting for instinct born of 160-million years, to tell them to come ashore and lay their eggs.

In some countries, sea turtles are slaughtered for food, legally and illegally. Even where they are protected, egg poaching is a problem. In the United States, turtles drown in shrimp trawls and commercial gill nets or become entangled in fishing line thrown into the water by careless sport anglers. They also ingest discarded plastics and tar balls from oil spills. But the biggest obstacle for them is the development of the beaches on which they have nested for eons.

One morning in 1981, University of Central Florida professor Lew Ehrhart—everybody, even his wife, calls him Doc—rode a four-wheel drive vehicle from the south end of Melbourne Beach about 20 miles to Sebastian Inlet State Recreation Area.

He expected to see some turtle nests. It was summer, the season for nesting turtles, after all. But he hardly expected to see hundreds. He was delighted, stunned, completely flabbergasted. He and his students began checking the beach every night. Their numbers, their data, grew. Thousands of loggerhead turtles were crawling out of the ocean and building nests from May into October. And hundreds of greens. Even a few of the very rare giant leatherbacks—they can measure eight feet and weigh 2,000 pounds—were using the beach.

"Why is this beach so good?" Ehrhart asks himself. "It's difficult to answer. We can only proximate because we don't know what a female turtle actually senses. It could be the offshore approach, the slope of the beach, the texture of the sand, a smell."

It also could be that turtles have been returning to this small stretch of beach for hundreds, perhaps thousands, of years. Something about this particular beach may be stamped into their genetic makeup. There are many mysteries about sea turtles, many theories, unproven.

"Turtles return to their natal beaches," Ehrhart says. "I'm sure of it. They return to the beach where they hatched to lay their own eggs."

Other scientists agree. In one famous study, tagged greens traveled 1,400 miles over open ocean and found their natal beach, Ascension Island, only five miles long. How? It could be that turtles can read the magnetic field encircling the earth. They could be navigating by the stars. It could be something else. Nobody knows how they find one beach out of all the beaches in the world.

Yet.

Doc Ehrhart never thought he'd end up studying a reptile. At Cornell, where he got his doctorate, he was a mammalogist. Over at the space center, in the wilderness surrounding Cape Canaveral, he studied mammals. But he became interested in the turtles that nested on the beach, almost within the shadow of the launching pad.

In the summer, he and his wife live in a beach house with 14 of his students. At dark, students comb the beach, wait for a turtle to crawl up, wait until she has laid eggs, and then take out giant calipers and measure her. At 1 a.m., they return home and collapse into beds, bunks, sleeping bags, couches and mattresses on the floor. They wake at 5 a.m. and drive the beach in all-terrain vehicles, counting nests and eggs. After they count eggs, they carefully rebury them. Last summer's 13,000 nests produced more than a million eggs. About 60 percent hatched. Probably about one percent will survive to sexual maturity.

Sex, for turtles, takes place in the ocean off the beach. The few human beings who have witnessed turtle sex describe it as a violent affair. Competing males whip the sea into a froth as they bite each other. The winner catches the receptive female, bites her on the neck, hooks the front of her shell with the sharp claws of his front flippers and mounts her, sometimes damaging her shell in the process as he penetrates. He leaves; she stores his sperm. During summer, she may nest four to seven times, laying hundreds of eggs at a shot.

The sex of a hatchling turtle is determined by the temperature of the sand and the location of the egg. The cooler the sand, the more likely a male turtle will hatch. The warmest sand produces females. Nobody knows why. When hatchlings emerge, after dark, raccoons try to eat them. So do ghost crabs. If there's a bright light on the beach, it can disorient them, the reason they sometimes head for highways along developed coasts and get run over. A hatchling that makes the water probably will be eaten by a fish, which is why hatchlings don't stop swimming for about 24 hours. They hide in offshore lines of seaweed.

"Where juvenile loggerheads go is a mystery," Lew Ehrhart says. Talking, he leans back in an easy chair at his house. Then he leans forward. He is so enthusiastic about his work, so animated when he speaks of turtles, that he seems younger than 52. He never takes vacations. He and his wife just celebrated their 30th wedding anniversary at a turtle conference in Mexico, where Doc caught a cold.

Juvenile loggerheads may be pulled north by the Gulf Stream. Then they may be captured by currents that take them toward Europe. They may spend years off Africa, foraging and growing. When they're about 10, they show up off Florida again. About 10 years later the females begin crawling up on the beach within the Archie Carr refuge to nest.

"And green turtles!" Doc Ehrhart almost shouts when he mentions greens. Pictures of them decorate his T-shirt. "We don't know where they spend most of their lives. We see some juveniles in the Indian River and just offshore. But when they're about two feet long, they're gone. You just don't see them again until they're adults."

A sexually mature green sometimes weighs 400 pounds and may be 50 years old. A large loggerhead, about 300 pounds, may live that long too. The life span of loggerheads is another mystery.

A green turtle eats algae and grass. A leatherback, the giant of the turtle world, devours jellyfish. A loggerhead, the most common of rare turtles, consumes crustaceans and mollusks. Its huge jaws can crush a conch. Twice, by accident, Doc managed to place his hands into a loggerhead's jaws. Feeling returned to his fingers about two weeks later. Another time he stepped too close to a loggerhead and her jaws closed around his leg.

"I could feel the connective tissue in my shin begin to pop."

His shin healed too.

The moon, almost full, fights through the clouds. Suddenly, the beach is bathed in pale light. Up ahead, 100 yards or so, something huge, something ancient, is emerging from the surf.

"My God!" hisses David Godfrey. "Look!"

The turtle, from this distance, looks like a small Volkswagen. Godfrey, who works for the Turtle Survival League, a branch of the Caribbean Conservation Corporation, is thrilled. His office is in Gainesville, and he almost never gets to watch nesting sea turtles anymore.

Godfrey is 27, a University of Florida graduate, and a self-described sea turtle fanatic. He grew up in Orlando, only an hour away from the beach, so he spent much of his teenage years here. He saw his first turtle, a loggerhead, from his surfboard when he was 16. When he arrived this afternoon, his surfboard was parked in the back seat of his rented Mustang convertible. The waves didn't cooperate, but now that night has come, the turtles are. In the last hour, on a half-mile walk, Godfrey has seen 10 of them building nests.

As they lumber up to the sand dunes, they leave tracks that look as if they were made by small bulldozers.

"Get down!" Godfrey suddenly whispers, grabbing his companion by the elbow. They hunker next to the surf. Incredibly, only 30 feet away, another loggerhead is emerging.

She drags her enormous torso, probably 250 pounds or so, out of the surf. She raises her huge head—it could be mistaken for a log—and gazes around.

Godfrey and his companions freeze. She crawls another 10 feet. Her head comes up. She could be sniffing the air.

She crawls another 10 feet. Stops. Her head is up. Now she lowers it, plows ahead, as if she is sniffing the sand, searching for her natal beach.

"We're seeing something very few people have ever seen," Godfrey whispers.

He and his companions don't move a muscle, despite the sand flies and mosquitoes the size of wasps. If the humans make a fuss, the turtle will most likely return to the ocean. If they remain motionless, the turtle should continue to the dune, dig a hole and lay her eggs. Once she's laying, she is not easily disturbed.

She reaches the dune. She digs. Suddenly, she's heading back toward the ocean, without laying her eggs. Something about the beach simply felt wrong to her. Maybe it was those strange pieces of driftwood, whispering at the surf.

Godfrey expresses no disappointment. Already he has seen many turtles tonight. He walks north now, back toward one of only four "Mom and Pop" motels for 20 miles. The beach, except for the moonlight, is dark and deserted. But way ahead is the glow of Cocoa and the Space Center. He is afraid this beach, this prehistoric place, could look the same one day.

His gloomy thoughts vanish when he discovers the spectacular turtle tracks. They're four feet wide, at least. They are different from the other tracks. "They're not made by a loggerhead," he says. "A green made them!"

Few greens nest in the United States, except here. In 1992, 608 nests were counted along the Archie Carr, a national record. Greens, more than loggerheads, require quality darkness, the kind that has all but vanished from coastal Florida. Straining to see, staring at the dune ahead, Godfrey lays his eyes on the first green he has ever encountered on a Florida beach.

He creeps behind her, on his hands and knees, and aims a flashlight covered by a red lens. She's laying her eggs. He stands and gestures, come on. It's safe to watch; we won't scare her.

She measures at least four feet, probably weighs 300 pounds, smells of the sea. She lies in a pit of her own making. With her back flippers, she constructed a chamber, shaped like a flask, wide at the bottom and narrow at the top. Eggs, one at a time, and in twos and threes, now drop into the hole. It takes a good half hour for her to lay about 100 leathery eggs.

Then she starts covering. With one rear flipper she scrapes sand into the hole. With the other, she packs it down, hard. Then she repeats the process again and again. Next she moves up in her pit and knocks sand around. She moves again and flips more sand. Godfrey is uncertain where she laid her eggs. She has disguised the location well.

She also has gotten herself into a jam. She's in the middle of a narrow footpath that leads to a parking lot. As she digs, her head butts up against the sea oats growing on the side of the path. Her hole grows deeper and deeper, as if she is excavating a cave.

But she knows her business. She emerges from the pit and plunges down the rim like an avalanche. She turns, instinctively, toward the sea. She lumbers down the slope, stopping every few feet, for rest, and then drags herself forward again, sniffing the air, watching the horizon, heading for the Atlantic, home.

She's in the surf now, but you can see the top of the shell. Now even her shell is gone.

The beach seems suddenly empty, except for tracks that tell you nothing, and everything.

Bone Man

Ruskin
July 1993

He knew his time was at hand. All his experience, every feeling in his gut, everything he knew about justice, told him as much. It was going to happen. Dodging raindrops, he jumped into his truck and bounced toward the machinery in the far pit. They had to be there. They just had to. He hopped from the truck and slipped down into the hole the crane had excavated.

He looked up.

They were there, protruding from a wall of shell-bones, shiny, black, ancient, glorious. An ice-age paradise. As the rain stung his cheeks, as the lightning lit his discovery, he felt positively, wonderfully, alive.

Then tears fell.

Luck has nothing to do with it. Talk to Frank Garcia, or people who know him best, and you'll hear the refrain again and again. Luck has played no role in his success as one of the world's great fossil hunters.

"Luck, hell," says Garcia, who lives in a little community on Tampa Bay. "I agree with what Edison said about genius. It's ninety-nine percent perspiration and one percent inspiration."

Garcia, 47, has no formal training in paleontology, the study of prehistoric animals through their fossilized bones. He barely graduated from high school. But he studied paleontology books when he was a boy, and he picked the brains of professional paleontologists when he was a teen-ager. As a man he continues to outwork other fossil collectors.

While they sleep, he looks for fossils. While they socialize, he looks for fossils. As they go about making a secure, comfortable living in mainstream professions, he lives modestly, lecturing or leading fossil collecting tours, making just enough money to do what he loves.

"I have such a desire, and so much enthusiasm, about wanting to know about the unknown," he says, dark eyes flashing. "Discovery is what life's all about."

In 1983, he discovered the world's greatest collection of ice-age fossils in a Hillsborough County shell mine known as the Leisey Shell Pit. He had predicted their presence based on the location and appearance of a mine he had been monitoring for years. Still, when he came across the mother lode of 1.5-million-year-old bones during a summer thunderstorm, he broke down and cried.

Over the years he has discovered more than 20 new species of animals, including two named in honor of him. Thousands of his important finds are in the Florida Museum of Natural History in Gainesville and the Smithsonian's American Museum of Natural History in Washington—all this from a former asbestos worker who used to regularly skip school.

"I'm always out there looking," Garcia says. He is a muscular man with coal black hair, a thick moustache and a dimple on his chin big enough to hide at least a small shark's tooth. "Looking is the key. A fossil hunter has to be dedicated."

When other fossil collectors flinch at danger, he presses forward. Looking for fossils, he once got trapped in a muddy pit that threatened to become his grave. He's been menaced by snakes and alligators, mosquitoes, lightning and Southern sheriffs. One puzzled lawman threatened to take Garcia to a mental hospital when he caught him at a construction site stuffing a pillowcase with fossilized feces.

When he is not hunting fossils, he talks about them, reads about them or writes poetry about them. When he listens to a piece of classical music, at bone-shattering volumes, he wonders how the music might serve as a soundtrack to one of his ambitious fossil slide shows. When he got married last summer, he and Dixie spent their honeymoon looking for fossils. They dug up the shell of a prehistoric turtle.

"You have to have enthusiasm," says Garcia, whose sentences, when he is excited, change course. Words tumble from his lips like bones from a ruptured sack. "You have to be . . . You know . . . I once . . . You have to want to make discoveries. Understand?"

He wrote a poem about his philosophy once.

Desire creates
Vision, and
Vision leads to
Great discoveries

"My mission in life is to excite people about what we had here in the past," says Garcia, who has spoken to thousands of Tampa Bay schoolchildren, over the years, about his favorite subject. "Fossils are a window to the past."

He goes through those windows like a cat burglar.

"In each generation there are only a very few fossil collectors like him," says Daryl Domning, a research specialist for the Smithsonian. "He just has this talent for finding extraordinary fossils, not just once in a while, but again and again."

In 1988, Domning took Garcia on an expedition to Jamaica. Domning hoped to find fossils from the original sea cow, a relative of the modern manatee. The sea cow Domning wanted lived 50-million years ago and probably crawled on land.

It took Garcia only two days. He was standing with Domning on a mountain when he noticed a small rock under their guide's foot.

"Move over," Garcia told the startled guide.

With a glance Garcia knew the rock was actually fossilized bone. Looking closely, he determined the bone was part of a sea cow skull. The men started digging. They found the rest of the skull, ribs and backbone.

"That's why I brought Frank with me," Domning told the guide, a geologist.

"I've been looking at sea cow bones since 1966," Garcia explains. "I don't have the education or the background of the two gentlemen, but I know how to find fossils."

Next year, Domning and Garcia hope to return to Jamaica. They want the rest of that sea cow, the part with legs. Acquaintances of Garcia say that if anybody can find it, he can. They have watched him do impossibly amazing things before.

"Sometimes I think he's psychic," says Don Ward, who has known him for decades. One time, years ago at the Leisey Shell Pit, Ward and other men were terribly discouraged after a fruitless afternoon of digging. Garcia walked up, cheerfully greeted the men and threw his heavy hunting knife into the ground.

"That's where we'll find something!" he announced.

They dug up the jaw of a cave bear.

Frank Garcia was born in New York in 1946, but moved to Tampa when he was a baby. One grandfather came from Spain, the other from Cuba. He inherited their culture and their passion for living. He spoke no English until he started school.

He failed first grade. He hated being in a classroom. "Boring," he says now. He daydreamed about dinosaurs. On summer vacations to Payokee, a farming community near Lake Okeechobee where his grandfather was mayor, he looked for dinosaur bones.

He was disappointed to learn Florida was under water when dinosaurs ruled the Earth. But one day he found a fossilized sand dollar shell. He thought it was mind-boggling that oceans had covered even Lake Okeechobee.

After Florida emerged from the sea 28-million years ago, mammal life blossomed, and back in Tampa Garcia looked for their bones, often during hours he should have been in school. His father complained about the growing collection of fossils filling up their West Tampa house. His friends called him "The Bone Man."

He graduated from Tampa Jefferson—Thomas Jefferson, who collected fossils, was his hero—and spent a few years in the Naval Reserve. He got married and divorced. "Immaturity on my part," he explains now. He could have gone to college, on the G.I. Bill, and possibly studied paleontology, but he had unpleasant memories of school. Anyway, professional paleontologists often spend their lives in institutions, teaching or writing papers. Frank Garcia intended to get his hands dirty. Construction work was good enough for him; after hours he had time for fossils.

He found the teeth of ancient horses and bison at Apollo Beach. He found the huge triangular teeth of *Carcharadon megalodons*—60-foot great white sharks—in the phosphate mines of Central Florida.

During summer, temperatures can exceed 110 degrees in the desert-like, moonscape conditions. Garcia loved phosphate mines. Mining exposed fossils.

At phosphate mines, he found jaws of ancient rhinos and the sea cows called dugongs. He found the jaw of a sperm whale. He found the skull of a long-beaked dolphin. He found the jaw of a new genus and species, *Pliocyon robustus*, a strange animal that was a combination dog and bear.

He dug out the upper jaw of a rare, dog-like, Hyanea. Only one other specimen had been found in North America. He discovered a new species of antelope, which the Florida Museum of Natural History named after him, *Sub-Antilocaptra garciae*.

He found the world's only two skulls of a rare shoved-tusked elephant called the Ambelodon. Sometimes, when he found something so astonishing, he wept. Sometimes he sang. Sometimes he danced a jig.

"He's an emotional man," says Jack Weldon, a good friend. "He's the type of guy who's not afraid to tell you how much your friendship means to him."

Sometimes, after a day of installing asbestos insulation, he would tank up on Cuban coffee and drive to the phosphate mines and look for fossils by moonlight. On days when he felt he was on verge of a great discovery, he'd telephone work and say he was sick. Once he called his boss and said he was having trouble with a tooth. He never explained that the tooth was actually a six-foot tusk from a prehistoric elephant, a mastodon.

One day, while visiting a mine, a tremendous thundershower swept him into a clay pit that quickly turned into a muddy bog. The only possible handhold, a bush, was occupied by a coral snake. Miles from civilization, with mud up to his armpits and a venomous reptile flicking its tongue at him, Garcia wondered if a future fossil hunter might one day discover his bones. By sheer luck, a phosphate worker drove past the remote area, heard his cries, and pulled him out with a shovel.

By the time he got home, the clay-mud covering his body was as hard as a plaster cast. He literally rolled out of his car and across the lawn to reach the hose. For Garcia, the comedy was a small price to pay: He'd collected 25 teeth from three-toed horses, a rhino tooth and a perfect tooth from a Gomphotherium, an unusual elephant with upper and lower tusks.

On some early-morning trips, he was met by mosquitoes so fierce they turned his white t-shirt black. Sometimes he dodged lightning bolts. Once, when he needed cloth to wrap up an important fossil, he cut his blue jeans into strips and spent the afternoon working in his underwear. Worried about grumpy sheriffs, he was careful to drive the speed limit on the one-hour drive home.

He would go anywhere, anytime, anyplace, even dangerous places, to pursue fossils. In Central Florida, he was diving in the Peace River, looking for prehistoric elephant bones. Concentrating hard, he bumped into a submerged 14-foot alligator. The memory that haunts: "I dropped a mastodon tooth and didn't go back for it."

He made one of his best discoveries when his leg was broken. He packed his equipment into his Ford Torino and used a crutch to work the gas pedal. At a phosphate mine, at a wide lake, he somehow managed to launch a rubber raft. He threw himself awkwardly into the raft and paddled across the lake to a promising-looking phosphate hill. With fear and difficulty he wobbled up the hill on his crutches.

Bones were sticking up out of the hill as if they had been waiting for him since the beginning of time. With his hunting knife he carefully dug around them. The bones were from some kind of skull he had never seen before. It looked like a cross between a moose and a reindeer and a camel. It had Y-shaped antlers on its nose that reminded him of a slingshot.

Later, a professional paleontologist at the Florida Museum of Natural History named it the *Kyptoceras amatorum*. It meant the horned wonder-amateur. The amateur part honored Garcia and other hobbyists who have contributed so much to the science of paleontology. The *Kyptoceras*, which lived about three-million years ago, was a completely new animal to science.

His extraordinary talent has failed to make him rich.

He continued installing insulation for a living—"I did okay"—but routinely turned down overtime opportunities because extra work cut into fossil time. The Smithsonian gave him a small grant to look for marine animal fossils, and he worked occasionally for the Tampa Museum of Science and Industry, leading tours to phosphate mines. He wrote and sold a small booklet full of tips about finding fossils. If he lived frugally, most of the time he could pay his bills.

He lived, alone, in a dusty trailer that positively bulged with bones. He drove a string of old cars—a Nash Rambler, a Hornet, a Malibu—all he could afford. He dreamed of fame.

In the late 1970s, a teen-ager showed him fossils collected from a shell mine in western Hillsborough. The owners of the mine—a family named Leisey—were selling the shell as roadfill. Garcia visited the mine and found horse teeth. On a subsequent trip, he dug out a mastodon jaw.

More significantly, he noticed a layer of yellow sand containing fossils from both land and sea animals. He wondered if part of the mine stood on an ancient riverbed, a riverbed that might be the resting place for prehistoric animals that had drowned or washed down for thousands of years.

As the months went by, and he found more bones, his excitement grew. He predicted, to friends, that the site sooner or later would yield something truly spectacular. Then he went on a vacation to look for fossils in Nebraska.

It was June 27, 1983, a Monday morning, when he next visited the Leisey Shell Pit. He drove over and asked if anyone had seen anything unusual. The man who operated a crane that dug shell had noticed something. He'd shoveled into a bunch of bone, and quit to go on vacation. Otherwise, he'd have worked through the bone, crushing it into oblivion.

Garcia thought his heart might explode. This could be the big one, he told himself, the mother lode he had yearned to find. He ran for his truck and sped toward the crane. It was parked in the spot Garcia had long expected to yield a discovery that would make him famous.

In the rain, he leapt from his truck. He winced when lightning struck nearby. He jumped into a cavity made by the crane and looked at the wall of shell that had been exposed by the digging. He rubbed his eyes, because of the rain, and because of disbelief.

There were more than 20 ice ages during the last two-million years. But Florida never froze. Animals that disappeared elsewhere thrived here.

At the Leisey Shell Pit, hundreds of blue-black bones stuck out the wall for about an acre. Not just little bones. Some bones were as thick as tree trunks. He saw mammoth jaws, camel jaws, saber cat teeth, horse skulls, horse feet. He backed away from the wall and sat down. Tears streamed down his face. He remembered what a famous archaeologist said upon entering the tomb of King Tut:

"I saw many wonderful things."

He jumped back into his truck and raced for a telephone.

In the months that followed, history was made. Paleontologists throughout the world descended on Hillsborough County. Dr. Clayton Ray of the Smithsonian told reporters: "Discovering this site was like discovering a new chapter in life."

At the Leisey Shell Pit, 200 species were uncovered, including 20 new to science. There was a condor with a 15-foot wingspread and a kind of vulture that was 18 feet from wingtip to wingtip. There were grand sloths and beavers. There was North America's best collection of the elephants known as mammoths. There were llamas, from infants to adults, hundreds of them, more than anybody had ever seen.

About 1.5-million years ago they had washed down a river into a bayou. The bayou eventually became dry land. In the 20th century, the land became a tomato field. In 1972, it became the Leisey Shell Pit. In 1983, Frank Garcia came along. The Florida Museum of Natural History filled two trailer trucks with 30,000 bones.

"It can be said that the Leisey Shell Pit is the richest well-studied early ice-age site anywhere in the world," says S. David Webb, a University of Florida paleontologist.

For a while, Frank Garcia was the most celebrated paleontologist on the planet. Every major newspaper and magazine covered his discovery. *The Today Show* did an eight-minute segment on him. His father timed it. Fossil clubs donated money so Garcia could quit construction and work the site. But as years passed and the publicity died down he eventually ran out of financing and went back to construction work again.

He has asbestos in his lungs. For years he installed it before anybody knew about the dangers. Friends in the business have died from asbestos-related lung diseases. He quit asbestos, and the construction trade, a few years ago.

"I'm a walking time bomb," he says.

If he coughs, he worries. Paleontologists know all about mortality.

He believes his enthusiasm for life and hard, physical labor have so far kept him healthy. He does not look like a man approaching the half-century mark. He has a flat stomach, sturdy legs and muscular arms. On a typical day of fossil hunting, he walks 10 miles, digs hundreds of holes and then carries heavy specimens back to his truck.

The truck is a red Toyota pickup with four-wheel drive and 140,000 miles. He has built a two-level camper in the back. He sleeps on one level when he's traveling. The other level is jammed with equipment. He has shovels, ice chests, water jugs, knives, plaster material for encasing fragile fossils and metal probes for detecting buried bones. The stereo is playing Bob Marley and the Wailers. The vanity license plate says: Ice Age.

"I don't know. We should get something today," he says. He's driving through Ruskin toward the Leisey Shell Pit, which is about five minutes from his house near the Little Manatee River. The pit is officially closed now to paleontologists, though he has permission to dig there. "That's the thing. You never know. You can find ANYTHING."

He drives past modest houses, tumbledown shacks and orange groves. And then there's the shell pit, on both sides of the road. On one side, the pit is filled with water. When digging stopped, and the pumps turned off, the water table came up. It's a lake. The other side is still relatively dry. But the Leiseys have turned off the pumps. Soon, whatever is under the ground will be lost to him.

He climbs out of the truck. The sun blasts the moonscape with white heat. He wears battered sneakers, running shorts, a tank top and a visor. He says he knows it's stupid, but he never wears sunscreen. He heads into the sunlight with a shovel and metal probe.

There are hundreds of holes dug by other paleontologists, adults and children, over the years. Over there somebody got a six-foot beaver. Over here a mastodon skull. In January, Garcia found the claw of a giant sloth. This sloth stood 21 feet high. Not long ago, in phosphate country, he dug up the skull of a *Gavialosuchus* crocodile. The skull was five feet long; the animal probably measured 32 feet. He keeps it at the small museum at his Ruskin home.

He does not look at you as he walks. His eyes are always aimed at the ground. He pokes at things with the probe. He stops, kneels, examines something. "Turtle shell," he says. He talks constantly to himself and whoever is with him.

"I look for teeth. They give away the presence of other things." Turtle shell. Shark's teeth. Here's a fossilized garfish scale. Here's the mouth parts of an ancient sting ray. He jams the probe three feet into the hard ground; his deltoids flex with the effort.

"Hear that?" he says. "You could hear a clicking sound when the probe hit bone. I think we got something."

With the shovel he digs in small bites so he misses nothing. Then he takes a huge hunting knife and carefully picks through the layers of sand he dislodged. He finds part of a turtle carapace, more than a million years old. It would be a nice find for a beginner. But he is looking for bigger game. A friend who accompanied him yesterday found a mastodon tooth. It weighed five pounds.

"I know there are great things here still waiting to be discovered," he says on the way home. He has a plan: buying unexplored property next to the mine and then searching for fossils, night and day, until he has uncovered every last treasure. He envisions a museum where children could visit and then head out into the field to dig fossils for school projects.

He did some figuring. It would cost $500,000 to buy the property he would like. He needs to raise the money somehow. Right now, the bone man, the poet of paleontology, is without a real job.

His last Smithsonian grant expired, and the Tampa Museum of Science and Industry has been using him less and less. A friend started a business in his name, Garcia Paleontology, which pays him to lead several fossil-collecting expedition tours a year, but it covers his expenses and nothing more. He also has a self-published book, *Sunrise at Bone Valley*, which he hopes to sell to a real publisher, but hasn't so far. He has sold a few of his fossils, something he has mixed emotions about.

"The best fossils should always go to museums," he says. "But, you know, I want to make a living at something I love. I'm not going back to the insulation business."

He charges for lectures and slide shows. His slide shows are interesting and flamboyant. In a Christmas show, where the thundering sound track is the *Nutcracker Suite*, he lectures about fossils while dressed as Santa Claus. In a future show, he will lecture as his hero, Thomas Jefferson. More than a president, Jefferson was a passionate paleontologist. He collected shark's teeth. Garcia once got to hold one of Jefferson's shark's teeth. It was a thrill.

"I had a dream about Jefferson," Frank Garcia says in his living room, surrounded by the bones of the long dead. "It was so vivid. He was right here in my house. We drank lots of Cuban coffee. And we talked, we talked all night about fossils."

A fishin' hole called Boca Grande

Boca Grande
June 1981

After the strike, the fish swims under the boat, leaps from the water, and lands, thrashing, in the stern. What a panicked 130-pound tarpon can do to a boat is awesome. With its tail it slaps two heavy fighting chairs to the bow. Then it breaks up the electronic gear near the console, chips some paint, pounds two holes in the deck, and somehow turns off the engine.

"A nightmare," says Gena Teachout, who is fishing with her teen-aged daughter on the night of the tarpon. "Blood and slime were everywhere, and all we could do is stand back and pray."

Prayers are answered. The monster calms down long enough to be thrown back, and the Teachouts survive the night at the world's only tarpon hole where fish regularly jump into boats.

The hole is actually a 400-yard-wide ditch or trench that sits in the middle of a wide pass separating Gasparilla Island from Cayo Costa Key at the mouth of Charlotte Harbor, in Southwest Florida. At 70-feet, the ditch is deeper than the rest of the pass, and tarpon like deep water. They also like the thousands of blue crabs that are swept through the pass with the tide.

"This place has got it all," says Van Hubbard, a grizzled fishing guide at the ripe old age of 32. "The tarpon have food and they have habitat. That's why there are more tarpon here than anywhere else."

We are floating over the hole in Hubbard's 39-foot boat, *Road Runner*. A large school of tarpon is rolling to our right. To our left, a school surfaces and a large fish spanks the water with its tail before diving.

"We can see a bunch of fish all around us," Hubbard says. "But look at this!"

He points to an electronic device that uses sonar to locate fish in deep water. Below us, according to the fish finder, is a great school of tarpon—several hundred of the spectacular silver gamefish that commonly grow heavier than 100 pounds.

"This is awesome," says Hubbard, who grew up in the Tampa Bay area. "And that's why I moved here. In Tampa Bay, I might get to cast to two or three fish at a time. Here I can cast to a school of five hundred fish. But you can't tell anybody that. They won't believe you. They got to see it themselves."

•　　•　　•

Fishermen began catching tarpon on rod and reel about 100 years ago. Tarpon were harpooned before that, because nobody thought it possible to catch one on primitive tackle. Who did it first nobody knows. By the late 1800s Boca Grande had become a fishing paradise for wealthy sportsmen. A steamer would tow into the pass a small fleet of rowboats containing fishermen, who would catch tarpon and then retire to mansions on the beach when mosquitoes came out at dusk.

Fishing was even better than now. So say records kept at the Gasparilla Inn, the island's elegant, old hotel. One angler caught 34 tarpon in a single day, according to figures written on a saucer-sized tarpon scale pinned to a wall. In a faded 1913 photograph, Nan Hunt poses with a 187-pound tarpon, largest ever landed at Boca Grande by a woman. In 1977, when Mrs. Hunter, was 82, she returned and caught a 90-pounder.

Not much of old Boca remains. For every old building, a new condominium or townhouse or houseboat has appeared—including one with a helicopter pad.

Boca Grande is changing. Miller's Marina is a good example. Destroyed in a 1975 fire, the rustic fishing camp was rebuilt completely. Now it is as modern and well-equipped as any marina in Florida. A successful angler might celebrate a tarpon with a tall drink and a video game. An unsuccessful angler might take out his frustration on the graffiti blackboard hanging in a restroom.

Down the water from Miller's stands one of the last relics of old Boca Grande. Whidden's Seafood Market Marina has changed little since the late Sam Whidden slapped some boards together in 1932. His daughters Isabelle and Barbara run the place now.

"We'll never change it," vows Isabelle, who started working in the marina as a third grader. "We might repair it a little, but nothin' else."

Whidden's was, and is, old and wooden and covered with a tin roof. Inside, an overworked fan pushes hot air. The only modern touches are an automatic coffee maker and a TV.

Everything else belongs to a different time, the sausage jars, the old gas stove, the stools, the cotton net, turtle shells, a player piano, and a sperm whale skull.

Sity Hall: Visters welcom to N corporate Boca Grande.

Their daddy put that on a sign years ago.

Plez rest in our hall. Sears Robuck and Air Conditioning for your comfort. Boca Grande es on the upp and up.

The air conditioning is gone. So is the monkey that used to be tied outside the door.

"This place was THE place to come," Isabelle tells me. "We used to have big dances here on Saturday nights. We had to put some old fish net over the beer in the dance hall to keep some of these fishermen from taking the warm beer."

Out in the hole, we are surrounded by boats of every size and value. One man fishes alone in a tiny Boston Whaler. Within a few feet of him is a 60-foot, air-conditioned Rybovitch equipped with every modern convenience. Boats drift so close together that each hooked fish becomes a threat. When an angler in a nearby boat strikes a fish, it fires out of the water and lands a few feet from our bow.

"When a fish hits, the captain puts the boat in gear," Hubbard explains. "There's two reasons for it. One is to help set the hook. The other is to get the hell out of the way from the fish. It'll come straight up and land in the boat and break a few rods—or legs."

Steve Soistman, a young rod builder from St. Petersburg, is Hubbard's first mate. He dip nets a small blue crab and impales it on a hook for Hubbard's mother, Eunice Claus. He puts a mutton minnow on my hook.

"When a tarpon hits a crab he's just gonna take it," Hubbard advises. "But he won't take a minnow right away. He's gonna kill it first, then come back for it. Both of you keep your rods absolutely still."

We make three drifts through the pass without a strike. On the fourth, I feel something tap my bait. The rod snaps down, then pops up.

"STRIKE!" Hubbard commands.

As Hubbard slams the boat into gear, and we move ahead, I strike. For a moment I feel the fish. Then nothing. The tarpon spit out the bait.

"This is too much like work," Hubbard finally says. "I don't like to fish this way. Let's go out on the beach, where we can cast to the tarpon."

Four days before, Hubbard had found tarpon away from the pass near the beach. His party had enjoyed seven strikes and released four fish before the arrival of Godzilla. Godzilla was king in a school of very big tarpon.

Hubbard had tossed a crab bait on an outfit equipped with line with a breaking strength of only 12 pounds. Godzilla inhaled the bait. Hubbard set the hook and asked if anyone in his party knew how to fight a big fish. Nobody did. Steve Soistman, the mate who had caught hundreds in his career, grabbed the rod.

For 45 minutes, the tarpon pretended it was not hooked, and stayed with the rest of the school. Hubbard finally gunned his boat and scattered the other fish. The fight began in earnest.

"It didn't make many long runs and only jumped once, so it didn't tire itself out," Soistman tells me now, as we head away from the pass. "It tried to run under the boat and I had to stick the rod in the water to keep the line from breaking on the prop. It was a very smart fish."

Thirty times Soistman drew the tarpon near the boat. Four times it was almost close enough to gaff. Then, after three hours, the line snapped. Godzilla likely weighed more than 175 pounds.

"I won't say I was broken-hearted," says Hubbard, who releases all of his tarpon anyway. "But I was disappointed. I didn't want to kill that fish, but I sure wanted to bring it in and show the other guides, who use heavy tackle and laugh about what they call my 'sewin' thread.' I would have loved to have seen their faces."

Off the beach, we encounter the largest concentration of tarpon I've ever seen, a school that is a hundred feet wide, at least, and another six feet deep.

"It's like a school of mullet," I whisper.

"Like a school of herring," Hubbard says. "That's all tarpon are. Giant herring."

He flips a crab in front of the school. Five hundred fish, at the very least, pass my bait without the slightest interest. It happens again. And again. Maybe we should have spat on our bait. It worked for the old-timers. Frustrated, Hubbard backs the boat away from the fish. We drift along in shallow water and wait.

"The tarpon are moving," he says, thinking out loud. "As long as they're moving, they ain't biting. I'll wait until they start circling a little. Then they'll eat."

The school moves closer and does slow down. Hubbard casts another crab and hands me the rod. Sweat drips into my eyes. I can feel my heart pounding in my chest, loud enough to drown out Hubbard's voice.

"Wait until that cork goes down, then strike. Smoothly now. That's only twelve-pound test."

The school inches toward my bait, closer and closer by the second. Then the great fish, all of them, pass it by. Just when I'm ready to moan, a fat tarpon turns around. My cork bobs once. Then it disappears.

"STRIIIIIKE!" Hubbard shrieks.

I strike and the fish heads for New Orleans. Line burns from the spool. Then, I make the fatal mistake. I brush my thumb against the spool to add a tad more pressure, something I would do to keep a snook away from pilings or a bass from swimming into the lily pads.

The line snaps. I have never heard anything as loud.

"MY GAWD!" Hubbard erupts. "Don't you EVER put your thumb on a spool to stop a tarpon! We've worked so hard for a crack at these fish! Tarpon ain't no bass! Gawd!"

For a moment, his hands are on my neck. For a moment, I find myself wishing I had a knife. Not for self defense, but to cut off my offending thumb.

A buck unlocks
the old Keys

Islamorada
August 1993

Traveling through today's Florida Keys can be a shock to an old-timer who remembers a more casual, more colorful, less prosperous place.

The tariff on even a modest motel room, where the air conditioner and toilet work indifferently, brings on a faint. At some eateries, even the mediocre ones, the arrival of the check induces cold sweat. The new-age tackle store wants $400 for a fly rod. The sign on the trendy gift shop's stained-glass window kindly requests that you wear shoes and shirt. Sadly, most patrons do.

Fortunately, there is an antidote to the modern Florida Keys.

Driving south on U.S. 1, you look for Mile Marker No. 78 on the side of the road. When you pass it, immediately check your odometer. You want to go about a half mile more. Cross the Lignum Vitae Bridge, then take an immediate right. Pass behind the Hungry Angler restaurant, then park your car under the coconut trees at Robbie's Boat Rentals.

The hand-painted sign is a sight for glazed eyes:

See the tarpon. $1.

You have found the last bargain in the Florida Keys.

Go ahead, walk inside the ramshackle building with the worm-eaten walls. It's not going to fall into the water; it has survived hurricanes. Say hi to the blond woman at the cash register, the one whose lips are never without a cigarette. Don't mind that she fails to greet you. That's how real Keys people are. Neither rude nor friendly, they tolerate you.

"You want to feed the tarpon?" she asks. You do.

"That's two dollars extra." Pay it. You're still getting a bargain. She hands you a bucket of dead minnows.

As you walk out on the 100-foot dock, you will notice tarpon in the water. To anglers, tarpon are Florida's gamefish prize. They pull hard and jump high. They have green backs, silver sides and a gaping, underslung jaw. They look exactly like pickled herring, only they are about 1,000 times larger.

At the end of the dock, prepare to be impressed. There are about 50 tarpon swimming about. The smallest might weigh 15 pounds. The largest might flirt with 150. This is no aquarium: These fish are free to come and go. They just hang out here.

You throw the first minnow. A five-foot tarpon, with the table manners of T. rex, inhales the minnow in an explosion of water. Now a truly enormous tarpon—it's a Harley-Davidson in scales—surfaces. It seems to be watching and waiting for you. Slowly, carefully, you lower your puny, minnow-filled hand.

The mighty mouth yawns . . . .

Sixteen years ago, Robbie Reckwerdt found a dying tarpon swimming in shallow water. Its jaw had been torn open after a tussle with an angler. Robbie, a fishing guide, put the injured tarpon in the tank where he kept bait. A friend of his, Doc Roach, sewed the tarpon's mouth with catgut. When the tarpon recovered, Robbie returned it to Florida Bay and named him Scarface.

Scarface refused to leave. Robbie fed him. Pretty soon, other tarpon arrived to keep Scarface company.

"They knew a good thing when they saw it," Robbie will tell you, "and they stayed. I think tarpon must be pretty intelligent."

Robbie has never bothered to advertise his feed-the-tarpon dock. Too many folks might scare the tarpon. But last year, several thousand people discovered his dock. By doing so, they got a taste of the old Keys, where things were simple, cheap and fun.

At noon, the dock is busy with customers. There's a blond woman in a silk pants suit. There's a shirtless guy who needed a shave yesterday. Several people, happily, risk splinters in bare feet.

Now a boat arrives. It's fishing guide C.C. Diggs. This morning, he took two clients tarpon fishing. They had two fish on, but they got away. Here, the mighty anglers will get the chance to put their hands on a tarpon, but they'll do it unarmed.

Robbie, 53, allows no fishing from his dock.

"When I was a fishin' guide," he explains, "I killed lots of tarpon. Feeding them, protecting them, is my penance to make up for the barbaric waste I did to them."

Every once in a while, somebody passing in a boat will throw out a line and try to hook one of Robbie's tarpon. Robbie, or his son or daughter, will thunder down the dock, shouting and waving their arms.

"Hey," Robbie will scream. "These are my pets!"

Sometimes, Robbie is too slow, and a fish bites a baited hook. Fortunately, there are lots of pilings in the water. Weaving among them like a figure skater, the tarpon always manage to sever the fishing line on the barnacles.

Diggs, the fishing guide, agrees that there should be no fishing. He always brings his clients to see Robbie's tarpon. They enjoy feeding them. He does, too. Leaning over the water, feeding them by hand, he says: "Sometimes they're more aggressive than at other times." Tarpon have no teeth, but the inside of their mouths is as rough as sandpaper. "During an aggressive time, one swallowed my hand to the elbow," Diggs says. "I got scraped a little bit, is all."

You don't want to get scraped, but you are interested in a closer relationship with a tarpon. You hold the minnow an inch above the water. The seven-footer rises, pauses, then opens that prehistoric kisser. Whoosh! The suction vacuums the minnow into oblivion. You jerk back your hand, exhilarated and surprised.

But not as surprised as the teen-age boy down the dock. Kneeling, he holds a minnow about two feet above the water. Momentarily distracted by the arrival of another boat, he forgets the matter at hand. He is unprepared for the three-foot tarpon that rockets out of the water, misses the minnow and crashes into his chest. Slime covers his t-shirt.

A few minutes later, back by the cash register, he takes a hearty slug from an ice-cold Mountain Dew. "That was something," he says. "That really was something."

The last bargain in the Keys.

Swamp loggers

Big Cypress
September 1994

Cesar Becerra is obeying the speed limit at this moment. But you can tell he wants to press pedal to metal and fly. Cesar seems to be a young man in a hurry, eager to catch up with all kinds of things, mainly history. Right now, he is driving through the Everglades to a ghost town called Jerome.

"It was an incredible place!" he almost shouts. Incredible is a word he often uses. "Most people have no idea what was here."

Cesar Becerra, lover of American history, can tell you: In the 1920s, after the first roads were built in the Everglades, logging companies rushed down to mine the last old-growth forest in Florida. Jerome was a lumber mill settlement, one of the South's busiest, for two decades. Thousands of ancient cypress trees were cut and sawed by rugged men who sometimes died in horrific accidents as they toiled in the dark swamps.

The Jerome mill, and other smaller mills nearby, eventually exhausted the best of the big trees and put themselves out of work. Time passed. The loggers got old or died, the trees started growing back, South Florida became modern, urban, cosmopolitan, changing, sometimes it seemed, by the hour. In with the new; out with the old. People forgot.

Cesar Becerra, a bloodhound in short pants, is on the trail of the old history.

He's driving a white government Jeep Cherokee on State Road 29 in South Florida. To his right is the Big Cypress National Preserve, where he has a weekend job. To his left is the Fakahatchee Strand State Preserve. Miami and Naples are about an hour away, but you wouldn't know it. Cesar is driving through a still daunting wilderness, an 800,000-acre swamp still home to bears and panthers and even a few grizzled human occupants who dislike civilization and civilized company. Old loggers.

Cesar pulls off the road, almost vibrating with enthusiasm. "Jerome!" he cries. The ghost town. He points to a blue building, made of cypress. "These were barracks," he says, parking. Two big mixed breed dogs run out howling.

He calms them.

He walks through weeds higher than his head, through mud, over rock piles, around swamp willow, Brazilian pepper and Australian pines.

"Right here," he says. "The mill was here."

The *Saturday Evening Post*, in one of the only stories ever published about what happened here, called the work "the toughest logging job in America, if not the world." The Jerome lumber mill once was among the most productive in the United

States. During the 1940s, loggers cut and finished about 100,000 board feet every day, enough to build five three-bedroom homes. About a thousand workers, mostly black men, kept the mill going. At night they retired to shacks along the edge of the clearing.

Right into the late 1950s, steam-driven locomotives, dinosaurs almost everywhere else in America, hauled log-filled cars over hundreds of miles of tracks laid, incredibly, in the swamps. Muscular men waded through waist-deep water past alligators and poisonous snakes to cut towering cypress trees with hand saws.

Now it is all gone, vanished, the shacks, the mill, the locomotives, the railroad tracks. Even the men who did the work, for the most part, are dead or old enough to think of mortality. What's left of the industry are dilapidated barracks and a couple of slime ponds and four concrete foundations that supported a 150-foot tall water tower that is no more.

The trees for the most part are growing back, though it will be another 700 years before they are as large as before. Inhospitable and mysterious, the domain of countless creatures of tooth and claw, the swamp remains a wilderness.

Cesar Becerra declares: "Man, it's right here, the least documented history in South Florida!"

He drives out of Jerome, turns down a gravel road, brakes for the swamp, leaps out of the Jeep and wades in. Stops and fishes around with his boots. Smiles. Bends down. As mosquitoes hover, he lifts a lost railroad tie. Then another and another.

"History is right under our feet!" he declares.

Cesar Becerra—the kid historian—is documenting it.

He's 21—something that inevitably surprises people who encounter him— and self-conscious enough about his baby face to have finally grown a wispy beard to make himself seem older. He's about six inches shy of six feet and stocky of build. His round eyeglasses give him a bookish air, but the park service uniform, which includes short pants, makes him look a little like a Boy Scout.

Last summer, as the history major began his senior year at Florida International University, he was commissioned by the Big Cypress National Preserve and the Student Conservation Foundation to trace the history of logging in South Florida.

"When I started my project, I figured I'd go into a museum and open a drawer and find a file all about the logging," he says. He found four photographs and a government report that mentioned the names of a couple of old loggers.

He had to do the detective work, tracking down old-timers, locating old pictures, wandering around Jerome with a metal detector hoping to find lost railroad equipment. Turned out he found more pictures and more old-timers than he thought possible. He put together an exhibition called *Jerome: Lost, Found—a Photographic Essay on South Florida's Last Great Sawmill.* It made the rounds of Florida museums.

"I've never known a young man to have more energy," says Niki Butcher, an artist who lives in the Big Cypress with her husband Clyde, a photographer. Cesar has become a frequent visitor to their home. He stops, chats—sometimes he gets so excited talking about his logging research that he forgets to eat the grilled cheese sandwich Niki has laid before him—and has to be reminded.

Cesar's parents came to Miami to escape Castro's revolution. His mother, a schoolteacher, took her young son to museums that showcased the history of their new country. Cesar's father, an architect, sometimes worried whether his son's interests would lead to anything productive. But he didn't discourage him. He eventually built a shed in the back yard so Cesar could house his growing collection of memorabilia.

"I'd save anything old," Cesar says.

In fifth grade, Cesar's class visited Miami's oldest house on a field trip. In 10th grade, when he got his driver's license, and his first car, he returned to the house, the Barnacle State Historic Site in Coconut Grove, for another look.

By age 15, he was among the youngest persons to ever lead historic tours at state parks. He worked his way through high school and Florida International University leading tours. When a national group of historians visited Miami, Cesar, still a teen-ager, was chosen to lead an expedition to Indian Key, the site of an important battle in the Seminole wars.

"Everything fascinates me about South Florida's history. Miami is not even one-hundred years old! It's young! Incredible! There's so much to know I'll never learn it all!"

He is on Miami's Centennial History Committee. He is a consultant with the Gold Coast Train Museum. He is treasurer for the South Florida Civil War Roundtable. He is historian for the Historical Reenactors Guild of Florida. He is secretary of the Miami Memorabilia Club.

"I just found an old Singer sewing machine!"

People who telephone him to find out more about his logging exhibit are unlikely to catch him at home. They leave messages on his answering machine. Cesar inevitably returns their calls late into the night, often rousing them from bed. "Sorry," he'll say sheepishly. "I just got home."

His last girlfriend broke up with him. She grew weary of dates that turned out to be history lectures and all the time he spent stalking retired loggers in the Big Cypress. Cesar tries to be philosophical. He says, "This friend of mine—he's a historian and archaeologist who's been married three times—he told me: 'Cesar, people like us are married to our work.' He might be right."

Cesar recently started his own small business leading historic tours. He also writes for the quarterly magazine of the Historical Museum of Southern Florida. Publishers wonder if he is interested in writing a book about logging in the Big Cypress.

Cesar still has to take a few courses to complete his college degree.

"I'm young," he says, a little defensively, "but I've been a historian for quite a while."

He likes to tell this story. One day he was out for a drive on the Tamiami Trail, the road that connects Miami to Naples through the Everglades and the Big Cypress. He stopped for a walk. When he returned to his vehicle, he heard a rumbling sound. He looked up in time to see an old building across the street collapse, just crumble to the ground, in an explosion of dust and rotting timber. Though it was a random event, it taught him a history lesson.

Time is fleeting. Time is the enemy.

Find the old men before they are gone.

Get their stories.

He started looking for the old loggers. Always they were surprised when he found them. They couldn't understand why anybody would be interested in their experiences. Sometimes the rural, elderly men even acted suspicious. Why did a young Cuban-American—and a city boy—want to know about them? Sometimes Cesar left his uniform at home and wore his own clothes. He'd knock on the door and introduce himself and let his enthusiasm win them over.

Sure they would talk.

"I always have a few specific questions for them, but mostly I just let them go, let them ramble."

Some gave him photographs. Some gave the names of other loggers. And those men typically gave him the names of others. One day someone told him about Frog Smith. Frog Smith lived in Fort Myers. Frog had worked at many professions during his 98 years on Earth, including gigging frogs in the Everglades and cutting trees in the Big Cypress. He was known as an amazing storyteller.

Cesar met Frog at Frog's house. Frog told many stories. He invited Cesar back in two weeks to look at his collection of logging photos. Frog died a few days later. Cesar has Frog's photos, but not the stories to go with them.

"A lot of the old loggers are dying," Cesar says. "When an old pioneer dies, it's like losing a library."

On a rainy Saturday, he heads into Copeland just down the road from Jerome, hoping to find Monroe Graham. Half a century ago, Copeland was a logging community and Monroe Graham was among its most skilled men with ax and saw. Now Copeland is an impoverished settlement in Florida's last great wilderness. Monroe Graham is 80, stooped and frail.

Copeland has a road prison, a grocery with sagging floors and a couple dozen ramshackle houses, shacks and rusty trailers. Monroe Graham lives on the black side of the settlement.

"Copeland is lost in time," Cesar says. "It's still completely segregated, except sometimes on Sunday. I came in to see Monroe on a Sunday once and there was a pulpit in his yard and a white preacher was preaching to an audience of whites and blacks."

Rain drips from an Australian pine. A pit-bull mix drinks from a puddle. A drunken man staggers across a clearing talking to himself. Cesar stops his vehicle in front of Monroe's trailer and shouts out a warm greeting. Monroe hobbles out, leaning on his cane, straining to see who's calling him. When he sees Cesar, he waves his cane hello.

"Good to see you," he says. "I was wonderin' when you was comin' back again."

Monroe was the first pioneer Cesar ever interviewed. He might be Cesar's favorite. Cesar has returned a number of times to hear Monroe's stories, which are mostly about hardship. For a decade, Monroe sawed and sweated and bled. But he survived and many did not.

Some men died, he'll tell you, crushed beyond recognition under the weight of falling trees. Some suffered skull fractures and brain injuries. Some lost legs and arms. Wading through the swamp, some stepped in rocky holes and snapped their legs. Some drowned. Some were bitten by venomous snakes, nipped by alligators.

"It was real rough work," he says, sitting in baggy overalls on a chair outside the trailer. "A hard, hard life."

Like many of the black men who did the brutal labor, he came to the Everglades out of desperation for a job. He hoped the $20-a-day salary might help pay the mortgage of a nice farm outside of Tallahassee, where he was born. He never made it back to the North Florida woods, never got the farm. In Copeland there was hardly money to support his family.

He lives alone now, in a leaky trailer with uneven floors. He has outlived two wives. His three daughters moved away. One son went to prison after shooting another man during a dice game in a jook-joint argument; after he was paroled he drowned in Copeland. Another son was shot dead in a domestic quarrel.

Monroe shifts in his chair and rolls up a leg of his overalls. The scar on his right knee? The ax slid off a tree and got me. This poor old crippled foot? Buried an ax in it by accident. One time a cypress tree fell and rolled his way. He ran but it caught him. He woke up, slumped against the log, head oozing blood. The white Boss Man— the one who wore a pistol in his belt—didn't tolerate malingerers. Monroe worked the next day.

His story is interrupted by the drunken neighbor, a slender man named Buck. Buck, for a reason Monroe doesn't understand, is enraged at him. Buck accuses Monroe of being evil, of being the devil. Buck reminds Monroe that he is old and will probably die soon. Monroe has a bad heart and a doctor has told him he has a spot on his lungs. Buck's words sting.

"Go home, Buck, you're drunk," Monroe shouts.

Monroe whispers that Buck is a good man, works hard, unless he drinks. Buck continues to taunt Monroe. Monroe hauls off and hits Buck with his cane. Buck laughs at the old man's blow and staggers away. Then he loses his balance and falls. He finds it hard to get up. As Buck struggles in the mud, Monroe's three dogs, including the pit bull, growl at Buck's throat. Monroe tells somebody to keep an eye on the dogs.

"They'll kill Buck," he sighs.

Life was difficult in the 1940s too. A whistle woke the loggers early. They boarded steam-driven trains that took them hours into the swamp. Sometimes water covered the tracks. Occasionally water flowed into the locomotives and extinguished the boiler fires.

When the tracks ended the men walked, pressing through bushes high and low, through vines and brambles, wading around alligators and cottonmouth moccasins, stumbling over the cypress roots called knees, then attacking the trees with crosscut saws, all the while trying to keep their balance in the water and mud and wondering what might happen next.

"Sometimes, when the trees fell, bees flew out, and they was mad, so we'd run, really run, and we'd jump into the deep water, go under and wait for the bees to leave."

Oxen and mules were brought in to drag the 125-foot logs back to the train. The train took the logs to the mills—there were hundreds of mills in the Big Cypress and Fakahatchee—and the mills converted the logs to lumber. During World War II, the lumber was important to ship building. After the war, lumber was shipped across the ocean to rebuild Europe. In the 1950s, the chain saw was introduced and all the big trees disappeared except at Corkscrew Swamp, owned by the National Audubon Society. Mills went out of business. Lumber companies looked elsewhere to exploit forests. Monroe Graham stayed.

He stands with effort, hobbles gingerly across the yard, accompanied by Cesar, who holds him gently by his arm. They head toward Monroe's cypress shack. It's the only logging shack left in Copeland. All the others were damaged by Hurricane Andrew, condemned and bulldozed by Collier County. Somehow, Monroe's shack was spared, though it seems poised to fall.

He sits in front of it, points at the high weeds, says he once had a pair of heavy tongs, the kind of tongs a strong man used to lift fallen logs, but he lost his tongs back in the grass or else somebody stole them.

"I wouldn't take any money for those tongs," he announces. "I wish I had me those tongs."

Cesar wishes he did too. He'd like to see the tongs in a museum. He and Monroe shake hands. Cesar returns to his Jeep. Buck staggers into the road, shouting curses, blocking the way. Cesar drives around him, youthful eyes as wide as the potholes on the road ahead.

The Bear

Great Smoky Mountains
August 1994

Standing in the wilderness, automatically looking around for bears, I eventually notice that my favorite gentle stream is no longer gentle. Swollen by heavy rains, it roars down the mountain, crumbling banks, carrying debris, nature unleashed.

I have brought waders and fly rod on this vacation to Great Smoky Mountains National Park. But now I picture myself losing my balance in the strong current, falling and tumbling down Cataloochee Creek, numbed hands reaching vainly for slippery boulders, lungs filling with icy water, my body becoming food for a lazy bear.

I decide to hike instead.

"You could drown in here," I say.

My son says he doubts it. Says he will be fine. At 18, he knows how to fool trout, is sure of foot and glows with the confidence of immortal youth.

I tell him my what-can-happen-when-you-are-wading story: Out in Utah, fly fishing in the snow-melt Logan River, I fell. The current swept me downstream so fast I couldn't regain my feet. I stopped myself by grabbing an overhead limb and hanging there, waders growing heavier as they filled with water, stretching my arms until they felt ready to leave their sockets. My brother-in-law had to rescue me.

"I could have drowned," I tell my son. I'm tempted to bring up my other fishing story—the one from my childhood that still fills me with horror—but I try not to think about that one. I hope the story of my near-drowning will suffice.

"Oh, dad," my son says.

I try not to be a worrywart back home in Florida, where I have lived, more or less comfortably, with the out-of-doors for more than four decades. Nor am I usually so anxious while visiting mountainous North Carolina, where I have taken vacations since childhood.

But the summer of 1994 has been different. My family has been reminded again and again that nature is completely indifferent to human affairs, that anything can happen, and sometimes what happens is fatal.

Driving up, we have to detour around Central Georgia, where tropical storm-generated floods have killed 31 people and damaged millions of dollars in property. In North Carolina, inclement weather makes for dangerous driving almost everywhere. Daily we seem to read newspaper stories about runaway trucks crashing on slick highways.

We also read about the elderly couple who stopped for a break on the nation's most beautiful highway, the Blue Ridge Parkway, and were injured when they fell off a cliff.

We read about lost hikers.

A 10-year-old Florida boy takes a walk with his dad to Clingman's Dome, one of the national park's most developed areas. For some reason the boy steps off the paved path. When his dad notices, the boy is gone. For two days a rescue team searches in vain and those of us following through newspaper accounts brace for the worst. On the third day the boy is found. He has survived by eating blueberries and drinking from a stream.

An elderly woman strolls from her state park campsite on Mount Mitchell, at 6,684 feet the highest peak in eastern North America. She vanishes. With awe I've hiked and ridden my bicycle throughout this raw wilderness. Perpetually wet, the mountain receives 100 inches of rain a year. Even in July, night temperatures drop into the 40s. I try to imagine this woman, wet, cold, hungry and totally unprepared for what has happened to her. Rescue efforts are called off after a week, my newspaper story says. She is presumed dead.

In Florida, sharks swim in our seas and alligators in our rivers, but only on the rarest occasions do they bother humans. We have no cliffs to fall from and almost never do we hear about vanished hikers—during my lifetime the state has lost its wildest edges.

Only once have I feared for my life. It was in a storm on Florida Bay, near the border of Everglades National Park, when the boat my father rented broke down and a tremendous squall overtook us. For an hour the wind howled and waves pounded and lightning crashed so near we could feel electricity in the air.

In Florida, I know what is worth fearing and what is not. I don't fret about sharks and alligators or about getting lost. I do avoid all boats in iffy weather.

In North Carolina, where I lack experience, where bears roam, where ice water roars down the mountains toward young anglers, I know what I don't know, and what I don't know is frightening.

My son and I argue about his fishing. But he persuades me that I am being overcautious and that he will be extra careful. Haven't I seen other anglers today? Yes, son, I have. Still, standing next to him as the stream boils past, I coach to the last, tell him the places least likely to get the strongest currents and warn him to pay attention to the weather. A hard rain could cause flash flooding. Get out of the water.

I tell him where I'll look for him in an hour. Be there.

I will, I will, he says, eyes rolling.

My wife and I start our hike.

We cross Cataloochee Creek, follow Caldwell Fork, and then climb Boogerman Trail. We slip and slide on the wet mud, slightly out of breath as we ascend through rosebay rhododendron heavy with blossoms. My anxiety fades as we pass through a never-logged forest filled with immense eastern hemlocks and even larger poplar trees. I look for the poplar I saw last year, the one blown apart by lightning, but I don't remember its exact location.

We see delicate Indian pipes, tiny white plants that grow out of decaying vegetation. We ascend through huge white pines and smell the fallen needles. Next we begin circling Den Ridge, which winds through great stumps of chestnut trees, killed by long-ago blight. I hear a pileated woodpecker hammering away, prospering among the death.

Below I hear something else.

For a moment I think I hear another hiker coming up. But then I realize it can't be. No trail is below us. Must be a deer. We have seen many on this vacation. Maybe we will get a good look at a buck.

I look down toward the noise.

I wave frantically to my wife and silently mouth one word:

Bear!

A black bear, untamed and unpredictable, is climbing in our direction. For the first time, we are seeing a bear on the bear's turf. We're not at a zoo, and we're not in a car, looking at him through safety glass.

All of this happens in an instant: I try to remember everything I have read about wilderness bears. They are unlikely to attack, most likely to run. But if they charge they probably are bluffing and will stop at the last instant. So don't run! Running is the worst thing to do. It can trigger the attack instinct. Back off slowly, talk softly.

Thirty feet below and he hasn't seen, smelled or heard us.

I clear my throat as loud as I can.

He stops. Looks up. I'd guess he weighs 300 pounds. He does not run. Meets our gaze.

My wife and I look at each other. We turn deliberately and walk steadily down the mountain, away from the bear, glancing back to see if he is following. He is not.

We giggle about our experience, our fear.

Then we stop. How often do we see bears? We do something incredibly foolish.

We go back to look at him again.

But the bear is gone. We start down the mountain, and I am thinking again about my son and whether he is keeping his balance in the heavy current.

My wife and I talk, excitedly, about the bear. But another part of me is remembering an outing from a long time ago. I'm remembering when I was 14 and as passionate an angler as my son is now.

I cajoled two boys, brothers, into fishing with me. One of them snagged his lure on the floodgate of a dam. He lowered his body onto the floodgate and tried to work his lure free. Suddenly, the tide, or maybe his own weight, triggered the automatic mechanism that worked the floodgate. It closed on him. We heard him scream and saw him kick. We watched as he was crushed.

Whenever I am anxious about my children, I remember how it happened, how anything can happen, however unexpected, to any of us, at any moment. And I wonder, irrationally, if I were somehow to blame for the death of my friend, because I convinced him to go fishing with me, and whether I will be punished for the deed by losing one of my own children.

We plow down the mountain to Caldwell Fork and I fight my way through the rhododendron to the creek and he is there in the dim light, casting calmly from a shallow place, perfectly safe.